WITHDRAWN

Dividing lines

CULTURAL POLITICS

Dividing lines: poetry, class and ideology in the 1930s

Adrian Caesar

MANCHESTER UNIVERSITY PRESS

MANCHESTER and NEW YORK

distributed in the USA and Canada by ST. MARTIN'S PRESS, New York

Published by Manchester University Press
Oxford Road, Manchester M13 9PL, UK
and Room 400, 175 Fifth Avenue,
New York, NY 10010, USA

Distributed exclusively in the USA and Canada
by St. Martin's Press, Inc.,
175 Fifth Avenue, New York, NY 10010, USA

British Library cataloguing in publication area
Caesar, Adrian
    Dividing lines: poetry, class and ideology in the 1930s – (Cultural politics).
    1. Poetry in English, 1900–45.– Critical studies
    I. Title II. Series
    821.91209

Library of Congress cataloging in publication data
Caesar, Adrian, 1955–
    Dividing lines: poetry, class, and ideology in the 1930s / Adrian Caesar
        p. cm. – (Cultural politics)
    Includes bibliographical references.
    ISBN 0-7190-3375-6 (cloth). – ISBN 0-7190-3376-4 (paper)
    1. English poetry – 20th century – History and criticism.
    2. Politics and literature – Great Britain – History – 20th century.
    3. Literature and society – Great Britain – History – 20th century.
    4. Political poetry, English – History and criticism. 5. Social
classes in literature. I. Title. II. Series.
PR605.H5C34 1990
821'.91209 – dc20   90-43717

ISBN 0 7190 3375 6 hardback
     0 7190 3376 4 paperback

Typeset in Joanna
by Koinonia Limited, Manchester
Printed in Great Britain
by Bell & Bain Limited, Glasgow

Contents

Acknowledgements

I would like to thank the many people who have helped me both directly and indirectly in the writing of this book. For their friendship and support at the beginning of the project I would like to thank Eddie and Felicity Hughes, and the members of the English department at the Flinders University of South Australia where I held a post-doctoral fellowship in 1982-3. Since then I have received encouragement from friends and colleagues at the University of New England, and the University College of New South Wales at the Australian Defence Force Academy. In particular I would like to thank Joy Hooton for reading various draft chapters, Margaret McNally for her cheerful patience and professionalism in preparing the MS, and my friends Victor and Alison Kelleher for their unstinting encouragement. I would also like to thank various members of my family: my parents for sharing their memories of working-class life in the 1930s with me, Richard and Karen for their support, and lastly, but not least, Claire, Ellen and Damian who put up with me whilst I wrote it.

Naturally, the shortcomings are all mine.

A.C.

For Mum and Dad

Introduction

This book had its beginnings several years ago when I was thinking about the poetry of the Second World War, and why that very considerable body of work was either dismissed in critical terms or simply ignored. It became apparent to me that literary historians had chosen to see the development of poetry 1930-60 as a series of actions and reactions, taking place with remarkable consistency decade by decade. In this model certain groups of poets (whether they considered themselves to be groups or not) are chosen as 'representative' of a decade. In this way Auden and his supposed acolytes are said to represent the 1930s, and the social and political interests of that decade. The poetry of the 1940s is then dismissed as an unfortunate reaction, both political and aesthetic, to Auden and the 'Audenesque', and is characterised by the words 'Neo' or 'New' Romanticism. The poets of the New Apocalypse movement are seen as indicative of this trend, as is the work of Dylan Thomas. Finally, we arrive in the 1950s where Larkin and the 'Movement' poets are seen in turn reacting against Neo-Romanticism, and their bête noir, Dylan Thomas; they vote Labour, espouse 'reason' and 'purity of diction'.

As I continued to read, I became fascinated with the way in which these ideas had been generated and perpetuated. It seemed that poets and editors in each decade, anxious to carve out a place and a career for themselves, had advertised themselves in these terms and succeeded, in so far as their not disinterested versions of what they were doing had been accepted and repeated by later literary historians. Furthermore, it became clear to me that to accept this pattern of literary historical development entailed a willingness to ignore or distort much that was being written in each decade; certain styles with their attendant aesthetic and political ideologies were being privileged at the expense of others that were not *necessarily* inferior.

I came to the conclusion that a process was at work which 'mythologises' each decade, in the sense that Roland Barthes uses the word 'myth'.[1] Ideas, images, and words are linked by habitual association and accrue significances not necessarily inherent in them, which can come to have the appearance of truth. It is in this way that it has become 'natural' when thinking of poetry of the 1930s to think immediately of Auden firstly, and then of Day Lewis, Spender and MacNeice. In this book I want to exert a critique of the matrix of ideas, words and images which constitute this myth of the 1930s. For if it can be shown that one decade is vulnerable to such re-writing, it may help to clarify our notions of the subsequent development of English poetry this century.

The first step in this procedure is to question the association of Auden with 'the 1930s'. Although I have so far been using a locution which suggests an endorsement of 'the 1930s' as some legitimate entity, it is worth remembering that to wrest a decade from the continuum, and treat those years as if they have some single, homogeneous quality by which they may be characterised is an artificial procedure, and one, I think, which lends itself to myth-making. And when 'the 1930s' are defined in terms of the work of a single poet, or even a single group of poets, I feel some lively interrogation is in order.

Since about 1975, critics and literary historians have often agreed to define Auden by use of the words 'the 1930s' or vice-versa. So we hear that 'Auden's devices of style and habits of feeling are the 'thirties or a large part of the 'thirties'.[2] Samuel Hynes entitles his influential study of the period, *The Auden generation: literature and politics in the 1930s*.[3] Bernard Bergonzi follows in his book *Reading the thirties*, by telling us that he will use 'the 1930s', not merely to refer to a 'period', but also 'to refer generically to a group of writers and the work they produced, mostly in that decade, occasionally later'. He goes on to identify this 'group' as largely corresponding 'to what Samuel Hynes . . . calls "the Auden generation"'.[4] Other examples are not difficult to find. We encounter David Wright asserting that Auden was the 'spokesman of the decade' and that 'as such he spoke for the left'.[5] Alice Prochaska's exhibition held at the National Gallery in 1976 was entitled 'Young writers of the thirties'. On its cover were portrait photographs of Auden, Spender, Day Lewis, MacNeice, and in recognition of prose, Christopher Isherwood.[6] The exhibition dealt almost exclusively with their work.[7] Most recently, despite its theoretical and methodological sophistications, Valentine Cunningham's massive *British writers of the thirties* (which appeared after much of my book had been written or drafted) has on its dust-jacket portrait photographs of Auden, Isherwood and Spender.[8] And although Cunningham wants to broaden the notion of 'the 1930s' somewhat, he admits that 'the Auden Generation remains canonical', and evidently feels there is no reason why this should not be so.[9]

In my early chapters I will be returning to some of the works mentioned above in order to scrutinise the development of this association of Auden with the 1930s, and to show that this construction of the decade is partial and ideologically freighted. The place of Auden, Spender, Day Lewis and MacNeice within the myth will be reviewed, as will the standing of Geoffrey Grigson's much-praised periodical *New verse*. In the later chapters I offer a reading of other poets in the 1930s whose work the literary historical myth ignores. My purpose in doing this is to demonstrate the heterogeneity of poetry in the 1930s, and to show that many of the writers themselves were aware of this heterogeneity. I also wish to discuss what I take to be a crucial relationship between class background, style and ideology in the work of the poets concerned. Thus far, Auden's centrality to the decade has been asserted with little or incomplete reference to the place he held within society, and tacitly has been promoted by implicit or explicit notions of some undefined 'literary value'. My approach is to place the poets of the 1930s into the context of their lived experience, and their position within society, thereby insisting upon the idea that both the production and the reception of poetry are inseparably bound to the structures of the society from which it springs.

As Cunningham acknowledges, there have been some previous attempts to penetrate the canonical view of the 1930s most notably in *The 1930s: A challenge to orthodoxy*, a book of essays edited by John Lucas. Cunningham goes on to note that the 'challenge' in this book constitutes an attempt to replace the 'Auden generation' with another group of avowedly left-wing writers who were associated with the magazine *Left review*, namely Edgell Rickword, Montagu Slater and Randall Swingler. Cunningham describes this procedure as 'daft' since the above-named writers do not 'comprise the whole, nor the central part of the decade'.[10] It is left to the reader to infer that Auden *et al.* are more 'central', a description which is also endorsed by Bergonzi.[11] It is crucial here to insist that I am not interested in 'centrality', rather my attempt is to de-centre Auden's place in the 1930s, and to show that the literary world was divided by class, style and ideology, and that the writers themselves were very aware of these divisions. Rather than wishing to merge text and context as Bergonzi and Cunningham do, in order to produce what they call a single 'text' of the 1930s, with all that this implies of homogeneity and hegemony, I wish to concentrate upon divisions and heterogeneity.

It is also important to add that I am not very much concerned in this book with judgements about 'literary value'. I take it that the poetry dealt with here, since it was published, was of some 'value' to both writers and readers, and therefore had a relationship to people's experience in the decade. And it is this breadth that I am anxious to articulate. I am not at all concerned with the construction of league tables, in displacing Auden by Dylan Thomas for instance. On the other hand, I am anxious to call into question the political and aesthetic ideologies which have elevated the liberal Audenesque, with its uneasy combination of Georgian and modernist influences, at the expense of other modes which do not share that comfortable and comforting middle-ground.

In discussing the relationship between class, style, and ideology in poetry, there are of course manifest difficulties which it is best to admit at the outset. In dealing with various groups of poets here, my starting point is the class and educational background from which each group emerges, and against which they react in varying degrees of ambivalence. The justification for such a procedure is not merely theoretical, but is in part based upon empirical observation. That is to say, that when I came to study the poetry and the little magazines of the decade, I found affiliations of young poets grouped not according to Hynes's notion of 'generations', but according to similarities in their poetry and poetics, which in turn seemed to have a relationship to their lived experience. And in their lived experience there tended to be coincidences of class and educational background.

It will be clear from these remarks that this study is based on an eclectic theoretical position which, whilst it acknowledges the power of literature to make or shape society, also wishes to insist upon the way in which the structures of society make and shape literature. In other words, I take it that the relationship between literature and society is one of dialectical exchange, and rather than attempting to produce a theoretical construct which demonstrates the relationship between class, style, and ideology, I have tried to look at the problem in terms of the poets themselves – how they viewed their art in relation to their education and upbringing, and how it embodies ideological perspectives arising from that experience and their subsequent careers.

Although it is difficult to prove empirically, it seems likely that the formation of a poetics may be related to social background in various crucial ways. First of all, the opportunity to experience and learn about poetry depends upon the kind and quality of education received both at home and at school. Quite clearly it is impossible to begin to write poetry without attaining a fairly sophisticated level of literacy. Furthermore, assuming that such a level is gained, an exposure to particular kinds of poetry has a direct bearing upon an early appreciation of specific writers and various traditions. These may then be emulated or later reacted against as the poet concerned struggles to find his or her own voice. At a more complex and necessarily more conjectural level, it may be posited that anybody in the struggle for self-realisation must either accept or reject the values and mores inherited from parents and the wider culture. This reaction to social background is not only an act of individuation with obvious psychological and political ramifications, but also, in the case of writers, must surely affect both the choice of poetic progenitors and their vision of the world. What I am suggesting here then, to borrow some of Eagleton's terminology, is that aesthetic ideology has an admittedly problematical relationship with inherited political ideologies.

Most poets of the 1930s sought, in their various ways, to build upon two distinct developments of nineteenth-century Romanticism: the modernism of Eliot, Pound and Yeats with its reactionary political flavouring, and the more liberal, specifically English, Georgian tradition through poets like Wilfred Owen and Edward Thomas. Despite the bluster of Eliot and Pound about the 'classical' orientation of their work, it seems to me clear that both their poetry and poetics derive in large measure from late nineteenth-century French Symbolism, which in turn may be related to earlier theorists of Romanticism. If we define Romanticism as an impulse to create order from chaos, harmony from division, through a metaphysics of integration predicated upon the healing powers of the imagination or art, then, I think, we are obliged to recognise, with critics like Northrop Frye, that all twentieth-century poetry is Romantic in origin.

At this point some further remarks are necessary about the competing claims of Georgianism and modernism. Literary history this century has privileged the latter at the expense of the former, just as it has privileged the poetry of the 1930s (or at least some of it) at the expense of poetry of the 1940s. It has become customary to write Georgian poetry off as sentimental, conservative, and trivial, whilst modernism is perceived to be serious, intellectual and innovative. The reputation of such poets as Edward Thomas has largely been established by claiming that they were not really Georgian.[12] In this study the word 'Georgian' is not by any means necessarily used in this way as a pejorative, but rather to denote a complex of stylistic and ideological attitudes which are at variance with those of modernism.

The nineteenth-century precursors of Georgianism are Wordsworth and Hardy. Accordingly the style of Georgian poetry rejoices in traditional, often balladic, forms, in largely conventional syntax and metre, in plain language and unelevated tones. Often the subject-matter accords with this 'low' style, and narrative elements are not uncommon. Stylistically modernism presents itself as more radical; it eschews stanzaic forms, adopts a fractured or tortuous syntax, habitually deploys irony, elevates the image at the expense of narrative, and is often tonally elevated and self-consciously 'difficult'.

Now there can be no question that modernists like Eliot, Pound and Yeats were also radical in their politics. They were, to give them their kindest appellation, radical Tories. But does this mean that Georgian poetry and poetics represent a bland, conservative acceptance of the status quo? And it is here that I wish to make a point crucial to the proper understanding of 1930s poetry. For the inaugurators of Georgian poetry were not wholly conservative in their politics. As Robert Ross has pointed out, most of them were Fabian Socialists or at least had sympathies in that direction.[13]

This liberal political tendency may be directly related to the aims of the Georgian movement promulgated by the *Georgian poetry* anthologies, edited by Edward Marsh, and published through Harold Monro's Poetry Bookshop between 1911 and 1922. These young idealistic poets wanted to popularise poetry, to find for poetry the audience they thought it deserved. By contrast Eliot and Pound took the opposite view: poetry was for the few, the intellectually élite, the uncompromisingly highbrow.

To return to the problems of the young poets of the 1930s: in changing social and political circumstances they were faced with forging their own poetry and poetics from their dual inheritance. Most of them produced hybrid styles combining elements of modernism and Georgianism. What is fascinating, however, is the way poets from differing class and educational backgrounds reacted differently to their shared aesthetic inheritance, and thus produced differing varieties of hybrid which expressed distinct ideological nuances.

Most published poetry of the 1930s was written by members of the middle class. But the complexities of the English class system are such that further distinctions are necessary in any analysis of a poet's social position. Here I have used the divisions of upper-middle, middle-middle and lower-middle class to characterise differences of social and educational background. It will be objected that such categorisations are hazardous because demarcations between them are very difficult to express definitively. But it seemed to me better to use such admittedly difficult terminology, rather than simply accept the literary historical precedent, which ignores such divisions, and relies upon a notion that the English middle class perceived no divisions within itself. My study seeks to make clear that the various poets dealt with were acutely aware, as most English people still are, of the nuances of social position within the middle class.

Such nice differences of origin are matched by equally nice distinctions in the ideology embodied in the various poets' work. And here we encounter difficulties of nomenclature when describing different degrees of conservatism. As my remarks about Georgian poetry imply, I take liberalism to represent a non-revolutionary critique of society; it seeks change within the existing structures of power and government. Liberalism is an active and humane conservatism. Alternatively conservatism accepts the status quo and applauds those historical institutions which uphold it. More radical right-wing ideologies are of two kinds. The radical Tory mounts a vehement critique of the status quo and seeks a further abrogation of power to traditional and hierarchical institutions. In its extreme form this, of course, leads to Fascism. The right-wing anarchist, on the other hand, is in vigorous opposition to society and its institutions, but offers no alternative system of government, extolling only individualism.

Liberalism then, in my view, has nothing to do with radicalism of the right or left. When speaking of left-wing ideology I am specifically referring to Socialism underpinned by Marxist thought. But it is only in the balladry of the working class, and in the pugnacious work of Hugh MacDiarmid, that we will find poetry in alliance with such thought. Just as English politics of the 1930s is dominated not by the much publicised minority groups of the left, but by an overwhelming conservatism, so too we will discover that the poetry of the decade is dominated by varying degrees of conservatism.

In trying to identify 'groups' of poets who share similar class and educational backgrounds, and similar aesthetic and ideological orientations, there are various dangers. Firstly, there is the problem of determinism, of implying that because a writer experienced a particular social background, he or she necessarily wrote in a particular way. Of course such an idea is unsatisfactory; the formation of style, of poetics, of ideology is infinitely complex and one would not wish to discount the parts played by individual pyschology and individual experience. What I am concerned to do in this study is to redress a perceived imbalance in previous accounts of the decade by stressing what I consider to be the importance of these social factors in the production and reception of art. Secondly, by grouping the poets as I have, there is a danger of obliterating the individual voice of each poet dealt with. I have tried to avoid this difficulty by outlining, at the beginning of each chapter, the characteristics shared by a particular group and have then proceeded to look at individual manifestations of style. In this way I hope to present a version of the 1930s which suggests a pattern, yet challenges the dominance of Auden by demonstrating the range of styles which were assayed in the decade. Thirdly, there is the problem of gender and class which I have not attempted to deal with here. The fact that very few women poets are dealt with in this study follows from the infrequency with which their work was published and discussed in the major literary periodicals of the decade. The literary world of the 1930s was male-dominated, and this study reflects that fact without wishing to condone it.

The obvious objection to any revisionist attempt such as this aims to be is that one myth is destroyed merely to create another which is equally vulnerable. In some serious senses there is no answer to this problem. But it seems to me, that if we are committed to poetry and to its continued relevance to our culture, then criticism must be prepared to seek an understanding of the mechanisms by which literary reputations and traditions become enshrined. If, in attempting this, it is admitted that there are no final definitive answers, this does not necessarily rob the pursuit of value or importance. History and literary history may be defined as the imposition of an individual's present sensibility upon the difficult, sometimes intractable, materials of the past. And, like any other historian or literary historian, I embark in the hope that the arguments presented and the evidence adduced here, might challenge received notions and stimulate further thought about poetry, not only of the past but also of the present and future.

In order to revise a myth, clearly it is imperative to establish exactly what that received system of ideas and images constitutes. In order to do this, it seems to me necessary to first of all look at the history of the decade. For the history and the literary history are of course subtly intertwined, and the history of the decade has been mythologised as much as its literary history. When we think of the 1930s certain images immediately spring to mind usually aligned with notions of crisis and political turbulence. In my first chapter then, I look at the history of the decade and try, to some extent at least, to penetrate historical myths about the period, and to give some idea of the social and political realities through which the poets lived and with which they attempted to grapple in their different ways.

Notes

1 R. Barthes, *Mythologies*, trans. A. Lavers, New York, 1972.
2 J. Symons, *The thirties: a dream revolved* (revd. ed.), London, 1975, pp. 75, 142.
3 S. Hynes, *The Auden generation: literature and politics in the 1930s*, London, 1976.
4 B. Bergonzi, *Reading the thirties: texts and contexts*, London, 1978, p. 1.
5 D. Wright, 'A life paid on both sides', *Times educational supplement*, 7 March 1980, p. 27.
6 A. Prochaska, *Young writers of the thirties*, London, 1976.
7 There were some few exhibits relating to Edward Upward and John Lehmann, writers who were friends of the Auden 'gang'.
8 V. Cunningham, *British writers of the thirties*, Oxford, 1988.
9 *Ibid.*, p. 17.
10 *Ibid.*
11 Bergonzi, *Reading the thirties*, pp. 8 and 144.
12 See J. Reeves, 'Introduction', *Georgian poetry*, Harmondsworth, 1962, pp. 11-23.
13 R. Ross, *The Georgian revolt*, London, 1965, p. 12.

1

The myth of the hungry decade

The word 'hungry' is applied to the 1930s in the same way that we hear of the 'roaring 1920s' or 'swinging 1960s'. Such characterisation of a decade by a single adjective is part of a process of mythologisation which begins when history is decimalised by artificially wresting a decade from the continuum. Then, certain words, images and ideas, are habitually associated with each other accruing significances not necessarily inherent in them, until in the absence of further information or criticism, these associations come to have the appearance of truth. Thus we are encouraged to think of the 1930s, neatly framed by the Wall Street Crash and the outbreak of the Second World War, as a time of 'crisis' dominated by extremist politics. Other images and events come easily to mind: dole queues, the Jarrow Crusade, Moseley and the British Union of Fascists, the 'King and Country' debate at Oxford, the Peace Pledge Union and the Peace Ballot, the activities of the Left Book Club. All these contribute to the notion that the 1930s was a time of widespread political agitation and activism. At this point the historical and literary-historical myths intersect. For it is a commonplace of literary history that young poets of the 1930s belonged to a radical, left-wing intelligentsia deeply involved in the issues of the day. And, just as major political events demarcate the beginning and end of the decade, so in literary history Auden's career provides a parallel structure. His first commercial publication appeared in 1930 and he left England for America in 1939 thus occasioning the 'English Auden' to be entirely distinguished from the 'American'.

But before going on to discuss further the lineaments of the literary-historical problem it is necessary to take a closer look at the history of the decade. If it can be shown that there are perspectives which call into question the myth of England tottering on the brink of revolution or about to sink under the depression, then this clearly has implications for a discussion of the supposedly radical 1930s poets.

Any rehearsal of international occurrences between 1929 and 1939 clearly indicates why the idea of 'crisis' is endemic to the times.

Hitler became Chancellor of Germany in 1933, and in March assumed dictatorial powers. Two years later Italy attacked Abyssinia, and by 1936 had completed the conquest of that country. In the same year Germany re-militarised the Rhineland, and in July Fascist insurgents began their rebellion against the Republican government in Spain. In 1937 the Japanese resumed their hostilities against China by taking Peking, Nanking and Shanghai, the Rome–Berlin–Tokyo axis by this time being virtually cemented. In March of the following year, Germany occupied Austria and, after the infamous Munich Agreement in September, went on to annex the Sudetenland of Czechoslovakia, a country which was finally overrun in March 1939. In the same month the disunited forces of the left and centre finally succumbed to Franco's Fascists in Spain. The Nazi–Soviet pact in August 1939 and the German invasion of Poland a month later were the final preludes to a World War that several European powers had struggled to avoid for some years.

The manifest turbulence on the continent of Europe encourages visions of England in the same throes. Some historical accounts have chosen to dwell upon those aspects of the decade which propound a view of Britain in the grips of 'crisis' and left-wing fervour. The social history of the period written by Margot Heinemann and Noreen Branson tends in this direction. Britain is described as suffering, with other industrial nations, the 'devastating impact' of the 'worst slump ever known'.[1] A rhetoric of dramatic exaggeration informs other generalisations made without adequate supporting evidence. It is said, for instance, that a widespread feeling came into being that the slump signified a 'mortal disease' which 'called in question the continued existence of the capitalist system itself'.[2] The unemployed are described as being 'engaged in bitter and massive conflict with the state', whilst the population as a whole, 'the casual observer and the most cursory reader of the popular press' is credited with an awareness of the situation.[3] All this is very impressionistic indeed and leads one to wonder amongst whom the 'feelings' that capitalism was a 'mortal disease' became widespread and, more importantly, what any such people did about their feelings? And one must surely question the very generous impulses implicitly atrributed to the popular press here. For myself I find it very difficult to imagine the cursory reader of Lord Rothermere's *Daily mail*, *Evening news*, *Sunday dispatch* or *Sunday pictorial*, being forced into political observations of a nature contrary to the extreme right-wing bias of these publications.[4]

Relatively recently historical research has sought a less emotive assessment than that of Heinemann and Branson. Taking his lead from a review in which A.J.P. Taylor was prompted to ask of the 1930s, 'which was more significant for the future – over a million unemployed or over a million private cars', John Stevenson published an invaluable essay, *Myth and reality: Britain in the thirties.*[5] This was followed by a book, *The slump,*[6] which elaborated the arguments advanced there. These closely documented accounts, whilst not wishing to minimise the importance of unemployment or the deprivations it gave rise to, are also concerned to demonstrate other aspects of the decade. The authors show that unemployment reached its peak in the winter of 1932-3 when the figures reached almost the three million mark . Although there were never less than one million unemployed throughout the 1930s, and between 1931 and 1935 there was an average of over two million, it is salutary to remember that there was never less than seventy-five per cent of the population in work, that new industries were developing in the South of England, that the suburbs were prosperous and standards of living were rising. Against the regional unemployment affecting Northern Ireland, industrial Scotland, the North-East, South Wales and Lancashire, one has to balance the new industrial structure which was being established predominantly in the South of England. The basis of this was the electricity supply industry. A boom in supply not only transformed methods of production, but also what was being produced. Electrical appliances such as mains radio, gramophones, irons, vacuum cleaners and lighting equipment were manufactured and made available to an ever-increasing market. This expansion together with the development of construction, chemicals and motor industries resulted in a rise of real living standards for those in work calculated for the decade at between fifteen and eighteen per cent. By 1939 there were over two million private vehicles licensed in Britain and between 1935 and 1940 35,000 houses were built, a figure only exceeded between 1945 and 1964.

As Stevenson and Cook demonstrate, these figures help towards an understanding of the most pertinent political question of the decade as far as Britain is concerned, that is, 'Not why the swing to political extremism was so great, but why it was, in fact so small'.[7] That the swing was indeed small is clearly indicated by the dominance of the national government throughout the decade and the comparatively small membership of activist radical organisations. The Labour Party was routed in 1931, and for the rest of the decade was unable to provide adequate alternative policies, confining itself to a sympathetic attitude to unemployment and a questioning of the government particularly over the means test. It was not a successful decade for the Communist Party of Great Britain either. Only one Communist MP was elected in 1931 and the membership was at a low ebb during the worst years of the depression, paradoxically increasing from six thousand to 17,756 in the latter half of the decade as economic recovery began. This increase was largely due to the reaction of the intelligentsia to the rise of Fascism in Europe.

The Communist-dominated National Unemployed Workers Movement was formed to promote agitation in the class war, and by December 1932 had a membership of fifty thousand, but after 1933 the movement began to decline. The TUC's Unemployment Association could boast a similar maximum membership, but was ideologically opposed to Communism and, like the Labour Party, adopted a supportive rather than an activist role. Only minorities supported such hunger marches and demonstrations as there were. The NUWM inspired marches of 1932, 1934, and 1936 each involved only between one and two thousand participants. The famous Jarrow Crusade, which is 'almost synonymous' with working-class agitation in the 1930s,[8] was one of the smallest, involving only two hundred men. This was organised independently of the NUWM and indeed was politically opposed to extremism; one man was expelled from the march because he was a Communist. The march was effectual only in terms of publicity. A.J.P. Taylor offers the opinion that middle-class consciences were aroused, and cites the generous reception of marchers in various places as evidence for this.[9]

Clearly there was some sympathy for the marchers among the middle classes, but this was only translated into political action by a very few. Generally the reaction of the middle classes was traditional in that their pity was never strong enough to overcome their fear of working-class agitation, a fear which had been entrenched in English culture since the industrial revolution.[10] This, together with Labour's weakness, the British working-class distrust of Communism, the easing of the economic situation after 1934, the highly regionalised nature of unemployment and rising living standards, lead one to the conclusion drawn by Orwell in 1936 that there was no political turbulence left in England.[11]

Orwell, here and elsewhere, supports the thesis that conservatism was the most important political feature of the decade. In 'England your England' Orwell writes: 'However much one may hate to admit it, it is almost certain that between 1931 and 1940 the National Government represented the will of the mass of the people'.[12] This applied as much in foreign affairs as it did in domestic policy. The traditional insularity of most British people was exacerbated by an overwhelming desire to avoid another World War. Support for movements like the Peace Pledge Union and the Peace Ballot was widespread, and as Orwell says, 'In spite of the campaigns of a few thousand left-wingers, it is fairly certain that the bulk of the English people were behind Chamberlain's foreign policy'.[13] The desire for peace was one of the rare attitudes which for a time was shared by all classes, but with the outbreak of the Spanish Civil War some of the intellectual left and some radicals of the working class abandoned the pacifist position, thereby departing from majority feelings.

It is precisely this minority movement which has gained most publicity and become part of the myth of the 1930s. Undoubtedly the Spanish Civil War was a crucial event for some intellectuals. Having been engaged in a paper debate since the beginning of the decade, the conflict between left and right was now rendered in immediate physical terms; a focus was provided for ideology to be transformed into action. The extent of British involvement in Spain, however, can be easily over-estimated. Only four thousand volunteeers reached Spain from Britain. Of these some were militant workers, others middle-class intellectuals, and one suspects that a proportion of these were less motivated by politics than a need for belief, escape and adventure: the 'swimmers into cleanness leaping' of Rupert Brooke's famous sonnet, 'Peace'.[14] Apart from the heroics of the few, internationalism did not thrive. Once again it is Orwell who provides the most telling description of this when he remarks upon the lack of support given to the Spanish workers by the British working class. But when England was threatened by Germany, men rushed to join Local Defence Volunteers in huge numbers.[15] And of course it was not only the working class who reacted in this way. When the population as a whole is taken into account nationalism in Britain always seems to have been a stronger emotion than internationalism.

But we should beware of taking Orwell's essentially negative view of the 1930s as definitive, just as we should be on our guard against any implication that Stevenson and Cook's version of the decade corresponds to any absolute 'reality'. I have used the work of the last-named historians as a corrective to received ideas about the nature and extent of the depression, and of the political dissent it gave rise to. And predictably Stevenson and Cook offer an alternative view to Orwell's pessimism. They argue that the 1930s provided an 'indirect legacy' which 'conditioned the shaping of war-time and post-war policy'. In other words they believe that the years of the Second World War which led to the Labour victory of 1945 and the evolution of the Welfare State, were conditioned by the experiences of the 1930s. Stevenson and Cook demonstrate that the historical significance of the 1930s can only be fully understood by relating the decade to the continuum.

What the bald rehearsal of facts and figures which I have presented so far does not, however, do is to illustrate in any forceful manner the way in which the political and economic events and conditions of the decade impinged upon the lived experience of various sections of the population. Since I am interested to place the poetry of the decade into the context of the society in which it was produced and received, it is, I think, useful to flesh out this raw data in order to show the heterogeneous nature of that society. Despite the rising living standards for those in work, Britain in the 1930s was a society in which distinctions between class affected every area of experience. Nowhere can this be more readily shown than in matters concerning education, housing and employment. To take these three areas in turn, let us begin with education.

In the 1920s and 1930s, and indeed until the Education Act of 1944, elementary schools provided the basis of education for the lower classes. These schools catered for children aged 5-14, and as Arthur Marwick notes, they were 'quintessentially working class'.[16] Many elementary school teachers were impressed not with their pupils' ability or aptitude for learning, but rather with 'the inadequacy of their clothing, their diet, and their personal hygiene'.[17] The only alternative secondary education, apart from the public schools, were the maintained and aided secondary schools, sometimes called grammar schools, more often referred to as 'county' schools. In order to get to such a school a competitive examination had to be passed at the age of ten, and the child's parents had to be able to afford books and fees. A quantity of free places were available, but in some local authorities those who sought them had to face a tougher exam. It followed then, that such schools were predominantly middle-class, although it was possible for highly intelligent children of the working class to win a place there.

The maintained, county schools (we may call them grammar schools for convenience) provided some little opportunity for class divisions to be crossed, but the number of people who so benefited was very small indeed. In 1934, for instance, only six per cent of those educated in such schools reached tertiary education, and of those who began their careers in elementary schools only four in every thousand went to a university, and one in 1,000 to Oxford or Cambridge.[18] During the inter-war years, the vast majority of children left school before they were sixteen. As L.C.B. Seaman has noted, seventy per cent of all children began earning at fourteen years of age, and ninety per cent at fifteen. He goes on to point out that this was 'indicative of the hard economic fact that working-class and lower-middle-class earnings were unequal to the cost of maintaining an adolescent who, by staying at school, added to the expenses of a household while contributing nothing to its income … The sixth form was, therefore, reserved for a tiny minority who would enter teaching, the civil service, nursing and university courses'.[19] If this is true of the grammar schools then it becomes quite clear that it was only the aspiring middle-middle class, and the solidly wealthy upper-middle and upper classes who could avail themselves of the benefits of preparatory and public-school education, and in turn of the universities, in particular Oxford and Cambridge. It is this fact which gives rise to a paradox articulated by Seaman when he says that the grammar schools tended to sharpen class divisions, because they made an intelligent minority more aware than they might otherwise have been of 'the contrast between the deprivations endured by the many and the privileges enjoyed by the few'.[20]

In the 1920s and 1930s class and educational background were intimately related. I leave it to the reader to judge how far this situation has changed today. But in 1956 it was possible for a historian of the 1930s to remark: 'Only in England is education, still, quite strictly, a matter of social class, in that it is normal for children of the upper-middle and upper-classes to go to a special kind of school in which children of the lower-middle and working-classes are rarely met with'.[21] The implications of all this for the reading and writing of literature of the 1930s are not difficult to infer. In elementary schools and grammar schools before the sixth form, if poetry was met with at all, it was by way of rote learning passages from Shakespeare, or poems of the 'literary war-horses of the Nineteenth Century'.[22] On the other hand, pupils at the public schools not only imbibed a classical education, with all that that implies of appreciating grammar, syntax and metrics, but also were taught English poetry from a relatively early age. As the testimony of poets like Auden, MacNeice, and Day Lewis makes clear, apt pupils also benefited from associations with enthusiastic masters and older pupils who introduced them to the writings of contemporary poets. And, although it would be silly to deny the possibility of transcending the limitations of one's education, at least to some extent, the ideological assumptions gained in one's formative years should not be under-estimated. If it was taken for granted in the public schools that the pupils would form the political and artistic élite of the society, then it was equally sure that the elementary schools were teaching the sons and daughters of the working classes to know and recognise their place in the scheme of things.

The three-tiered education system consisting of elementary, grammar and public schools catering roughly for working, middle, and upper classes has an analogue with respect to housing. Terraced, semi-detached and detached, accommodation provided immediate physical evidence of the same broad social divisions. Nicer distinctions between sections of the population could be easily perceived from the precise dimensions of the dwellings concerned. At one end of the scale were the huge country houses with their attendant estates inhabited by the landed and titled gentry, then sliding down slightly there were the four or five-bedroomed homes of the suburban upper-middle-class ('Stockbroker tudor'),[23] then there were the smaller detached or large semis of the middle-middle class and so on down to the terraces of the working class. At this end of the scale too, there are important, and too frequently ignored distinctions to be made. Not all of the working class in the 1930s were slum dwellers. The families of skilled and semi-skilled men who had employment lived in the relative comfort of terraces with two downstairs rooms and a back kitchen, with two or three rooms upstairs. But the slide down the scale from here to two-up, two-downs in back to back rows or one-up, one-downs in similar arrangements is swift and dramatic and by this route we arrive at the slum tenements of the urban poor.

The best way to illustrate the distinctions I am identifying is photographically,[24] but some idea of the yawning chasm between the very rich and the very poor may perhaps be rendered in words. Here is P.G. Wodehouse describing Bertie Wooster's arrival at 'Totleigh Towers', the home of 'Sir Watkyn Bassett', in his novel, *The code of the Woosters* (1938).

... Old Bassett, I noted, had laid out his money to excellent advantage. I am a bit of a connoisseur of country houses, and I found this one well up to sample. Nice facade, spreading grounds, smoothly shaven lawns, and a general atmosphere of what is known as old world peace. Cows were in the distance, sheep and birds respectively bleating and tootling, and from somewhere near at hand came the report of a gun, indicating that someone was having a whirl at the local rabbits. Totleigh Towers might be a place where man was vile, but undoubtedly every prospect pleased ...

The cup of tea on arrival at a country house is a thing which, as a rule, I particularly enjoy. I like the crackling logs, the shaded lights, the scent of buttered toast, the general atmosphere of leisured cosiness ...[25]

Despite the fictional context, and the whimsicality of tone here, this passage provides a neat and telling contrast with a number of case-histories designed to highlight the problem of slum-dwelling, published in the *Architect's journal* in 1933. Here we find the stark realities of a man, wife and six children living in one room in Manchester, or of four families inhabiting one house in Liverpool, of father, mother and six children living in two upstairs rooms with a leaky roof and no running water.[26] Examples like this were not difficult to find. In 1934 the BBC broadcast a series of talks by unemployed men and women, the published record of which is a trenchant documentation of the worst kinds of poverty. Here again we learn of families living in two or three rooms with no sink, water closet, pantry, copper or cooking stove, where water had to be carried up several flights of stairs. Large numbers of children had to share a bedroom with one or two adults, and the sharing of a bed by five persons or a bedroom by ten was not unheard of. Sir E. D. Simon writing in his *Anti-slum campaign*, although acknowledging that it was difficult to determine precisely the full extent of the slum problem, estimated that there were probably four million dwellings in England and Wales which came into that category.[27]

It will be recalled that the 1930s was a time when many new houses were built, but this was private enterprise housing designed for purchase by those who could afford the market price. So countryside gradually gave way to ribbon developement and suburbs, where the salaried workers of the middle-middle and lower-middle classes could now afford their own homes and gardens. There was some building of council houses and flats for the more prosperous members of the working class, but such accommodation was clearly demarcated from the wealthier privately-owned homes by size, quality and geographical location. Arthur Marwick makes this plain: 'Class distinctions were very clear in the dwellings which arose out of the housing boom of the period . . . The classic instance of the class divide is the case of the Cutteslowe Wall in Oxford, where a wall was actually built to divide a working-class local authority housing estate from a middle-class private developer's estate.'[28] Such segregation not only divided working from middle class. Only marginally more subtle than building walls between people was the Town and Country Planning Act of 1932 which proposed 'zoning' of houses at 1, 8, or 12 to the acre, thereby ensuring that the middle classes would be clearly divided by income difference.[29]

But who cared? As Seaman says, 'For those who had regular work and a steady income, the 'thirties were serene years'.[30] Perhaps 'serene' is going a bit too far. We should not forget that working-class life as a whole was extremely difficult. But relatively, working people were better off than their fathers had been. And the prosperous working class were rightly proud of their clean, warm homes with their arduously donkey-stoned door-step and gleaming brass fender in the parlour. The front room would be maintained in a state of pristine readiness for entertaining the vicar, priest or for other special occasions. They were used very rarely. It was in this room too that aspidistras were regularly dusted.[31] A greater variety of foods, clothes and leisure activities were available to the inhabitants of such homes than had ever been known before. The 1930s saw the working class beginning to emerge not only as mass-producers but also as mass-consumers. It was the decade of Woolworths stores and of mass advertisements.

In leisure hours the local pub provided a solace for many working men, and on Saturdays there was the association football match, greyhound or pigeon racing. The 'pictures', dance-halls, and music-halls provided theatrical, social and courting opportunities for both men and women. There was even the very remote possibility of owning a battery-operated radio and listening to the BBC's Dance Orchestra or, later in the decade, to Arthur Askey in Band waggon.[32] At Bank Holiday for some there would be day-trips to the seaside by train. For a few there might be a week's holiday each year or every other year (holidays with pay began in 1938).

The middle classes had more time, space, money and leisure than the working class to enjoy the various commodities and pastimes on offer. They were able to dress more fashionably and expensively, to eat more sumptuously and to live more variously than their less privileged contemporaries. The middle-middle to upper-middle classes would, perhaps, listen to their radiograms rather less than the lower-middle-class, for the former could afford to attend concerts, theatre, the opera, restaurants, and for some, society balls. The men could also play or watch amateur sport, cricket or 'rugger'. To be an *amateur* was very important socially as it signified that one had the time and money to 'play-up, play-up and play the game', for its own sake. Professionalism in sport was equated with poverty and with the working class.[33] Hence the development of semi-professional rugby league in the industrial towns of the North – the sport of miners, rather than the sport of kings. For the women, meanwhile, there were morning-teas, charity functions, at-homes and bridge-parties.

In the home, the trials of domestic life for the middle classes were alleviated by the presence of servants or new electrical domestic appliances or both:

To have at least one servant was so essential a mark of respectability that in 1931 nearly one in every five households still had at least one full-time domestic living-in, and the employment of a daily-maid complete with cap and apron, was not beyond the means of a grammar school teacher who had paid off his mortgage or reached his maximum salary. Servants were increasingly difficult to get in the towns, above all in the South East, but as late as 1939 a well-off family of three in the West Country might employ a cook, a housemaid, and a chauffeur gardener ...[34]

Even if the household budget could not run to a servant, the new gadgetry – electrical washing machines, irons, vacuum cleaners – considerably improved the lot of the housewife. And for the wealthier woman there was the promise of holidays, of drives in the motor, or at least a sit-down in the assiduously tended garden on a sunny day. (Even the lower-middle class prided themselves upon their gardens; the cultivation of roses was a particular vogue of the 1930s.) In working-class homes, a woman's work was likely to be as physically arduous and mentally stultifying as her husband's.

It is of little purpose here to further rehearse the leisured lifestyle of the very rich. Suffice it to say that their opulent, leisured existence looks sadly decadent when one turns to consider the poverty at the other end of the scale. Here we encounter the greatest social divide of the period: that between the employed and those who were either unemployed or casually employed. Those people that we might call the non-working class formed a kind of sub-group whose sufferings were largely ignored by the population as a whole. Despite the attempts of various middle-class writers and journalists to publicise their plight, their lot would only be improved by the return to full-employment engendered by the war, and the instigation of social welfare in the post-war years. The published testimony of the 1934 BBC talks by unemployed men and women provide scarifying documentation of the worst aspects of the decade. The following words of a Mrs Pallas may be said to speak for several million people who because of the slump were consigned to an under-class through no fault of their own:

If only he had work. Just imagine what it would be like. On the whole, my husband has worked about one year out of twelve and a half. His face was lovely when I married him, but now he's skin and bones. When I married he was robust and had a good job. He was earning from eight pounds to ten pounds a week. He's a left-handed ship's riveter − a craft which could be earning him a lot of money ...

He fell out of work about four months after I was married, so I've hardly known what a week's wage was. Through all the struggling I've still not lost my respectability ...

My husband never changes his dole money, but although he doesn't keep a halfpenny pocket-money, still we can't manage. And we don't waste nothing. And there's no enjoyment comes out of our money − no pictures, no papers, no sports. Everything's patched and mended in our house ...

We very, very rarely get cheese. We all like it, but it is a bit of a luxury. When there are birthdays we have it. I can't manage more than one box of matches a week − that's all we ever use. Many a time we've sat in the dark it is gas light, and we haven't a penny for the slot, maybe, or we haven't a match. Rather than let people know, we sat in the dark ...

I don't know to whatever I'll put the boys. I've no idea whatever. I think they ought to know what's happening in the world, but we can't afford any newspaper ... What's gone is past, but I wouldn't like to live a minute of my life over again. All the struggling is just for food ... I have no hope that my husband will ever work again.[35]

It should not be thought that this is unusual or exaggerated. Other personal accounts like this, and further independent testimony, demonstrate that such hardship was a commonplace amongst the unemployed. Their diet consisted of bread, margarine or dripping, tea, and the occasional can of condensed milk. The already established physical differences between the working class and the rest of the population due to poor diet and hard physical labour were thus exacerbated, and many children of these impoverished families grew up with rickets. It was also a cruel paradox that the poorer the family, the larger it tended to be. Practising contraception was a matter of both education and wealth. So families of five, six and seven lived off the pittance allowed to them by the dole. The average weekly expenditure on food for such a family would be about 2s 6d a head, whereas it was calculated that the 'average' expenditure on food per head in the 1930s was 9s.[36] As Seaman has aptly remarked, 'for the working class, tragedy was not enacted on a stage by hired mimic sufferers whom one could observe as one pleased. It was something in which they were involved, and which was as inevitable as pregnancy, sickness and old age.'[37]

One cannot hope in such a limited space to do justice to the complexities of a social history of the 1930s. What I have tried to illustrate here are some of the salient characteristics of the decade. There is a fairly clear consensus amongst social historians that class was a major determinant in the way that life was lived. I have tried to give some idea of this. I have also tried to illustrate the most telling paradoxes of the decade; whilst for the majority living standards were steadily improving, conditions for the unfortunate minority were appalling; political conservatism dominated the decade, electorally obliterating the radicalism of the few. It was against this background that young poets of the upper-middle class created a myth of themselves as socially concerned, left-wing poets. It is a myth which liberal commentators have perpetuated, ignoring other poets who were not part of the myth and did not come from the same class and educational background. This literary-historical myth privileges a certain kind of poetry which arises from a particular set of circum-stances and from particular lived experiences. By contextualising their writing in terms of the society as a whole, and by looking beyond the upper-middle-class poets of the decade, this study seeks to redress a perceived imbalance. The next step in this pursuit is to move from the historical myth of the thirties, to that of literary history, in order to see how this myth came into being, what it represents, and how it has been perpetuated in recent years. This is a step which inevitably removes us from the historical details articulated here, into the rarefied air of intellectual, aesthetic and academic debate. But this excursion will be relatively brief. When I come to deal with the poets and poetry of the decade it is hoped that what has been said here will shed further light on my discussion, and enable the reader to judge more precisely than other commentators have done so far, to what extent Auden's poetry 'represents' or 'is' the 1930s.

Notes

1   M. Heinemann and N. Branson, *Britain in the nineteen-thirties*, London, 1971, p. 1.
2   Ibid., p. 2.
3   Ibid., p. 5.
4   J. Stevenson and C. Cook, *The Slump: society and politics during the depression*, London, 1977, p. 203.
5   J. Stevenson, 'Myth and reality: Britain in the nineteen-thirties', *Crisis and controversy*, ed. A. Sked and C. Cook, London, 1976, pp. 90-110.
6   Stevenson and Cook, *The Slump*.
7   Stevenson, *Crisis and controversy*, p. 95.
8. Stevenson and Cook, *The Slump*, p. 184.
9   A.J.P. Taylor, *English history 1914-45*, Oxford, 1965, p. 349.
10 R. Williams, *Culture and society, 1780-1950* (1958), Harmondsworth, 1979, pp. 99-136.
11 G. Orwell,'The road to Wigan pier diary', *Collected essays, journalism, and letters* (1968), Harmondsworth, 1976, Vol. 1, p. 207.
12 G. Orwell, 'England your England', *The lion and the unicorn*, London, 1941, p. 31.
13. Ibid.
14 R. Brooke, 'Peace', *1914 and other poems*, London, 1941, p. 11.
15 Orwell, *The lion and the unicorn*, p. 27.
16 A. Marwick, *Britain in our century*, London, 1984, p. 100.
17 L.C.B. Seaman, *Life in Britain between the wars*, London, 1970, p. 102.
18 Ibid., p. 108.
19. Ibid., pp. 106-7.
20 Ibid., p. 111.
21 J.D. Scott, *Life in Britain*, London, 1956, p. 169.
22 Seaman, *Life in Britain between the wars*, p. 103.
23 The phrase was coined by the cartoonist Osbert Lancaster. See Marwick, *Britain in our century*, pp. 94-5.
24 See, for example, J. Symons, *The angry 30s*, London, 1976; J. Symons, *Between the wars: Britain in photographs*, London, 1972; Marwick, *Britain in our century*.
25 P.G. Wodehouse, *The code of the Woosters*, London, 1938, pp. 46-7, 67.
26 M. and N. Ward, *Home in the twenties and thirties*, London, 1978, p. 80.
27 Ibid.
28 Marwick, *Britain in our century*, pp. 99-100.
29 Ward, *Home in the twenties and thirties*, p. 74.
30 Seaman, *Life in Britain between the wars*, p. 188.
31 I thought that the aspidistra might be a 'mythical' property, but I am assured by several people who lived in working-class terraced housing in the 1930s that they were very popular. Certainly I remember my grandmother's!
32 A. Jenkins, *The thirties*, London, 1976, p. 132.
33 Seaman, *Life in Britain between the wars*, pp. 160-3.
34 Ibid., pp. 158-9.
35 Quoted by P. Mauger and L. Smith, *The British people 1902-1968*, London, 1969, pp. 119-20. See also Seaman, *Life in Britain between the wars*, pp. 174-6.
36 Seaman, *Life in Britain between the wars*, p. 176.
37 Ibid., p. 171.

2

The making of a literary-historical myth

In 1933 Julian Bell, then an undergraduate at Cambridge, wrote a letter to the *New statesman* in which he established Auden and his 'group' as the leaders of a literary and political cabal:

> By the end of 1933, we have arrived at a situation in which almost the only subject of discussion is contemporary politics, and in which a very large majority of the more intelligent undergraduates are Communists or almost Communists. As far as an interest in literature continues it has very largely changed its character and become an ally of Communism under the influence of Mr. Auden's Oxford group. Indeed, it might, with some plausibility be argued that Communism in England is at present largely a literary phenomenon – an attempt of a second post-war generation to escape from the Waste Land.[1]

Although in the rest of his letter, Bell shows himself to be acutely aware of the mixed motivations his peers had for adopting Communism, and is able to document the 'prevalent hysterical enthusiasm', he is already clearly committed to the notion that Auden is the leader of a group of Communist poets who are already said to constitute a particular 'generation'. How had Auden achieved such a reputation so quickly? After all, by 1933, he had only published one commerical volume of poems,[2] one play, and that curious *mélange* of prose and poetry, The orators. And these books were by no means reaching a vast audience. By the end of 1933, Auden's *Poems* (1930) had sold about a thousand copies, and The orators rather less than that number.[3] That such sales are not bad as far as poetry goes is not in question. But for the 'spokesman' of a generation to be reaching such a small audience is surely very telling. And, as I shall demonstrate when we come to look at Auden's 1930s work, one turns in vain to *Poems*, The orators (1932) or The dance of death (1933), for evidence to suggest that Auden was writing from a Marxist perspective. In the cramped, elliptical early poems one detects an aesthetic ideology largely inherited from T.S. Eliot. The style, which expresses a thematic concern for Lawrentian love and strong leadership, bespeaks the position of a radical Conservative rather than that of a Communist. The orators is so ideologically confused that at least two critics have found traces of Nazism there,[4] but this does not seem to have impinged upon the literary-historical idea of Auden as a left-wing sympathiser. It is true that Auden's play, The dance of death, which was produced by the experimental Group Theatre, hints in a highly ambivalent way at an interest in Marx, but as some contemporary reviewers pointed out, the play was both artistically and ideologically unclear, and very far from being engagé.

The establishment of the Auden mythology, then, does not lie so much in the import of his creative writing, as in the company he kept, and the publicity so readily given to what was hailed as a 'new' poetry. Michael Roberts's two anthologies, New signatures (1932) and New country (1933), played a vital role in this respect, for it was in these books that Auden, Spender, and Day Lewis, together with other young Oxbridge-educated writers, first found a collective platform. They were bound into a group not so much because of shared concerns or styles, but more so because of Roberts's polemical introductory statements wherein he presumed to speak for all his contributors.

In the preface to New signatures Roberts attempts to define what is different about the poets included. But, without acknowledging the fact, he concludes by attaching them all to the Romantic tradition. The 'problems' of the young poets, he says, are 'aspects of an emotional discord' which can only be resolved 'by a new harmonisation such as that which may be brought about by a work of art'.[5] A more succinct account of the central metaphysic of High Romanticism would be difficult to find. Roberts's tentative remarks concerning politics, however, were new. Here he says that, 'recognition of the importance of others' on the part of the poets, sometimes 'naturally' leads 'to what appears to be the essence of the communist attitude'. It hardly needs to be said that recognising the importance of others simply will not do as a definition of Communism. In the troubled political atmosphere of 1932, however, despite Roberts's language of evasion and qualification, the very use of the word 'communist' was apparently enough to sway an audience. And in New country, which was published in the year when unemployment reached its highest level for the decade,[6] references to Communism, to Lenin, and to revolution are liberally scattered throughout the prose contributions. Day Lewis's 'Letter to a young revolutionary', and Spender's essay 'Poetry and revolution', though both politically naive, clearly fostered the notion that the Auden group were committed to the left. And it was in New country that Auden published his poem, 'A Communist to others', which, by virtue of its title alone, was enough to fuel the 'prevalent hysterical enthusiasm' for Communism mentioned by Bell in his letter.

Any reading of Auden's poem now is surely bound to acknowledge its condescension and uncertainty. But in 1933, with high unemployment at home, and the rise of Hitler in Germany, it cannot be entirely surprising that the audience (or at least some of the audience) mistook confusion for commitment. As Samuel Hynes has rightly remarked, 'new poets become a renascence when a public wants and needs a renascence'.[7] And it is worth considering for a moment the quality and dimensions of the public who were colluding in the creation of the nascent mythology.

It is important, first of all, to reiterate how small an audience it was. Only one thousand copies of New signatures were sold in its first year of publication, and less than two hundred in its second.[8] Secondly, the main source of interest in a poetical-political renaissance was Oxbridge. Young men from similar class and educational backgrounds as 'MacSpaunday'[9] found in these poets' writings an expression of their own dilemmas. Christopher Gillie writes of the impact of Auden's poetry thus: 'The imagery, the diction, the scene of these first poems made us feel that this was a poetry of our country expressing a state of mind that was also ours; their compression and obscurity gave the less discomfort because they seemed an assurance against facile answers to our large and haunting problems.'[10] This sheds light upon the process of myth-creation. For there is a tacit admission here of a distinction between the poems themselves (compressed and obscure) and what the poems are taken to represent (answers to our large and haunting problems). Plainly it was the 'state of mind' that was important. And it is surely not fanciful to suggest that this had much to do with a class and cultural background shared by poet and audience. Significantly the young poet George Barker, who left school at sixteen and did not attend a university, in a review of New signatures remarked that he did not consider the poets published there to be 'poets of their time' at all.[11]

Nevertheless, it was Auden, Day Lewis, Spender and MacNeice who rose rapidly to fame during the decade. The bulk of their output contributed to this. They were nothing if not prolific. But the reputation of the group cannot have been unaffected by their own critical writings about each other. Auden stood aloof from this, but Spender, Day Lewis and MacNeice in their books, The destructive element,[12] A hope for poetry[13] and Modern poetry[14] respectively, all wrote in praise of Auden and of each other. And in Spender's book we find Auden's name once again linked with Communism.

Auden also gained publicity from Geoffrey Grigson's *New verse*, a magazine for which various large claims have been made. It is widely held to be the best poetry periodical of its time. Because of his celebrated, vitriolic style of reviewing, it was assumed then, and has been assumed since, that Grigson had some exact editorial principles which Auden's work somehow exemplified. A double number dedicated to Auden in 1938, and Grigson's essays on 'objectivism' published late in the magazine's life, have encouraged this point of view. It is, however, one which, as we shall see in a later chapter, cannot bear close scrutiny. What may be said with certainty here is that the magazine consistently promoted Auden's career to its one thousand regular readers. One cannot help wondering if these were the same thousand people who bought copies of Auden's *Poems* (1930) and *New signatures* in their first years of publication.

However this may be, Auden's ascendancy continued to be encouraged until the outbreak of the Second World War. In January 1939 Auden and his friend Christopher Isherwood had left England to take up residence in the United States. With the outbreak of war in September, this emigration was equated by some with the 'failure' of the 1930s poets. In an editorial of 1940 for the second issue of his magazine *Horizon*, Cyril Connolly writes:

... the departure of Auden and Isherwood to America a year ago is the most important literary event since the outbreak of the Spanish Civil War ... two of our best writers, who were also two of our most militant left-wing writers, have abandoned England ... The flight of Auden and Isherwood to a land richer in incident and opportunity is also the symptom of the failure of social realism as an aesthetic doctrine ... We believe that a reaction away from social realism is as necessary and salutary as was, a generation ago, the reaction from the ivory tower.[15]

Connolly clearly subscribes to the idea of Auden as a doyen of the left, and attributes to him, as well as Isherwood, the aesthetic doctrine of 'social-realism'. And, having accepted this premise, Connolly antici- pates a 'reaction' which will eventually become enshrined as part of the myth of 1940s poetry. In a later issue of *Horizon*, Connolly reiterated his opinion that the 'academic socialism' of the 1930s was not strong enough to revive poetry, and goes on to say, 'we are waiting for a new romanticism to bring it back to life'.[16] 'Neo-Romanticism' has since become a catch-all term of abuse by which the poetry of the Second World War has been dismissed.

Connolly was not, of course, alone in identifying the poetry of the

1930s as a failure, and contributing to the idea that poetry of the war years would constitute a reaction to the previous ten years' work. George Orwell, in his famous essay *Inside the whale* (1940), articulates the view that Auden, Spender, Day Lewis and MacNeice were the poets of the 1930s, and that their work was part of a 'left-wing orthodoxy' amongst the intelligentsia during the decade. But he is by no means a celebrator of their work. He writes a very cogent critique of Auden, and pungently describes much of the 'left-wing orthodoxy' as 'nonsense from the start'. He concludes that: 'On the whole the literary-history of the thirties seems to justify the opinion that a writer does well to keep out of politics.' The lucubrations of Henry Miller (which doubtless at the time were perceived by many to be appropriately Neo-Romantic) are upheld by Orwell as possibly the starting point of a new school which 'would get right away from the political animal'.[17]

Some poets themselves found Neo-Romanticism a convenient platform from which to promote their wares. J.F. Hendry and Henry Treece were largely responsible for the New Apocalypse movement which, as its name implies, openly espoused Neo-Romanticism. The representatives of this movement, being the only 'group' to emerge in the 1940s, have since been taken to characterise all that is worst about the poetry of the war years. In attempting to carve a niche for themselves, Hendry, Treece, and other 'theorists' of the movement like G.S. Fraser and Nicholas Moore, extolled the Romantic virtues of imagination, integration and organicism. But the irony of their 'new' Romanticism was that it had grey hair. We have already noticed that Roberts's position in *New signatures* (1932) may be directly related to Romanticism, and the case of Dylan Thomas is also instructive in this connection. He is often identified with Neo-Romanticism in the 1940s, but he published three volumes in the 1930s, and his work may be found in all the leading literary periodicals of the decade. The idea that Thomas suddenly became a Neo-Romantic in 1939 is simply not true. The place of Surrealism, that apotheosis of Romanticism, also threatens to render the idea of Neo-Romanticism meaningless. For Surrealism reached the height of its vogue in England in the mid-1930s. For the Apocalyptics to describe their work as 'a dialectical progression from Surrealism'[18] may have some little truth in it, but for them to claim that this development constituted a 'new' Romanticism was a nonsense.

If a New Romanticism was vaunted as the way forward at the

beginning of the war, it did not take long for a reversal of opinion to begin. 'Neo-Romanticism' was soon to be stigmatised and the reputation of the Audenesque revived. The beginnings of this process may be witnessed in the pages of Tambimuttu's Poetry (London). The first issue of this magazine appeared in February 1939, just three months before the last issue of New verse. Just as New verse has become identified with Auden, left-wing politics, academic socialism and objectivism, so Poetry (London) has become identified with a supposedly right-wing Neo-Romanticism. The editors of the two magazines played an important role in the establishment of this binary schematisation. Writing in the early numbers, Tambimuttu is anxious to secure a place for his magazine and so explicitly differentiates it from the endeavours of New verse and Twentieth century verse.[19] He also remarks that a reaction to the 'objective reportage' of the 1930s has taken place, a reaction to which he declares himself to be 'sympathetic', but has not initiated.[20] Tambimuttu thus substantiated the myth of 1930s 'objectivism', and by admitting that a reaction to this chimera had taken place, laid himself open to attack on the grounds that he was promulgating Neo-Romanticism. In several issues of the magazine Tambi (as he was universally known in the 1940s) specifically denied this charge, saying that he was not serving Neo-Romanticism or any other 'hen coup or clique'.[21] I have argued elsewhere that the poetry Tambimuttu printed showed both his talent and catholicity as an editor.[22] He served poetry rather than any particular group of poets. But Grigson's attacks on Poetry (London) and upon 1940s poetry generally have until now prevailed in literary history.

Grigson and Tambimuttu crossed swords in print initially over the issue of Dylan Thomas, a poet whom Tambimuttu admired. Grigson published a typically swingeing and vitriolic critique of Thomas in the magazine Polemic. Tambi defended Thomas in Poetry (London), not only asserting the quality of Thomas's writing, but also deploring Grigson's acerbic approach. It was also made abundantly clear that whatever 'standards' Grigson thought himself to be upholding, Tambimuttu considered them to belong to a lifeless past which was irrelevant to the problems of the day.[23] It is much to Tambi's credit that he published Grigson's riposte, which amongst other barbs made mention of 'that faith in muddle and contradiction which has made Poetry (London) the most foolish (if representative) periodical of its time'.[24]

The row between Grigson and Tambimuttu took place in 1947-8. At the same time the writings of the emergent 'Movement' poets began their reinforcement of the myth which endorses the Audenesque, and denigrates 1940s poetry as being uniformly Neo-Romantic. The 'Movement', another group of Oxbridge poets, rose up to denounce Dylan Thomas (whom they chose as the representative of all that was 'bad' about Second World War poetry), and to point to Auden as the purveyor of a 'discipline' which they thought salutary.[25] Although the poets in this group (Larkin, Davie, Amis and Wain amongst them) were later obliged to distinguish themselves from Auden and the Audenesque,[26] their studied attack on Thomas is a crucial stepping stone to later critical affirmations which laud Auden as the figurehead of the period 1930-45, and dismiss those poets who did not follow him.

The Movement poets continued their campaign through the 1950s. Their poetry, which relied upon strict forms, 'purity of diction', and a wariness of emotion, created a climate which made any revisionist reading of 1940s poetry extremely unlikely. Indeed it was in the 1960s that a vogue for Audenesque writing of the 1930s was further encouraged. In 1964 Robin Skelton edited an anthology, The Penguin book of thirties poetry. Writing in the introduction he says:

We come back then, finally to Auden. He is the clear Master of the period. He dominates it from first to last. His sovereignty is never seriously in doubt, though from the vantage point of 1963, many of these poems appear less accomplished than some by his contemporaries. The satirical note is often shrill, and there is often a note of schoolboy knowingness, an eager relishing of the audience's probably shocked response. And yet these aspects are all subordinate to Auden's main virtue, which was his assumption that poetry actually did have an audience, and that poetry could be changed into a valuable instrument of social health.[27]

This is very telling. For here we have a clear distinction being made between Auden's poetry itself, and what are said to be his assumptions about poetry. Skelton pertinently criticises the former, but subordinates such objections on ethical grounds. Auden's 'virtue' is said to reside in his poetic, which Skelton identifies as both public and political. Auden's strictly 'literary' achievements are put at the service of ideology. The reasons for Skelton's procedures are intimated at the close of his introduction when he relates the situation of the 1960s to that of the 1930s: '. . . threatened by war as we are threatened, troubled by social and racial conflicts as we are troubled, [we are led] to wonder whether or not an anthology of this kind is a piece of literary history, or an illumination of our own present discomforts.'[28]

In England in 1963 unemployment reached its highest point since 1947.[29] This was also the year of Profumo and Kim Philby, the Beatles and Bob Dylan. America's disastrous escalation of its involvement in Vietnam in 1965 already seemed likely. The production and reception of Skelton's anthology (it was reprinted five times to 1975 and a further six times to 1987) must be seen in this context. Skelton's continuation of the myth of 1930s poetry, and the ready aquiescence of an audience, is, I suggest, at least in part due to middle-class consciousness of material inequalities and social injustice on a massive international scale. There was, and still is, a need to identify, in the canon of English literature, a supposedly 'radical' poetry which, though it might 'illuminate present troubles', also acts as a palliative by justifying the very act of reading poetry, and providing the middle classes with a vicarious sense of 'caring'.

In 1968, Skelton edited another anthology, this time of 1940s poetry. Although in his introduction he attempts to give the best of 1940s poetry its due, he also invokes the terms 'social objectivity' and Neo-Romanticism to distinguish between poetry of the 1930s and 1940s. Whilst it is admitted that 'the best work of the forties is formidably good', the lack of discipline, pretension, excess and vagueness of much 1940s poetry is alluded to.[30] The latter view has become enshrined, the former ignored. Poetry of the 1930s has become fashionable, 1940s poetry, until very recently, has been dismissed. Skelton's anthology of 1940s poetry, in significant contrast to his 1930s collection, was not reprinted at all between 1968 and 1981.

The idea that 1940s poetry is marked by a retreat into subjective individualism in contradistinction to the public, socially-oriented poetry of the 1930s, was promoted from the 1950s through to the 1970s by writers of the Auden group who can hardly be said to be disinterested in the matter. Spender, Day Lewis, MacNeice, and John Lehmann all drew retrospective comparisons between their situation in the 1930s and that of the Romantic poets of the nineteenth century. Spender writes of the '1930s generation': 'They had taken a bet that a world order of peace and social justice would emerge in their time, just as Wordsworth, Coleridge and Shelley had done in their day. They lost as the Romantics had done, and were forced to spend their next phase searching for an attitude which would be independent of external events.'[31] Other explicit comparisons which suggest that the 1930s poets simply turned from politics to the comforts of the 'egotistical sublime' may be found in both Day Lewis's autobiography, and in an interview he gave in 1972 where he likens himself and his generation to 'the young Wordsworth at the start of the French Revolution'.[32]

MacNeice, always somewhat more sceptical, and not prone to this kind of self-congratulation, makes his comparison more caustically. He writes that young men in the early 1930s were 'swallowing Marx with the same naive enthusiasm that made Shelley swallow Rousseau'.[33] This remark, no less than those of Spender and Day Lewis, indicates their writers' tendency to mythologise themselves through self-aggrandising and untenable comparisons with Wordsworth and Shelley. It is difficult to feel that either Spender or Day Lewis are poets close to the stature of either Wordsworth or Shelley, and to make analogies between poets writing over one hundred years apart falls into the fallacy of historical recurrence. Such comparisons ignore the enormous political, philosophical, social and aesthetic shifts between the time of the Romantic revolution and that of Spender and Day Lewis. We may be grateful that the self-commentary of the latter poets accurately brings the '1930s generation' within the ambit of Romanticism, but their descriptions of how their poetry changed clearly contributes to the idea that these poets were seriously commited to the left during the 1930s and reacted against this tendency in the following decade. As we shall see in a later chapter, the case is hardly as simple as this.

Geoffrey Grigson's recollections, though less politically weighted than those of his contemporaries I have quoted, nevertheless follow the by-now familar pattern. In contradistinction to his own magazine, little magazines of the war years are accused of 'wangling', 'compromise', 'mental masturbation' and 'dotty inclusiveness'.[34] And poetry of the 1940s is described as: 'Unbraced, unbra'd, no body belt, saddles slipped under the belly. Dead guts instead of empty shell. A revelation of sprawl.'[35] The 1940s are written of as an unfortunate interregnum between the braced, belted, and presumably bra'd poetry of the Audenesque and the Movement.

Academic criticism of the 1970s and 1980s has not, by and large, held up such obvious expressions of personal animus to scrutiny. Rather, the dominant myth has been reinforced by major studies. In what have become very influential works, both Samuel Hynes and Bernard Bergonzi have encouraged the idea that the 1930s were dominated by the Audenesque. It is important to consider the premises upon which these studies are built in order to demonstrate that certain poets are excluded from consideration for reasons which are not above question.

The authors and texts discussed in Hynes's book, The Auden generation: literature and politics in the 1930s, are selected in accordance with an idiosyncratic (and to my mind untenable) definition of what a 'literary-generation' constitutes. In his preface Hynes says that he is concerned with 'a generation of writers', the 'men and women born in England between 1900 and the First World War, who came of age in the 'twenties and lived through their early maturity during the depression'.[36] He goes on to say that 'almost every work of importance' produced by this 'generation' is 'demonstrably related to its historical moment in mood and tone'.[37] This tacitly defines 'importance' for us; implicitly works overtly unrelated to public events, the historical moment, are not important. And yet as early as 1937, interest in the importance of Dylan Thomas's poetry (which, with one or two notable exceptions, cannot be related directly to public events) was such that Henry Treece began writing a book-length study of his work.[38]

To return to Hynes's value-judgements; we find him further refining his notion of a literary generation:

To write about the literary existence of a generation is to accept a necessary restriction of subject: you will be writing almost entirely about the middle-class members of the generation. English literature has been middle-class as long as there has been an English middle-class, and the generation of the 'thirties was not different in this respect from its predecessors; most of the writers I deal with here came from professional families, and were educated at public schools and at Oxford or Cambridge. Virtually no writing of literary importance came out of the working-class during the decade.[39]

This is very suave indeed. What it fails to take into account, however, is the complexity of the English class-system. To implicitly define the 'middle class' as public school and Oxbridge educated neatly ignores the lower-middle class and the grammar-school-educated middle-middle class from which writers like Dylan Thomas and George Barker emerged in the 1930s.

Hynes adds a further gloss on his phrase 'the making of a generation': 'I assume that a generation grows in definition by the interaction of consciousness and circumstance. One might say that a generation does not really exist until it has been made conscious of its identity, and that for such consciousness it must depend on the special awareness of its artists, and their ability to create the forms appropriate to their own particular circumstances.'[40] It should be clear from these quotations that Hynes's definition of a 'literary generation' is both reductive and tautological. In order to belong to the 'Auden generation' one has to be born between 1900 and 1914 (fourteen years, of course, does not correspond to anyone else's definition of a generation), one has to belong not merely to the middle class but to the public-school and Oxbridge-educated middle-middle to upper-middle class. And then, since one shares a particular set of attitudes towards past events, historical and cultural (Hynes actually chooses the First World War and T.S. Eliot's *The waste land*), one has the credentials to create one's own generation by writing works of 'literary importance' in 'forms appropriate to one's particular circumstances'.

There is no question that 'MacSpaunday' and prose writers like Rex Warner and Isherwood did share similar backgrounds in terms of class and education, and that this informs their writings of the 1930s. It also informs the kind of myths they helped to establish and perpetuate about themselves. What, to my mind, is radically wrong with Hynes's account is that he does not penetrate but perpetuates these myths at the expense of other writers who do not share the same background and have a different aesthetic orientation. He makes his chosen writers representative of a decade and a 'generation' when in fact they are only representative of a particular class and a particular style of writing which, of course, Hynes assumes to be of 'literary value' without ever defining or attempting definition of what that means.

The treatment (or non-treatment) of poets like David Gascoyne, George Barker and Dylan Thomas is symptomatic of Hynes's proce-dures. Significantly none of these poets share the same class or educational background as the Auden 'generation' though they were born in 1913, 1914, and 1916 respectively. None of them share the Auden style. Hynes therefore puts them beyond the pale of his 'generation' even though their first volumes were published in 1932, 1933, and 1934 respectively, and the leading literary magazines of the 1930s published their work. Other poets who do not fit Hynes's prescription are also left out of account; one thinks of Kathleen Raine, Bernard Spencer, Kenneth Allot and Norman Cameron, who all somehow do not quite qualify for the 'generation'. The list of prose writers excluded by Hynes might begin with Walter Greenwood and go on to James Hanley, Walter Brierley, Willy Goldmann and Lewis Grassic Gibbon. But one cannot wonder at the exclusion of these five writers; they are presumably too proletarian to have any of Hynes's 'literary value'. Although the same cannot be said of the omitted poets that I have mentioned, what may be asserted is that the middle-class to lower-middle-class background of some of them crucially affected both their stylistics and poetics in the 1930s, and that the work of all of them erases the notion of any single stylistic homogeneity in the decade.

Following Hynes however, there is a determined resistance to more inclusive views of the decade as Bernard Bergonzi's book, *Reading the thirties: texts and contexts*, amply indicates. Although one might cautiously applaud the self-consciousness with which Bergonzi plots his tentative steps beyond 'Anglo-Saxon empiricism', the validity of his approach to literary history is more questionable. Bergonzi is interested to demonstrate the way in which the 'texts of literature' intersect with the 'texts of history' by finding correspondences of image and motif between the two. The problem with this is the way in which the 'texts' are selected. Bergonzi makes it clear that his use of the word ''Thirties' 'largely corresponds to what Samuel Hynes ... calls the Auden Generation',[41] and goes on to speak of a 'fascination' with the 'mythology of the decade'.[42] He admits that survivors of the 1930s may find his account of the decade questionable, but justifies his pursuit as an attempt to find 'categories and models' which 'make sense' of the literary activities of the decade. But the categories and models thus set up render a version of the 1930s seen through the eyes of a group of upper-middle-class writers. The 'text' of the 1930s which emerges is partial and fraught with ideological implications which Bergonzi seems reluctant to discuss. Indeed there is a deliberate avoidance of 'political' contextualisation. Bergonzi quotes Arnold Rattenbury as an example of a 'survivor's' distortions. Rattenbury writes: 'That the thirties were made of Auden and friends is as unlikely a notion as daft.'[43]

As much of my book is intended to show, I agree with Rattenbury, but Bergonzi bravely and unrepentantly admits to this 'daftness' on the grounds that no other poet is of sufficient stature to effect Auden's 'centrality in the literary life of the 'thirties'.[44] It is important I think to notice that despite his adoption of a less than traditional methodology in his book, the argument for Auden's 'centrality' is based on notions of 'literary value'. Writing of why he finds some writers more important than others, we again hear that Auden is 'central' because his 'very individual vision and tone were in balance with his capacity for general statement and taking a large view of things . . .'. Auden was 'a dazzling verbal performer' with 'skill and brilliance'.[45] The qualities

Bergonzi attributes to Auden may readily be conceded. What is in question here is why those skills constitute 'centrality', why do they so overpower other writings and other visions?

In concluding the introduction to his book, Bergonzi alludes to Gascoyne, Barker, Thomas and to Lewis Grassic Gibbon, whom, he suggests, had little other than political interests in common with the writers he has chosen to discuss. Although he says he 'loves' some of their writings, those who do not subscribe to the Audenesque, 'belong on different maps are to be sought on different expeditions'.[46] The pertinent and unanswered question is why? Why do the contemporaneous writings of other authors belong on a different 'map'? Surely to deliberately omit texts which do not fit into a predetermined pattern, to choose to discuss, and see as representative, only those works which have things in common, is not the way to understand fully the writing of a 'period' or 'generation'. It seems to me that the selectivity of accounts like those of Hynes and Bergonzi, their willingness to agree upon a 'myth' of Auden and the 1930s, is a product of value-systems which are no longer a matter of course, which masquerade under the title of 'literary value', and which are open to the same charge of distortion that Bergonzi levels at Rattenbury.

Much of what I have said about Bergonzi may also be applied to Cunningham's book, British writers of the thirties. Cunningham goes much further than Bergonzi, but his pursuit is essentially similar. He wishes to collapse text and context, and draw analogies between the texts of literature and the texts of history. He chooses certain metaphors and motifs and then traces their incidence in a huge variety of texts and contexts. His study then, in some ways looks beyond Auden et al. to popular literature, film, sport etc. Cunningham argues that these texts and contexts constitute 'in large something like a connected field, a whole text, a set of diverse signs adding up more or less, to a single semiotic'. In order to 'decode' the single semiotic one must 'grapple with as much of the components of that scene, that text, as he can ...'.[47] This, no doubt, is why the book is 530 pages long. The problem, however, is again one of selectivity and principles of selectivity. The 'dominant' images and metaphors that Cunningham chooses to discuss occur in the writings of some writers more than others. Auden, Day Lewis, Spender and MacNeice are alluded to hundreds of times; they are a massive, if not a dominating presence in the book. This is justified by arguing that 'Auden and his group were regarded by very many of their contemporaries as the central figures',[48] and that 'the influence of Auden on his time was extreme'.[49] Cunningham is also willing to subscribe to Hynes's notion of 'generation'. He refers to authors 'flowering in the shade of Auden's output', who constitute a distinct 'generation' and these writers almost inevitably include Thomas, Barker and Gascoyne.[50] Although there is much to be admired in Cunningham's study, and though he wishes to broaden the 1930s to include more than the Audenesque, his book does little to displace the centrality of Auden and friends.

What emerges from the literary-historical myth of the 1930s then, is a preference for the poets of the upper-middle class, who in the 1930s often advertised themselves as left-wing but could not escape the English liberal tradition. This preference represents the artificial establishment of a canon which holds the liberal middle ground. Under the auspices of an inevitably ideological conception of 'literary value' the mythical view of the decade tends to exclude Surrealism (and writers associated with that movement in the 1930s) and omits the relatively plain, personal style, adopted by some writers in the second half of the decade, which may be treated as a kind of Neo-Georgianism. It also excludes the 'Agitprop' (for want of a better word) poetry, and the balladry written by the working class.

By thus elevating the Audenesque, the literary histories of Hynes, Bergonzi, and to some extent at least Cunningham, also implicitly secure the supremacy of 1930s poetry over that of the 1940s. There have been, in recent years, books which have dealt with poetry of the Second World War. But none of these has challenged the literary-historical myth. Robert Hewison, in his much praised book *Under siege*, writes:

Looked at as literary-history the period 1939 to 45 has a definite pattern, both in terms of schools and generations. The established poets of the 'thirties continued to work along the themes they had chosen before the war, though they developed further and further away from the original matrix of Marxist and Freudian theory; on the other hand a new generation of poets reacted away from the outwardly directed and 'classical' viewpoint of pre-war poetry of the Auden school towards a romantic and inwardly directed extreme.[51]

Here is the mythology writ large. Poetry of the 1930s is said to be public, classical, and through association with Marx, left-wing. The work of the following decade is conceived as a crude antithesis of all this.

Linda Shires, writing of British poetry of the 2nd World War, is acutely aware of the part played by the Movement poets in mis-representing poetry of the 1940s. But she is still prepared to accept several tenets of the mythology. For instance, she does not 'underestimate Auden's influence on British poetry after 1939',[52] but delicately side-steps the issue when she remarks that 'this is not part' of her subject. Shires goes on to say that 'by emphasising the subjectivity of the 'forties, the members of the Movement correctly identified the decade's major artistic shift'.[53] And, almost inevitably, we hear of the 'Apocalyptics' reacting against the 'Auden School'.[54] From an ideological point of view perhaps the most telling moment in her book occurs when she remarks that: 'The problems for the poet in wartime were exactly those which Virginia Woolf exposed . . . in *Between the acts*'.[55] The attempt to see the poets of the 1940s through the upper-middle-class lens of Bloomsbury is surely a grave mistake. Auden, Spender and other upper-middle-class poets of the 1930s certainly had connections with the aestheticians of West London, but Keith Douglas, Alun Lewis, Charles Causley and other young poets of the 1940s most certainly did not.

I have explored the genesis and development of the literary-historical myth of the 1930s and 1940s in order to make clear how deep-rooted and pervasive certain ideas about the period are. The oppositions of Classicism and Romanticism, objectivism and subjectivism, left wing and right wing are all wielded in a schematisation which in my view ignores the poetry these labels are intended to describe. The idea of Auden and an 'Auden generation' looms large over the whole period, he and his group are considered to be 'central'. And often this centrality is defended in terms of a 'literary value' which pretends to be ideologically innocent. But I have tried to show how ideology and literary value are conflated by the myth. If we set one of Auden's finest poems against one by Dylan Thomas, we are surely bound to admit that both are well-written. The preference for Auden exhibited by the myth is not a matter of pure literary merit but of ideological bias. It is Auden's appeal to the liberal middle-class conscience which dominates the literary history of the period, not some timeless standard of poetic craftsmanship. But this is perhaps too pre-emptive a statement. It is time to look at the poetry and poetics of Auden and his followers, so that my reading of them may be measured against the myth that I have outlined here.

Notes

1 The letter is quoted in P. Stansky and W. Abrahams, *Journey to the frontier*, New York, 1966, pp. 108-9.
2 A second edition of Auden's *Poems* (1930) appeared in 1933. Seven new poems replaced a similar number which Auden deleted in revising the first edition.
3 J. Symons, *The Thirties: a dream revolved*, (revd. ed.), London, 1975, p. 33.
4 See G.S. Fraser, *Vision and rhetoric: studies in modern poetry*, London, 1959, pp. 150-1, and Symons, *The thirties*, pp. 29-30.
5 M. Roberts, Preface to *New signatures*, London, 1932, pp. 12-13.
6 J. Stevenson,'Myth and reality: Britain in the nineteen-thirties', *Crisis and controversy*, ed. A. Sked and C. Cook, London, 1976, p. 91.
7 S. Hynes, *The Auden generation: literature and politics in England in the 1930s*, London, 1976, p. 98.
8 Ibid., p. 83.
9 This was Roy Campbell's less than flattering label for the 'Auden group'. See R. Carter ed., *Thirties poets: 'the Auden group': a casebook*, London, 1984, p. 12.
10 C. Gillie, *Movements in English literature 1900-1940*, London, 1975, p. 128.
11 G. Barker, *The Adelphi*, No. 4, June 1932, p. 642.
12 S. Spender, *The destructive element: a study of modern writers and beliefs*, London, 1935.
13 C. Day Lewis, *A hope for poetry*, Oxford, 1934 (revd. ed. 1936).
14 L. MacNeice, *Modern poetry: a personal essay*, Oxford, 1938.
15 C. Connolly, 'Comment', *Horizon*, No. 2, Feb. 1940, pp. 68-71.
16 C. Connolly, 'Comment', *Horizon*, No. 4, Nov. 1941, p. 301.
17 G. Orwell, 'Inside the whale', *Inside the whale and other essays* (1957), Harmondsworth, 1975, pp. 9-50.
18 G.S. Fraser, 'Apocalypse in poetry', *The white horseman*, ed. J.F. Hendry and H. Treece, London, 1941, pp. 153-79.
19 J.M. Tambimuttu, *Poetry London*, No. 2, April 1939, p. 34.
20 J.M. Tambimuttu, *Poetry London*, No. 6, May-June 1941, p. 164.
21 *Poetry London*, No. 2, April 1939, p. 34; No. 7, Oct.-Nov. 1942, p. 6; No. 10, Dec. 1944.
22 A. Caesar, 'Poetry (London)', *British literary magazines, vol. IV, the modern age 1914-1984*, ed. A. Sullivan, New York, 1986, pp. 358-64.
23 See J.M. Tambimuttu, *Poetry London*, No. 11, Sept.-Oct. 1947, pp. 5-8.
24 G. Grigson, *Poetry London*, No. 13, June-July 1948 , p. 46.
25 B. Morrison, *The Movement: English poetry and fiction of the 1950s* , Oxford, 1980, pp. 24-5.
26 Ibid., p. 21.
27 R. Skelton, Introduction to *Poetry of the thirties*, Harmondsworth, 1964, pp. 33-4.
28 Ibid., p. 37.
29 B. Gilbert, *Britain since 1918*, London, 1967, p. 200.
30 R. Skelton, Introduction to *Poetry of the forties*, Harmondsworth, 1968, pp. 16-17, 26-7.
31 S. Spender, *World within world*, London, 1951, p. 287.
32 C. Day Lewis, 'Shortly before his death C. Day Lewis talked to Hallam Tennyson', *The listener*, 88, 27 July 1972, pp. 108-10.
33 L. MacNeice, *The strings are false*, London, 1965, p. 146.
34 G. Grigson, *The crest on the silver*, London, 1950, p. 163.
35 'A conversation with Geoffrey Grigson', *The review*, No. 22, June 1970, p. 25.
36 Hynes, *The Auden generation*, p. 9.
37 Ibid., p. 10.
38 D. Thomas,*The Collected letters*, London, 1985, pp. 272-3.
39 Hynes, *The Auden generation*, pp. 10-11.

40 Ibid., p. 11.
41 B. Bergonzi, *Reading the thirties: text and contexts*, London, 1978, p. 1.
42 Ibid.
43 A. Rattenbury, 'Total attainder and the Helots', *Renaissance and modern studies*, XX, 1976, pp. 103-119, is quoted by Bergonzi, pp. 8-9.
44 Bergonzi, *Reading the thirties*, p. 8.
45 Ibid., p. 144.
46 Ibid., pp. 8-9.
47 V. Cunningham, *British writers of the thirties*, Oxford, 1988, p. 2.
48 Ibid., p. 17.
49 Ibid., p. 20.
50 Ibid., p. 22.
51 R. Hewison, *Under siege: literary life in London 1939-45*, London, 1979, pp. 100-1.
52 L. Shires, *British poetry of the Second World War*, London, 1985, p. xv.
53 Ibid., p. 24.
54 Ibid., p. 25.
55 Ibid., p. 5.

3

Auden and the Audenesque

W.H. Auden was born in 1907 into a conventional, upper-middle-class family in York. Both his parents were children of clergymen in the Church of England. This secured their status despite the socially suspect fact that Auden's father earned most of his living as a doctor.[1] They lived in some style in a large detached house where two maids and a cook helped Mrs Auden contrive comfortable domestic arrangements, whilst Dr Auden did the rounds of his private practice driven by his own coachman. In 1908, however, the family moved to Solihull, then a village on the outskirts of Birmingham, as Dr Auden gave up his practice to take up the job of Birmingham's first medical inspector of schools. This entailed a drop of salary, but bolstered by his small private income, family life continued much as it had done in York. Although his parents moved house several times over the years, ending up in the village of Harborne, the environs of Birmingham were 'home' to Wystan Auden both in his childhood, and at various periods in his adult life until he left England for the United States in 1939.

The atmosphere at home was devout, learned and cultured. Auden's mother led daily family prayers with the servants in attendance. Her tastes were for High Anglican ritual, with its sumptuous vestments, candles and incense.[2] This clearly influenced Auden in his later devotions. His mother's musical abilities and enthusiasms were also to make a lasting mark upon the poet. Auden retained a serious interest in classical music, particularly opera, for the rest of his life. As he grew up, he also had access to his father's library which was that of a polymath. As Auden says himself, this not only taught him to read but also dictated his choice of reading which was wide and casual rather than scholarly.[3]

Auden's education, then, began at home. In 1915 his more formal learning commenced at St Edmund's preparatory school, Surrey. From there he progressed, in 1920, to Gresham's public school in Norfolk where he spent five years before going up to Oxford. Auden, in later life, greatly appreciated the positive influence that both schools had

had on his development as a poet. The curriculum at St Edmund's was heavily weighted towards Latin and Greek. Auden felt that this had been highly advantageous to him, believing that the hours spent translating as a boy had taught him things about the English language that could not be learnt in other ways.[4] In various writings about schooldays, Auden also affectionately remembers several schoolmasters, testifying to their influence upon his education in poetry.[5]

Auden won an Exhibition to study natural sciences at Christ Church, Oxford, but he arrived amidst the 'dreaming spires' already a practising poet and with a secure conviction that this was his vocation. He spent his first year half-heartedly studying biology, zoology and chemistry, writing poems and exploring his self-confessed homosexual preferences in what seem to have been relatively uninhibited ways. In 1926 he changed courses to English Language and Literature, and it was at this time that Auden 'discovered' and fell under the influence of T.S. Eliot's poetry. It was also at this time that certain aspects of the Auden mythology had their genesis.

As Stephen Spender recalls, Auden would hold court to other talented undergraduates in a room with the curtains or blinds always shut. Here he would make categorical pronouncements on a variety of subjects, casting himself in the role of leader and healer:

Already at the university, Auden's relationships with his fellow human beings had fallen into a pattern. They were really of two kinds – teacher to pupil and The Colleagues. Those of us who automatically fell into the role of pupil went to him for instruction about poetry, our psychological ailments, the art of living and so on. The Colleagues – consisting pre-eminently of Christopher Isherwood (at Cambridge), Day Lewis and Rex Warner – were a little group (sometimes called 'The Gang') who were rather like a shadow cabinet, the successors to the literary governments at this time: we were governed it seemed by J.C. Squire and a group of Georgian poets – more like a cricket team than literary figures. The honourable opposition was Bloomsbury, amongst whom could be loosely counted Virginia Woolf, E.M. Forster and T.S. Eliot.[6]

Doubtless there is some truth in the description of Auden's pedagogic manner, and it cannot be questioned that he was the leader of his own small 'gang' (the cabinet looks very shadowy indeed in opposition to Woolf, Forster and Eliot). What may be legitimately scrutinised, however, is the relationship of this to the *poems* Auden was writing at the time, and over the next few years, which found print in his first commercial volume *Poems* (1930). For in many of these the persona of leader, diagnostician, and healer is projected through belligerently confident tones. But this illusion of authority, created primarily by a statemental manner, is not substantiated by the totality of the utterances. It seems likely that the public, dogmatic pronouncements of the young poet conceal as much uncertainty as they reveal self-confidence. The need to be part of a 'gang', and the styling of one's literary progenitors as the 'opposition' are indicative of insecurity rather than conviction. And, as I hope now to demonstrate, Auden's earliest published writings are characterised by conflict and tension, by images of defeat and failure, rather than of integration and success.

On leaving Oxford in the summer of 1928, Auden was granted an allowance by his father, which enabled the poet to spend the next eighteen months travelling and writing. He spent a considerable amount of this time in Berlin, a city to which he was attracted by the availability of beautiful boys. When in England during this period, Auden stayed either with his parents in Harborne, or at the cottage in the Lake District that his parents also owned. It was a time of considerable productivity as Auden grappled with the artistic, psychological, and social problems that beset him, and which form the subject of Poems (1930). A key to understanding the central concerns of this volume is provided by a diary Auden was writing in 1929. Here he expresses, amongst other things, his diagnosis of the class into which he was born: 'The middle class: an orphan class, with no fixed residence, capable of snobbery in both directions. From class insecurity it has developed the family unit as a defence. Like the private bands in the tribal migrations. It is afraid of its fortunate position . . . The real 'life-wish' is the desire for separation, from family, from one's literary predecessors.'[7] Auden laments the divisions he perceives within society, and the guilt and insecurity that these give rise to, but he also locates the 'life-wish' in a deliberate act of separation, of individuation. The implications of such a life-wish, not only pertain to family and literary progenitors, they also impinge upon politics and love. As an isolated individual it is difficult to espouse a politics other than the anarchistic, it is also difficult to praise Eros. For erotic love and a concern for society imply attitudes of joining, rather than separation: a joining which inevitably threatens isolation.

These are the tensions which inform Poems (1930); they express different aspects of Auden's struggle to liberate himself from his personal, social and literary past. Nowhere is this clearer than in the longest poem in the volume, 'It was Easter as I walked in the public gardens'. The poem was written in four parts between April and October 1929. Each part constitutes a meditation upon the relationships between death and love, between the past, present and a possible future. In keeping with the dates of composition, the poem moves us from spring, through summer to autumn and intimations of winter. This seasonal progression provides a structural principle, binding the parts together, as well as suggesting a counterpoint between patterns of growth and decay in nature, and those in the life of man. The poem opens with the persona contemplating spring in a traditional way; it is a season of renewal and regeneration in which both poet and lover are implicated: they will discover new ways of love, new ways of writing. It is a season of 'fresh power'. But this celebration is soon cut short as Auden, following Eliot, expresses his own intimation that 'April is the cruellest month'. Solitary man is not in consonance with nature, but is a victim of arrested development. This idea is introduced in a deliberately shocking and violently reductive metaphor which likens man to an 'embryo chicken'. The opposition of style so created, between the clear, bucolic tones of the opening lines, and the rather ugly, anti-romantic, Eliotic, metaphor of the close, indicates a conceptual and emotional tension. The poet's contemplation shifts from life towards death, from a vital future to a moribund past.

The second verse paragraph is replete with a sense of ennervation. The poet recalls winter and 'all those whose death / Is necessary condition of the season's setting forth'. The isolated speaker thinks of the success and failure of various friends and lovers, but this contemplation does not afford solace or guidance. In powerfully suggestive imagery, Auden describes an impasse in which not only are death and life contrasted, but also those conditions are associated with the mechanical modern age on the one hand, and on the other with the healing procreative power of nature. The choice between these seems to the poet 'a necessary error'; the modern, mechanical age spells death to the imagination, whilst a return to Romantic pastoralism takes the poet back towards literary progenitors from whom he is anxious to separate himself. Auden wants 'an altering speech for altering things', but finds his speech poised between the self-consciously modernistic, with its deathly intimations of Eliot's *Waste land*, and a Georgian pastoralism from which he feels equally alienated.

Parts 2 and 3 of the poem develop more explicitly the problems raised in part 1. The poet's alienation from nature is reiterated, and the need for progress is assumed. The concentration is upon psychological analysis and the desire to find a way of loving that is creative rather than destructive. Part 2 has the poet a 'homesick foreigner' suffering from 'intercepted growth'. We are located in Germany where there is 'shooting and barricade in street', and talk of 'final war / Of proletariat and police'. Further atrocities are described, though it is not made clear whether it is the proletariat, the police or both who are commiting them. What we are told is that the poet is 'angry' with all this. We then proceed somewhat incongrously to a meditation upon a landscape seen from a hill-top:

Smoke rises from factory in field,
Memory of fire: On all sides heard
Vanishing music of isolated larks:
From village square voices in hymn,
Men's voices, an old use.[8]

Auden turns from the political violence of the present to the attractions of the past. But the Promethean fire, the lark song of Romanticism, will not do, they are an 'old use'. And so the poet turns inward to a psychological analysis which implies that the political divisions and violence described are symptomatic of mental sickness on a wide scale.

Auden describes the child's separation from the mother, which leaves the grown man alone, fearful and friendless. The Freudian and Lawrentian answer to this fall into division lies in the sexual relationship. But in this poem, Auden's concern is with the failure of sexual relations; they provide no answer to current problems:

Body reminds in him to loving,
Reminds but takes no further part,
Perfunctorily affectionate in hired room
But takes no part and is unloving
But loving death. May see in dead,
In face of dead that loving wish,
As one returns from Africa to wife
And his ancestral property in Wales.

Merely sensual love is equated here with spiritual death, and such death is, in turn, specifically related to the property-owning classes and to imperialism. It seems likely that Auden's sexual experiences in Berlin are pertinent here. He was in the habit of picking up boys and of frequenting brothels. In his diary is a list of 'Boys had Germany 1928-29'.[9] There are several on the list whose names are 'unknown', and who are identified merely by the place in which they were 'had'. It would seem then, that Auden's sexual encounters were indeed perfunctory and emotionally impoverished. He implies in the lines quoted that such impoverishment is an ancestral curse inherited from the English ruling classes. And he may have felt too, that the power relations involved, the sexual exploitation of the working class, had a wider political analogy.

However this may be, certain it is that Auden considered himself and his class to be incapable of right-loving. This becomes ever more transparent in sections 3 and 4 of the poem. In section 3 the poet dwells upon the necessity for a psychological 'weaning' from the past so that the individual may participate in the creation of 'a new race / And a new language'. This act of separation and creation, however, is continually baulked by insecurity which transforms erotic pleasure into neurotic disease. The only answer Auden has to this is figured in the fourth and last section where an apocalyptic winter is envisaged in melodramatic tones. Auden here departs from his lived experience to speak of the future in terms of 'the dragon's day, the devourer's'. The poem becomes overwrought. In order to find a way forward 'Love' is said to need,

... death, death of the grain, our death,
Death of the old gang; would leave them
In sullen valley where is made no friend,
The old gang to be forgotten in the spring,
The hard bitch and the riding-master,
Stiff underground; deep in clear lake
The lolling bridegroom, beautiful, there.

In order to create a new way of loving and of life, the middle class must be destroyed. The weakness of this conclusion lies in its glib abstraction. The word 'death' is wielded far too easily, and the question is begged as to what kind of 'love', what kind of society is envisaged succeeding. The 'lolling bridegroom' suggests the end of bourgeois marriage and by extension family life. But apart from the buried implication that homosexual love might be superior, there is little of positive alternative to be found.

I have dwelt on this poem at length because it seems to me that the rest of Auden's first collection plays variations upon the themes assayed here. Some of the poems concentrate upon the inward psychological problems of right loving. The significantly titled 'No trenchant parting', 'Love by ambition', 'Before this loved one', 'This lunar beauty' and 'Upon this line between adventure' are of this kind. With their abbreviated line and syntax, their use of polysyllables and abstract nouns, they advertise themselves as 'difficult' and 'modern'. They are centrally concerned to probe the validity of a Lawrentian view of sexual love. In some of the poems the abandonment of constraint and intellect to instinct is considered positive. In others this position is found wanting. Another common concern is the notion that the protagonist's inherited modes of loving are destructive, deathly.

The other characteristic mode in *Poems* (1930) has a less resistant surface, and by introducing us to the famous Audenesque landscape of frontier lands peopled by spies and incendiaries, tends to have a wider social application. Though the manner in such poems as 'Who stands, the crux left of the watershed', 'Control of the passes was, he saw, the key', 'Having abdicated with comparative ease' and 'Consider this and in our time', is more expansive, nevertheless Auden's fondness for ellipsis, for abstract nouns, and for definite articles placed against indefinite nouns, ensures a 'difficulty', a 'mysteriousness' which, like the concluding lines of 'It was Easter', strike one as the product of strained over-writing than the expression of deeply felt conviction. And, it should be further urged, the landscapes in these poems have nothing to do with 'objectivism', much less with 'social realism'. Nowhere in Auden's canon is there any attempt to figure the industrial landscapes of the Northern urban conurbations, of Birmingham, Manchester, Leeds or Liverpool. Rather, as Humphrey Carpenter makes clear, Auden's attraction to industrial machinery stems from his boyhood feelings for the lead mines of the Pennines, and it is this Lawrentian fascination for the impositions of industry upon a rural landscape that is incorporated into the figurative landscapes of the Audenesque.

It has not been sufficiently recognised that the frontiers in these landscapes are metaphors not only for social division, but also for psycho-sexual divisions. Crossing over boundaries may apply to sexual experience as much as to strictly political activity. In 'Who stands the crux left of the watershed', the bourgeois protagonist is imaged alienated from the industrial landscape and its inhabitants, alienated from nature, and implicitly incapable of 'natural' love. He stands at the crux, unable to move forward. He can only go back to his landed inheritance. It is a vision of the middle class as alienated and defeated. Similarly in 'Control of the passes was, he saw, the key', the 'spy' who has glimpsed the new district has been captured 'seduced by the old tricks'. He dreams of a lover, but will be shot before such a relationship can be achieved. Again, we have an image of defeat, death and failure. In this poem Auden seems to implicate himself, whilst in others like 'Consider this and in our time' and 'Since you are going to begin today' he prophesies the destruction of the bourgeoisie from an elevated, though isolated position.

There is nothing in *Poems* (1930) to suggest that Auden was left-wing. The attack in these poems is upon his own class, his inheritance. And the poems, when they are not resistantly private, are addressed to members of his own class. But in rejecting the upper-middle class Auden does not seek a 'negative identification'[10] with the working class. Rather, in their individualism and in their defeatism, the poems tend ideologically to the right, albeit in a rather anarchistic fashion. This is embodied stylistically in a tempering of Eliot's modernism by some Georgian influence, with Auden's voice emerging from the struggle with these two distinct strands of his aesthetic inheritance.

In 1930, the allowance from his father having run out, Auden took a job as a master at a private school in Scotland. He was to spend the next five years of his life teaching in various preparatory and public schools. This constituted a return to a schoolboy ethos of adolescent, homoerotic intrigue which fascinated Auden and exercised a considerable influence upon his thinking and writing. Certainly his next volume, *The orators* (1932) is steeped in what Auden called elsewhere, 'the prep-school atmosphere'.[11] In various prose writings of the 1930s Auden discussed his attitude towards prep and public schools.[12] More than once, in a context of criticism, he drew an analogy between such schools and a Fascist state.[13] But his attitude to these schools was not one of simple opposition. He admitted to having been happy at school, and as we have already observed he celebrated various aspects of his formal and informal education. Furthermore, his biographers agree that Auden was happy as a teacher (the role of leader and healer may again be pertinent here). School may have represented some values that he despised, but it also had qualities to which he was deeply attracted. This, I think, helps to explain the difficulties of reading *The orators*.

Most critics agree that the thematic concerns of this collage of prose and poetry revolve around the problems of leadership, power, group solidarity and right loving in a society characterised as 'this England where nobody is well'. The idea of bourgeois neurosis explored in *Poems* (1930) is taken up, and Auden seems to be investigating various Lawrentian panaceas to this problem. But finally the text defies strict exegesis because of what Edward Mendelson has aptly described as its 'bafflingly elusive tone'.[14] This problem is encountered throughout *The orators*, and nowhere more so than in the final section which comprises 'Six odes'. These balladic poems are full of private references to Auden's friends, of jokey public-school language, and of 'camp' suggestion. The second 'ode' is addressed to 'Gabriell Carritt, Captain of Sedburgh School XV, Spring 1927'. The 'ode' celebrates the first XV in what appears to be a parody of pre-1914 public-school enthusiasts like Newbolt:[15]

Symondson – praise him at once! –
Our right-wing three-quarter back
Sergy, bulwark of every defence,
      Mainspring of attack:
When aligned like a squadron of bombers they flew downfield
Over and over again we yelled
'Let the ball out to Sergy!' They did, he scored, and we dance.[16]

The tone of this, and the stanzas which precede it seems to be affectionate, yet if we place those 'bombers' in the context of the First World War we are led to the sinister implication that the ethos which produced 'play-up, play-up and play the game' may also induce the horrors of the Somme and Passchendaele. Any such irony, however, is not pursued, and the poem in its joyful acknowledgement of physical prowess and team spirit often reinforces the power of Newbolt's imprecations rather than deflating them. The poem closes with a plea that the boys may be allowed to express themselves as freely sexually, as they are allowed to express themselves on the games field. They will then come to the 'right sleep', which I take it is post-coital, fulfilling and implicitly homosexual. There is little irony here.

The poem then returns us, as so much in *The orators* does, to Auden's ambivalent attitude to public schools. They may separate boys from the rest of society, and impose upon them a hierarchically ordered society, they may repress sexuality, but on the other hand they offer community as against loneliness and provide the ground for homoerotic and homosexual experiences then outlawed by the society at large. *The orators*, by its form and language leans towards an endorsement of the positive aspects of public-school life. It is Auden's most radically modernist work. He experiments with collage, with diagrams, with oblique references and above all with the reproduction of a closed public-school tone and language. It is as if he wishes to speak to a small community of like-minded colleagues, to be the pedagogic leader and healer of his own upper-middle-class, small school.

We seem to be a long way from Communism here. Yet in the 1930s, though some discerned the extreme right-wing implications of parts of *The orators*, others 'took it for granted' that 'the implied politics were more or less Marxist'.[17] Why this should be so can only remain a matter of conjecture, but it seems likely that the appearance of Auden's poem 'A Communist to Others' in *Twentieth century* a few months after *The orators* appeared may well have been influential. Some detailed attention to this poem is therefore salutary in order to challenge the idea that Auden had any left-wing political convictions.

The poem opens by ostensibly addressing the working class. Immediately there is a tonal problem as Auden speaks from a superior height, and depicts working people as mindless sensationalists who are passively 'directed' by 'cops' to indulge in 'talkie-houses' or 'hugs' by the canal. The stanzaic pattern adopted has a triplet rhyme (fug/drug/hug) and bouncing metre which ensures that the experiences alluded to are both scorned and trivialised, as the poet continues to claim a knowledge of working-class fears:

We know the terrifying brink
From which in dreams you nightly shrink.
'I shall be sacked without', you think,
    'A testimonial.'

We cannot put on airs with you
The fears that hurt you hurt us too
    Only we say
That like all nightmares these are fake
If you would help us we could make
Our eyes to open, and awake
    Shall find night day.[18]

There are difficulties in the argument here which belie any Marxist commitment on the writer's part. The stance of superior wisdom sits uncomfortably with 'we cannot put on airs with you', and the force of this contradiction is exacerbated in the lines, 'If you would help us we could make / Our eyes to open.' Implicitly 'our' eyes are already open since 'we' know so much. The positioning of the pronouns in these lines is also telling.The effect is to wrest the primary impulse for change from the proletariat, and secure it for Auden's royal 'we'. Of course this openly contradicts Marxist doctrine which speaks of a section of the intelligentsia 'going over' to support a proletarian revolution. In Auden's poem the position is, at least in the first four stanzas, inverted. We might also legitimately question just how 'fake' the 'nightmare' of unemployment was to working-class people in 1932/3 when the numbers out of work reached their heighest for the decade.

The problem of Auden's privileged stance within the poem, and the attendant puzzle of exactly to whom the first person plural pronoun refers, is further complicated from stanza five onwards where suddenly the 'we' and the 'you' are apparently reversed:

O splendid person, you who stand
In spotless flannels or with hand
   Expert on trigger;
Whose lovely hair and shapely limb
Year after year are kept in trim
Till buffers envy as you swim
   Your Grecian figure:

You're thinking us a nasty sight;
Yes, we are poisoned, you are right,
   Not even clean;
We do not know how to behave
We are not beautiful or brave
You would not pick our sort to save
   Your first fifteen.

It may be tempting to read this as an indication that the upper-middle-class poet of the opening stanzas has 'gone over' to join the working class. There are, I think, two serious difficulties with such a reading. Firstly, although the pronouns are switched, the voice of the poem does not change; 'we' are as knowing and superior in 'our' vilification of the upper-middle classes as 'we' have been in 'our' treatment of the working classes in the first four stanzas. Secondly, it seems unlikely that Auden would go so far as to describe the working class as 'poisoned' or 'unclean'. Rather, these adjectives, and indeed the whole of stanzas five and six are more convincingly read as suggesting a distinction between 'hearties' and 'aesthetes' of the upper-middle class. In other words the 'we' appears to refer to a group of writers who, like the persona, see themselves as superior to, and isolated from the 'masses' of both working and middle classes.

The poem continues from the dismissal of the 'splendid person' in 'spotless flannels' to offer a blunt critique of 'dare-devil mystics', and of 'wise' men who are later characterised as the 'great malignant / Cambridge ulcer / That army intellectual / Of every kind of liberal'.

There follows a puerile curse directed against all those that have been satirised: Auden wishes illness, sterility, mental illness and death upon the bourgeoisie. He attempts to stand as aloof from the middle class here as he did from the working class at the beginning of the poem. In the final stanzas, Auden's position is further refined as he apostrophises an 'unhappy poet'. Romantic solitude and escapism are satirised against the ostensible 'tenderness' and engagement of the persona's stance. But there is irony here too, for in the course of the poem, the persona has dislocated himself to speak from a position of superior isolation. The insistent use of plural pronouns does not resolve this problem since we are never convincingly vouchsafed to whom they refer. And in the closing lines there is further inadvertent irony:

Comrades to whom our thoughts return,
Brothers for whom our bowels yearn
    When words are over;
Remember that in each direction
Love outside our own election
Holds us in unseen connection:
    O trust that ever.

Having previously satirised the 'army' of liberal intellectuals, and those who rely upon mystical notions to combat political problems, Auden now calls upon a 'love' which is beyond our 'election' to bind 'us' all together. This either constitutes a retreat into the liberal tradition which the poem is supposed to be satirising, wherein 'love' is posited as a catch-all panacea for political problems, or, more pruriently, through 'our yearning bowels' it suggests an instinctual, homosexual coupling of the classes. Whichever way one cares to read the stanza, it does not convince as the expression of a committed Marxist. As in the other works we have discussed, Auden here is quite capable of mounting a scathing critique of his own class, but has immense difficulty in articulating a coherent alternative position.

'A Communist to others' is, ironically, a poem which expresses more about the division of classes than it does about their possible integration. In 1934 Auden wrote of the way in which class differences are cemented by public school education: '. . . the public schoolboy's attitude to the working class and to the not-quite-quite has altered very little since the war. He is taught to be fairly kind and polite, provided of course they return the compliment, but their lives and needs remain as remote to him as those of another species. And I doubt very much if the same isn't true of the staff as well.'[19] A familiarity with public-school 'types', and a huge distance from the working-class is given expression in 'A Communist to others', and there is further evidence to suggest that Auden, despite his homosexual adventures with 'rough trade',[20] was fully aware of this distance. In a letter of autumn 1932, Auden wrote to Rupert Doone saying, 'No. I am a bourgeois. I shall not join the C.P.'[21]

Nevertheless, in 1933, Auden published a play, *The dance of death*, which has been taken by some critics to be signal of Auden's Marxism. In fact the play suffers from similar conflicts and paradoxes to those we have observed in all of Auden's work so far. Samuel Hynes has argued that *The dance of death* constitutes a 'parable of Marxist econom-ics'.[22] In support of this thesis he quotes the opening announcement of the play and its closing chorus. The former, according to Hynes, is an 'explicit' statement of 'a concept that is central to Marxist theory – the inevitable decline of the bourgeoisie'. And the latter speech is said to be advocating the 'force that matters . . . economic determinism and control of the instruments of production'.[23] But if we turn to the play, and place the speeches Hynes refers to in context, no such neat account suffices. The introductory announcement says that the play will present: '. . . a picture of the decline of a class, of how its members dream of a new life, but secretly desire the old, for there is death inside them.'[24] This need not be interpreted in terms of either Marx or Freud (the other 'parable source' cited by Hynes). Rather, I think, the announcement demonstrates Auden projecting his own divided consciousness onto the whole of his class. Auden himself is precisely in the position of wanting change, but cleaving to his liberal inheritance. The opening statement argues that the middle classes cannot resolve this predicament, and so are defeated. But the Marxist dialectic holds that rebel middle-class intellectuals have a role to play in the revolution. Auden side-steps this proposition through a reversion to Romantic metaphysics. The idea that we carry our own death within us may be more easily attributed to Rilke than it can to Marx or Freud.

As the play progresses we see the middle classes seeking various palliatives to their malaise. We see them indulge in the kind of cult of sun and athleticism fostered in Weimar Germany, we see them worshipping a Nationalist demagogue, and lastly we see them celebrating a Lawrentian principle of instinctual vitality. At the close of the play with the 'dancer' (an emblem of the middle classes) finally dead, the chorus introduces 'Marx' to the tune of Mendelssohn's 'Wedding march':

O Mr. Marx, you've gathered
All the material facts
You know the economic
Reasons for our acts.[25]

Marx duly appears on stage with 'two young communists', and speaking of the dancer says, 'The instruments of production have been too much for him. He is liquidated.' Buell has cogently remarked that this conclusion 'raises as many problems as it solves', and speaks of the 'patent absurdity of Marx's entrance to the "Wedding March"'.[26] The last detail surely implies a satire of Marxist enthusiasm, and is given further weight by the rest of the drama. For throughout the play the chorus has been marked by its gullibility, and its desperately fickle adherence to false doctrines. There is nothing to make us feel that middle-class adherence to Marxism is of a different order to the other decadent Romantic idealisms that we have witnessed them clinging to. There is nothing to give Marx's words any authority. The play is not so much a 'parable of Marxist economics' as a critique of Romantic self-indulgences as possible answers to an overwhelming spiritual malaise.

In these works of the early 1930s then, Auden may be seen reacting against his own class background, but finding when he does so that he is left with no secure position to hold. The ideas concerning leadership, instinctual love, and power, given incoherent expression in *The orators* are satirised in *The dance of death* but the conclusion of the play leaves one in doubt as to Auden's position. The entrance of two young Communists to the 'Wedding march' is somewhat 'camp', and reminds one of the 'we' in 'A Communist to others'. There is a feeling in these works, and in *The orators*, that the only group Auden wishes to adhere himself to is a gang of public-school chums, who share the same homoerotic or homosexual tastes. Nowhere in these works do we find any serious interest in Communism, or in Marxist ideas about history or revolution. And these were Auden's most radical years.

Between 1932 and 1936 Auden wrote the poems which were to appear in *Look, stranger!* (1936). These are years in which Auden's vision became increasingly conservative. This is evident not only in the ideological orientation of the poems, but also in their style. The modernism of the early 'telegraphese', the experimentation of *The orators* is abandoned, and stanzaic patterns increasingly prevail. Although the syntax is sometimes difficult to read, in the majority of poems it is far more transparent than in the earlier work. The tenor of *Look, stranger!* is amply illustrated by Auden's epigraph:

Since the external disorder, and extravagant lies,
The baroque frontiers, the surrealist police;
What can truth treasure, or heart bless,
But a narrow strictness?[27]

'Strictness' in loving is the principle theme of the volume. Almost a third of the poems are personal love poems, some of them being addressed to Benjamin Britten. But here, as in the rest of the volume, we find not a Lawrentian celebration of Eros but a movement towards the advocacy of love as an agent for good in specifically social and political contexts. The increasing sense of foreboding and European crisis that Auden registers in his epigraph, and in many other poems in *Look, stranger!*, engenders in him a traditional middle-class fear of revolutionary violence. His response is equally traditional, and constitutes a reversion to notions of right loving which have their origins in Christianity.

As the situation in Europe deteriorated, and his inherited values seemed to be increasingly threatened, Auden also betrayed a defensive patriotism. A poem like 'O Love the interest itself in thoughtless heaven' is demonstrative of this, and is also of interest as it appeared in *New country* alongside 'A Communist to others'. It is possible then, that at the time, it was taken to be an expression of left-wing sympathies. The opening lines of the poem, however, demonstrate Auden's reliance upon a metaphysical notion of love as an answer to social and political problems. In tones reminiscent of Shakespeare's *Henry V* 'Love' is invoked to induce in the audience a patriotism of place. It is very difficult indeed to relate this effusion about England to a left-wing politics. But as the poem progresses, Auden juxtaposes the past with a possible future, and it is this procedure which might be taken as a progressive gesture.

Auden details the imperialist and industrialist 'dream which so long has contented our will'. This 'dream' is said to be 'retreating', leaving behind it an obsolete industrial detritus, and 'The ladies and gentlemen apart, too much alone', who represent a dying breed. All this is rendered in unambiguous image and statement, carried by a relatively straightforward syntax. But when Auden introduces the 'dream' of the future, he also introduces an accumulation of metaphors in a very tortuous sentence structure:

Yet, O, at this very moment of our hopeless sigh

When inland they are thinking their thoughts but are watching
                                                             these islands,
As children in Chester look to Moel Fammau to decide
On picnics by the clearness or withdrawal of her treeless crown,

Some possible dream, long coiled in the ammonite's slumber
Is uncurling, prepared to lay on our talk and kindness
Its military silence, its surgeon's idea of pain;

And out of the Future into actual History,
As when Merlin, tamer of horses, and his lords to whom
Stonehenge was still a thought, the Pillars passed

And into the undared ocean swung north their prow,
Drives through the night and star-concealing dawn
For the virgin roadsteads of our hearts an unwavering keel.[28]

It is difficult to wrest coherence from this. Like the conclusion of
The dance of death, these stanzas raise questions rather than offering any
satisfactory resolutions. The dizzying progression of oblique metaphors is signal, I think, of Auden's own uncertainty and ambivalence.
Why, for instance, does Auden choose the reductive image of children
and picnics in the first of the three stanzas quoted? If 'inland' placed
against 'islands' is taken to suggest Europe, then we have the surely
inappropriate idea of beleaguered Europeans looking to England for
guidance as children in Chester contemplate the possibility of picnics.
And how do these 'picnics' relate to the 'military silence' and 'pain'
of the uncoiling dream? If 'we' really are sighing hopelessly to begin
with, how can such violence and pain render hope? Why does Auden
use images of magic and ancient religion to figure the realisation of
the dream in history? And finally, what are we to make of the dream
driving a 'keel' for the 'virgin roadsteads of our hearts'?

It seems to me that Auden, in trying to figure a possible dream of
the future, fails because he is tied to the past. One feels in the 'military
silence', the 'pain', the 'star-concealing dawn', that Auden is registering his fear of the future. However this may be, it is clear that these
stanzas do not constitute a vision of a Socialist revolution. They hint
at a change of heart which constitutes a reversion to liberalism. But for
this reader the poem concludes in confusion rather than conviction.
Auden casts himself in the role of soothsayer, but the problem is he
has no sure prophecy to give.

'Out on the lawn I lie in bed', written a year later in 1933, has a similar structure to the poem we have just looked at, but is perhaps, rather more successful. In 'Out on the lawn', however, the poet is not so much concerned with the past, but locates the poem securely in the present before projecting, in the closing stanzas, an apocalyptic vision of the future. This poem is also significant because Auden was later to remark that it records his first experience of Agape.[29] Certainly the opening of the poem is not inconsistent with such a claim, for it expresses feelingly a state of beatitude. The poet celebrates his 'lucky' situation as a schoolmaster at a public school where he is allowed on summer evenings to sit, 'Equal with colleagues in a ring', with 'fear', the 'lion griefs' and 'death' banished at least temporarily. But as the moon rises over Europe, the poet's sense of private felicity is intruded upon by thoughts of the public and political world. 'We', he suggests, 'do not care to know' about violence abroad or about 'what doubtful act allows / Our freedom in this English house'. There is no doubt that the pronouns refer to those who enjoy employment, wealth and security within the walls of the public school; the same walls which also act as a buffer against social and political calamity. Auden is able to deploy self-irony effectively here since he has admitted his own culpability in a very straightforward way; he is enjoying himself but has a guilty conscience.

As the poem proceeds, Auden distances himself and his peers from the onward movement of history. The 'path on which we move' shows 'intentions not our own', and something will be achieved which '...our excitement could conceive / But our hands left alone'. This 'something' is an apocalyptic revolution. Auden admits his distance from action; he is insulated not only by public-school walls, but also implicitly by his imagination; a violent 'sea' of change is juxtaposed with the poet's gentler 'river dreams'. The poet's fear of revolution is transparently figured as Auden goes on to make a plea that the liberal values represented by his public-school background will surface in the new society, like the parent's voice rising through a child's. If there must be a revolution, Auden is saying, let liberal upper-middle-class values survive it.

May this for which we dread to lose
Our privacy, need no excuse
   But to that strength belong;
As through a child's rash happy cries
The drowned voices of his parents rise
   In unlamenting song.[30]

'Out on the lawn I lie in bed' is a very explicit statement of Auden's political and social position. However much he may have reacted against his own class, ultimately he could not separate himself from it or its values. There are several more poems in *Look, stranger!* which make this abundantly clear. 'Now from my window sill I watch the night', is also set in the public school at which Auden was teaching, and constitutes a prayer to the 'Lords of limit', to protect both boys and masters, whom the poet 'loves', from violent extremities. And in 'Here on the cropped grass of the narrow ridge I stand', Auden offers a panoramic vision of England. As in several 1930s poems Auden stands above the scene he is describing, and this is not only a spatial metaphor, but one in which Auden's class position is also implicit:

> I give
> The children at the open swimming pool
> Lithe in their first and little beauty
>   A closer look;
> Follow the cramped clerk crooked at his desk,
> The guide in shorts pursuing flowers
>   In their careers;
> A digit of the crowd, would like to know
> Them better whom the shops and trams are full of,
> The little men and their mothers, not plain but
>   Dreadfully ugly.[31]

Here is a stark expression of class divisions. Auden looks down, in every sense of that phrase, upon his class inferiors. He would like to 'know / Them better', but there is little chance of him doing so, particularly as he regards them as 'little' and 'ugly'. The poem continues to provide a critique of industrial society, wherein what has gone wrong is blamed upon a lack of 'disciplined love'. Auden concludes by invoking Wilfred Owen and Katherine Mansfield as examples of how to write, and how to achieve right action. What that action might be is left unsaid, but implicitly it involves a disciplined love which goes beyond the merely sensual.

Auden's panoramic vision is extended in 'Easily, my dear, you move, easily your head', to include Europe. The nightmarish world of Hitler, Mussolini, Churchill, and Van der Lubbe is described. The problem, and its possible solution, is once again expressed in terms of 'love':

> But love, except at our proposal,
> Will do no trick at his disposal;

Without opinions of his own, performs
The programme that we think of merit,
And through our private stuff must work
His public spirit.[32]

The moral imperative is that of Christianity: to love one another. Auden
wrote this poem in 1934. A year later he wrote an essay in which he
discussed the differences between Communism and Christianity.
Christianity, wrote Auden, is not 'a quietist religion', but it does argue
that 'a change of heart can and must bring about a change in the
environment'.[33] Communism argues the obverse; that only by
changing the environment can a change of heart ensue. It is quite clear
that in Look, stranger! Auden's position is much closer to the Christian
position. Auden, by this time, might not have fully arrived at the
conviction which led him to re-adopt the High Anglicanism of his
familial inheritance, but he is well on the way.

In 1935 Auden gave up school mastering, and worked for a year
with the documentary film unit in London. This proved unfulfilling,
and Auden spent the rest of the decade as a professional travel-writer.
He spent from late May to August 1936 in Iceland, the product of
which was his collaborative book with Louis MacNeice entitled Letters
from Iceland. It was in this volume that Auden's brilliant, witty, if
somewhat aleatory poem Letter to Lord Byron first appeared, in which
Auden significantly described himself as a 'selfish pink old liberal'. In
1937 he visited Spain, but did not stay long, later admitting that the
desecration of churches by Republican forces had upset him greatly.
Out of this trip came the poem 'Spain', which some critics have used
as evidence of Auden's left-wing position.

The poem in fact shows Auden to be anti-Fascist, but certainly not
pro-Communist. He uses Spain as an emblem through which he can
express his sense of the necessity for choice in moral action. The war
is described as the result of the moral conflict within each individual.
In Spain we are told, 'Our fevers menacing shapes are precise and
alive'. Each individual must choose either the 'Just City' or 'the suicide
pact / the Romantic death'. There is no certainty that good will prevail,
and no indication that the Just City might be built upon Marxist or
Socialist foundations. The very phrase 'Just City' is more reminiscent
of St Augustine than it is of Marx. And the Utopia of Auden's
imagination, given expression in the poem, enshrines the values of the
liberal bourgeoisie. 'Tomorrow', we are told, may see 'the rediscovery
of romantic love', 'walks by the lake', 'bicycle races through the

suburbs', the 'pageant master and the musician', and 'poets exploding like bombs'. Although this list is in some ways attractive, it is difficult not to feel that it constitutes a glib idealisation. And his treatment of the war is similarly romanticised and damagingly unfeeling:

> To-day the deliberate increase in the chances of death;
> The conscious acceptance of guilt in the necessary murder;
>   To-day the expending of powers
> On the flat ephemeral pamphlet and the boring meeting.
>
> To-day the makeshift consolations; the shared cigarette;
> The cards in the candle-lit barn and the scraping concert,
>   The masculine jokes; to-day the
> Fumbled and unsatisfactory embrace before hurting.[34]

These are the stanzas that Orwell attacked so trenchantly in his essay 'Inside the whale'. As Orwell says, the phrase '"necessary murder"... could only be written by a person to whom murder is at most a *word*'.[35] Mention of the 'flat ephemeral pamphlet' and the 'boring meeting' betrays Auden's scant respect for the practicalities of politics, whilst the portrayal of soldiers seems to be underpinned by a notion of homoerotic solidarity, rather than political ideology. It is tempting to suggest that the poem has rather more to do with the Romantic death than it has with building the Just City.

Before leaving for Spain, Auden had written to a friend attempting to explain his decision for 'visiting' the civil war:

> I feel I can speak with authority about la Condition Humaine of only a small class of English intellectuals and professional people and the time has come to gamble on something bigger.
> I shall probably be a bloody bad soldier but how can I speak to/for them without becoming one?[36]

In fact Auden never became a soldier, and in my view, 'Spain' does not show Auden speaking either to or for soldiers of the Popular Front. Auden's self-diagnosis, quoted above, is as true for his poems of the later 1930s as it is for his earlier poems. He spoke from his individual experience which was that of an upper-middle-class Englishman.

In 1938 Auden travelled with Christopher Isherwood to view the Sino-Japanese conflict. He came back with what he described as a 'tourist's aquaintance' of China. It was, he said, a country 'impossible to know'.[37] Nevertheless the experience gave rise to the sonnet sequence 'In time of war' which uses some of the incidents he had observed in order to express a panoramic vision of history wherein man has fallen and failed to achieve the 'Good Place'. Whilst in China, Isherwood suspected Auden of having distinct Christian leanings,[38] and this is borne out, both in the sonnet sequence and in such poems of 1938 and 1939 as 'Musée des Beaux Arts' and the 'Elegy for W.B. Yeats'. Both these poems are concerned to place art outside the world of action and event, and to question the relationship of art to ethics and to Christianity. Auden's slightly later interest in the Christian Existentialist thought of Kierkegaard is thus prefigured.

Auden's poems of the 1930s show a gradual movement back towards his liberal conservative, Anglican inheritance. In the first two years of the decade there is some flirtation with radicalism, but this is more often consonant with radical right-wing thinking than with the left. What then of claims that Auden was an 'objectivist', a 'Social Realist' or a 'Socialist Realist'? Those who have used such words to describe Auden rarely trouble themselves with definitions of their terms. Sometimes this is for the very good reason that those terms are derived from extremely incoherent theorising. This is the case with 'objectivism', which stems from two rather slight essays by Geoffrey Grigson, published in 1938 and 1939 respectively.[39] I shall be looking at these in more detail when I discuss Grigson and his magazine New verse in a later chapter. For now, suffice it to say that there is not a sufficiently defined theory of objectivism against which we might measure Auden's work.

This is true too of 'social realism' which presumably is a slightly less committed version of socialist realism. We have then to rely upon theories of socialist realism to advance our discussion. The two major and influential theorists who might have relevance to Auden's case are the infamous Zhdanov (whom Terry Eagleton has described as a 'cultural thug') and Bertolt Brecht. Zhdanov, in 1934, said of socialist realism: 'It means in the first place that you must know life in order to be able to depict it truthfully in artistic creations, to depict it neither scholastically, nor lifelessly, not simply as objective reality, but rather as reality in its revolutionary development. The truthfulness and historical exactitude of the artistic image must be linked with the task of ideological transformation, of the education of the working people in the spirit of socialism.'[40] Auden's work is neither scholastic nor lifeless, and clearly often goes beyond the bounds of 'objective reality'. One might also tentatively concede that on a few occasions Auden attempts to figure 'revolutionary development' although, as I have argued, when he does so, he expresses a very ambivalent attitude towards such development. But clearly Auden's work cannot be said to be allied to the 'task of ideological transformation', or to the 'education of the working people'. And so his work departs from Zhdanov's prescriptions.

Brecht's notions about socialist realism, however, are much less doctrinaire than Zdhanov's. Can we then relate Auden's poetry more closely to Brecht's ideas? Brecht says, 'Realistic means discovering the causal complexes of society/unmasking the prevailing view of things as the view of those who rule it/writing from the standpoint of the class which offers the broadest solutions for the pressing difficulties in which human society is caught/emphasising the element of development/making possible the concrete and making possible abstraction from it.'[41] Auden's work does not seem to me to demonstrate convincingly any of these features. Auden writes from the standpoint of the ruling class whose prevailing view is liberal at best. Rather than revealing the causal complexes of society or emphasising the element of development, Auden's poetry embodies tensions between past values and possible progress, tensions which are either resolved negatively by prophesying the death of the middle class, or positively by ideas of erotic, filial and finally Christian love. Neither his defeatism or his hope have much to do with socialist realism.

It might be thought that even if Auden's poetry itself does not show any trace of Marxist thought, and cannot be adequately described as 'socialist realist', then perhaps his ideas about poetry might offer some evidence of interest in developing a left-wing poetic. But this is not so. In fact Auden's writings about the nature of his own art betray the same tensions that inform his poetry. There are some gestures towards a progressive positon, but much more which attaches Auden to the central Romantic conservative tradition.

It should be noted, first of all, how comparatively little Auden contributed to the debate about the function of poetry in relation to public events and politics, which was conducted in books and magazines during the 1930s and early 1940s. Between 1935 and 1939, however, he did commit himself to paper on the subject. Various themes emerge from these utterances, but very little is innovatory. The furthest Auden goes towards a radical poetic is to assert the democratising value of pluralism. Poetry, he says, should be 'taken down from the shelf';[42] he does not believe in 'Poetry with a capital P';[43] poetry is 'memorable speech', and this includes riddles, nursery rhymes, and the like.[44] But these slightly forward-looking tendencies must be weighed against Auden's defence of the 'high-brow', his subscription to such Romantic notions as 'sincerity',[45] or poetry as the reconciler of 'the unwilling subject and object',[46] and perhaps most pertinently for my purposes here, his emphatic rejection of poetry as an instrument of politics. The poet, Auden avers in an essay of 1936, is not a good politician; he is not concerned with telling people what to do, but with extending our knowledge of good and evil.[47] The poet, unlike the social reformer, actively wants evils to write about; 'the slums or disease or hell' are his subject materials.[48]

The same essay concludes with Auden making a declaration of the kind of poetry he would 'like to write but can't', and that constitutes, 'the thoughts of a wise man in the speech of the common people'. In the context of the Workers' Educational Association publication, The highway, in which this essay was first published, Auden's remark is at once condescending and ingratiating. The literary provenance of the quotation, which has its source in Aristotle, but comes more directly from Yeats speaking of Lady Gregory's work,[49] is less deceiving; Auden's aspirations are akin to the conservative Yeats. In an essay about light verse, written in 1938, Auden argues that 'light' does not necessarily mean trivial, and that although light verse tends to be 'public' it is conservative in its orientation.[50] We need look no further than to Auden's self-confessedly 'light' Letter to Lord Byron to perceive the ac-curacy of Auden's remark.

In 1939 Auden left England for America. Precisely how and why he came to this decision is not entirely clear, but writing about it in a letter, he spoke of family life being a threat to artistic and intellectual endeavour and went on: 'I felt the situation in England was becoming impossible. I couldn't grow up. English life is for me a family life, and I love my family but I don't want to live with them'.[51] Without wishing to suggest that these remarks tell the whole story of why Auden emigrated, they do seem to me highly pertinent. Throughout the decade, despite his schoolmastering, and his various travels, he was always drawn back towards the family home in Birmingham. His poetry follows a similar pattern. It begins by expressing an ambivalent attitude to his class (and therefore his family) background, but finally is drawn back towards inherited values. The act of individuation which he desired so much in 1929, occurs in a paradoxical way ten years later with his departure from England and his family. On arriving in America he very soon began a relationship which he considered in terms of marriage, and he re-joined the Anglican communion. It is as if both the psycho-sexual dilemmas and the moral perplexities which are expressed in so much of his 1930s poetry, are made susceptible of resolution by a physical and corresponding psychological distance from his parents, and from the class divisions of England.

The style of Auden's poetry in the 1930s in terms of broad traditions juxtaposes the obliquity, syntactic difficulty, and startling imagery of modernism, with the plainer language and syntax, the more conventional metaphors and rhythms of the Georgians. A modernist disdain for an audience vies with the Georgian aspiration to court one. High Toryism vies with a more liberal conservatism, and as the decade progressed the latter began increasingly to dominate. The particular trademarks of the style, which have been dubbed the 'Audenesque' are indicative of the tensions in his position. Auden's use of the definite article either placed against a very indefinite noun ('the enemy', 'the antagonist') or used as a means of categorisation ('The little men and their mothers', 'The sallow faces of the city'), his fondness for inexplicable or inapposite adjectives ('vague woods', 'pansy railway', 'feather ocean'), his use of imperative opening lines ('Consider this and in our time', 'Get there if you can and see the land you once were proud to own') and his utilisation of reductive or bathetic similes in which the brain is likened to a 'poky nursery' or his father to 'an Airedale' are recurrent rhetorical devices. They are symptomatic of a pedagogical intent, and in this way are apparently directed outwards towards an audience, but they also confer superior knowledge and isolation upon the poet, sometimes deliberately obfuscating his meaning. In the later 1930s and in the 1940s these devices are seen less and less in his work.

In a letter of 1937 Auden wrote that 'the artist . . . can only tell the truth about things he knows and is interested in, and that depends on where and how he lives . . .'[52] It is my contention that his poetry of the 1930s demonstrates this proposition. It is poetry which expresses the dilemmas of an upper-middle-class homosexual with a tender conscience, who clearly perceives some of the social and political ills of his time, but can find no answer to them without reverting to the traditional values of his class. It might be supposed by some that Auden's sexuality led him towards a radical sexual politics, but I do not think this is the case. As some of the poems I have looked at here suggest, his homosexuality and homoeroticism were inextricably involved with the life of public schools; it was, in other words, part of an upper-middle-class tradition.[53] And when, in Berlin, his sexual preferences led him into brief liaisons with working-class boys, it did not, I think, engender further understanding of that class, but involved him in exploitative relationships in which he wielded power. That Auden perceived this himself is, I think, indicated by the lines I quoted earlier from 'It was Easter as I walked in the public garden'.

The qualities of Auden's best work of the 1930s, its wit, irony, comedy and liveliness, will always have its admirers. But it must be realised that he was not the spokesman of a generation, of a decade, or of the left. The world of his poems relates to his public-school and Oxford education, to his schoolmastering in various private and public schools, and to his extensive travels in a decade when overseas holidays were available only to very few indeed. His experience was of the upper-middle class, and in his writing he is often very self-conscious of that class and of class division. And, in the final analysis, however much one might admire his facility as a writer, his liberal conservative ideology should not be ignored but clearly understood for what it is.

Notes

1 For biographical details, here and elsewhere, I am greatly indebted to Humphrey Carpenter, *W.H. Auden: a biography*, London, 1981.
2 See W.H. Auden, 'The prolific and the devourer', *The English Auden*, ed. E. Mendelson, London, 1977, p. 397. This text will be referred to hereafter as *EA*.
3 'The prolific and the devourer', *EA*, p. 397.
4 W.H. Auden, *A certain world*, London, 1971, p. 146.
5 W.H. Auden, 'The liberal Fascist', *EA*, p. 323.
6 S. Spender, 'W.H. Auden and his poetry', *Auden: a collection of critical essays*, ed. M.K. Spears, Englewood Cliifs, New Jersey, 1964, pp. 26-7.
7 W.H. Auden,'Journal entries', *EA*, p. 299-300.
8 *EA*, pp. 37-40.
9 Carpenter, *W.H. Auden: a biography*, p. 97.
10 See R. Williams, *Culture and society 1780-1950* (1958), Harmondsworth, 1979, pp. 178-80.
11 'Journal entries', *EA*, p. 301.
12 See W.H. Auden, 'The liberal Fascist' and 'The prolific and the devourer', *EA*, pp. 321-7 and pp. 398-401 respectively.
13 Auden, 'The liberal Fascist', *EA*, p. 325, and 'The prolific and the devourer', *EA*, p. 400.
14 *EA*, p. 94.
15 I am thinking of poems by Newbolt like 'The best school of all' or 'Vitae lampada'. In the latter we find the famous imprecation to 'Play up! play up! and play the game!'
16 *EA*, p. 97.
17 G.S. Fraser, 'The career of W.H. Auden', *Auden: a collection of critical essays*, p. 82.
18 I am using the text of the poem as it appeared in *New country*, ed. M. Roberts, London, 1933, pp. 209-13.
19 Auden, 'The liberal Fascist', *EA*, pp. 322-3.

20 Carpenter, *W.H. Auden: a biography*, p. 90.
21 *Ibid.*, p. 153.
22 S. Hynes, *The Auden generation*, London, 1976, p. 129.
23 *Ibid.*, pp. 127-8.
24 W.H. Auden, *The dance of death*, London, 1933, p. 7.
25 *Ibid.*, p. 38.
26 F. Buell, *W.H. Auden as a social poet*, New York, 1973, p. 101.
27 *EA*, p. 111.
28 *EA*, p. 119.
29 W.H. Auden, Foreword to 'The Protestant mystics', *Forewords and afterwords*, London, 1973, pp. 69-70.
30 *EA*, p. 138.
31 *Ibid.*, p. 142.
32 *Ibid.*, p. 153.
33 W.H. Auden, 'The good life', *EA*, p. 345.
34 *W.H. Auden, Spain*, London, 1937.
35 G. Orwell, 'Inside the whale', *Inside the whale and other essays*, Harmondsworth, 1962, p. 37.
36 Carpenter, *W.H. Auden: a biography*, p. 207.
37 *Ibid.*, p. 239.
38 C. Isherwood, *Christopher and his kind*, New York, 1977, pp. 241-2, 306, 333.
39 G. Grigson, 'Lonely but not lonely enough', *New verse*, Nos. 31-2, autumn-winter 1938, pp. 16-17; Preface to the 1st edition, *New verse: an anthology* (1939), London, 1942, pp. 15-24.
40 D. Laing, *The Marxist theory of art*, London, 1978, p. 41.
41 *Ibid.*, pp. 56-7.
42 W.H. Auden, Introduction to 'The poet's tongue' (1935), *EA*, p. 328.
43 W.H. Auden, 'Poetry, poets, and taste' (1936), *EA*, p. 358.
44 Auden, 'The poet's tongue', *EA*, p. 327.
45 Auden, 'Poetry, poets, and taste', *EA*, p. 360.
46 Auden, 'The poet's tongue', *EA*, p. 329.
47 *Ibid.*
48 'Poetry, poets and taste', *EA*, p. 359.
49 W.B. Yeats, 'Dramatis Personae', *Autobiographies* (1965), New York, 1974, p. 264.
50 W.H. Auden, 'Light verse' (1938), *EA*, pp. 363-8.
51 Carpenter, *W.H. Auden: a biography*, p. 243.
52 *Ibid.*, p. 245.
53 See P. Fussell, *The Great War and modern memory* (1975), London, 1977, pp. 270-99, and *W.H. Auden: a biography*, pp. 47-9.

4

The Auden 'gang': Day Lewis, Spender and MacNeice

I

Cecil Day Lewis, Stephen Spender and Louis MacNeice were identified with Auden in the 1930s as a group of Communist poets. The association of their names has continued ever since. These are the poets that Samuel Hynes and Bernard Bergonzi concentrate upon in their studies of the period. They are also the poets who dominated Alice Prochaska's 1976 London exhibition, 'Young writers of the 'thirties'.[1] More recently, in 1984, a critical volume was published in the 'Casebook' series, *Thirties poetry: the Auden group,*[2] the title of which speaks for itself. In challenging such mythical perspectives it is not then enough merely to re-read Auden. We must look at the rest of the group to see whether in their writings we can find anything of the left-wing poetry, the revolutionary poetics, which they are said to have expressed. But before looking in turn at the poetry and poetics of Day Lewis, Spender, and MacNeice, we may identify immediately some aspects of their position within society that they shared with Auden.

All three of Auden's 'disciples' come from a similar class and educational background to their supposed leader. Although both Day Lewis and MacNeice were born in Ireland, they were sent to English prep and public schools.[3] And, just as Auden was directly related to the Church of England via his maternal grandmother, so too Day Lewis and MacNeice have close family connections with the establishment Church; they were both sons of Church of Ireland clergymen. Spender, however, was brought up in London, and his father was a Liberal politician. In his autobiography, Spender is anxious to stress that he did not attend public school, and that his family was relatively impecunious. But it is quite clear that despite such protestations he did belong to the upper reaches of the middle class. His family had servants. The school he did attend was not public but private and fee-paying; he did not attend a state grammar school.[4]

All three poets proceeded from school to Oxford University where they met Auden separately. They did not all know each other well until later on. Indeed it was not until 1947 that Auden, Spender and Day Lewis found themselves in the same room together.[5] Nevertheless, it is clear from the autobiographical writings of Spender and Day Lewis that on meeting Auden in the late 1920s, they both fell under his spell. And it is undoubtedly these two who have benefited most through their association with Auden. MacNeice was always more aloof, and, as I shall argue later on, his reputation has suffered rather than been enhanced by his involvement in the mythology of the decade.

However this may be, it is not surprising that Spender, Day Lewis and MacNeice, coming as they did from a similar background, share tensions and paradoxes to be found in Auden's work. They all, with varying degrees of intensity, react critically to their own class background, yet ultimately cleave to its values. They all explicitly or implicitly communicate a sense of guilt, and seek to articulate answers to contemporary social and political problems. And they all claim both Georgian and modernist literary progenitors. But because they share such broad similarities does not, of course, mean that their poetry has no individuality. I now hope to show that, despite sharing some of Auden's stylistic mannerisms, it would be exceedingly difficult to mistake Spender's poetic voice for that of Auden, or to confound MacNeice's work with that of Day Lewis. I begin my discussion here by looking briefly at Day Lewis's work for he undoubtedly owes more to Auden than either Spender or MacNeice.

II

Cecil Day Lewis was born in 1904. He lived for the first three years of his life at Ballintubber, near Sligo, Queen's County, Ireland, where he and his parents lived in a large and elegant detached house.[6] It is doubtful if the family accommodation was ever quite so sumptuous again, as his father left Ireland to take up a curacy at the Priory in Malvern, subsequently moving to Ealing, Notting Hill, Lancaster Gate, and finally to Edwinstowe in north Nottinghamshire where he was the parish vicar until his death in 1937. Nevertheless, Day Lewis's childhood was spent in relatively opulent surroundings. His world was one of servants, nursemaids, gardeners and relatives, the latter gaining in importance after his mother died when he was only four years old.

Indeed most of his summers between 1908and1914 were spent at the rectory in Monart, where his uncle the Reverend W.G. Squires was the vicar, and his aunt provided a surrogate mother-figure. Here the lifestyle was sumptous: 'Rude plenty extended some way indoors. We were always eating: breakfast, elevenses, lunch, early tea, high tea, late supper, with visits to the fruit trees and bushes in between, or to the earthenware crocks which held buttermilk and cold, cold water from the wells.'[7]

Day Lewis's first school was 'Wilkie's', a small, private preparatory establishment, described by the poet as 'humane and lively'.[8] Thanks to the tutorship of his aunt, Day Lewis was already an 'avid reader' at the age of six, so unsurprisingly he took well to school and the beginnings of a classical education. In 1917 he won a scholarship to Sherborne school where he entered the Lower Fifth Classical, and continued his studies until he gained a place at Wadham College, Oxford in 1923. Like Auden, Day Lewis remembers various masters at his public school with great affection, and attributes to them some of his early appreciation of English literature.[9]

During vacations from Sherborne, Day Lewis would return to Edwinstowe where his father, now re-married, practised his vocation. The younger Day Lewis has described his father's religion as being of the polite, unenthusiastic variety, and for the young poet Christianity was 'a tradition and a habit'[10] rather than a passionately held conviction. This was the typical theology of the Church of England. Despising the lavish ritual and vestements of Catholicism or High Anglicanism, as much as it shied away from the ranting evangelism of 'low' churches, it held the middle way. And there it also found a social analogue: it was inexorably middle class. Day Lewis recalls that his father's Christianity 'found nothing paradoxical in the rigid class distinctions of the time'.[11] Cecil was not allowed to join the church choir or the boy scouts because both groups of boys did not belong to his own class. Furthermore, when at Edwinstowe, Day Lewis was made aware of the insecurity of his social position:

... I lived at Edwinstowe between two worlds. On the one hand there were the great houses ... – which I entered rarely and always with a sense of *de bas en haut*: on the other lay an equally inaccessible terrain – the world of the miners, farm labourers, railwaymen, small shopkeepers. Class distinctions were still in force, so there was no question of my hobnobbing with the children of the working class or petty-bourgeois families ... I was limited therefore, to the professional-class families in the neighbourhood, who were few and far between ...[12]

We may recall that Auden's remark about belonging to an 'orphan class'. It is, I think, important to understand that these poets not only felt divided from the working class, but also felt keenly their separation from the more moneyed and titled reaches of their own class.

There is little doubt that attendance at Oxford University did little to allay this extreme class-consciousness. Day Lewis writes of arriving at Oxford feeling 'the same defensiveness about Wadham' that he had 'occasionally felt about Sherborne'.[13] Just as Sherborne was not one of the more renowned public schools, so Wadham was not one of the prestigious colleges. He goes on to speak of the 'opulence and leisure' of Oxford, but also notes that his allowance of £250 per annum meant that he 'lacked the means' to fully indulge in the 'gilded and well-oiled life'.[14] In other words, Oxford was hardly a socially broadening experience, and on leaving Day Lewis was obliged to find gainful employment in the same narrow world in which he had spent all of his life: he became a schoolmaster. From 1927to1935 he taught first at prep schools in Oxford and Scotland, and then at a public school in Cheltenham.

Day Lewis was nothing if not prolific as a poet. By the time he collaborated with Auden in editing the 1927 Oxford Poetry anthology for Basil Blackwell, he had already published one volume, and his second was about to appear. Day Lewis was later to disown these early works as 'juvenilia', but their respective titles, *Beechen vigil* and *Country comets* are very telling. For Day Lewis was more of a countryman than Auden, and having, as an adolescent, been steeped in the Romantic poetry of the nineteenth century, he produced early nature poems some of which rival the effusions of the most honeyed Georgians. Needless to say, there is nothing here which smacks of an interest in radical politics of any persuasion. The conservatism is quiet, unassuming and total.

Day Lewis's following two volumes, *Transitional poem* (1929) and *From feathers to iron* (1931), are lyrical sequences which display some stylistic development, but little in the way of political advance. As G.S. Fraser has remarked, Day Lewis was a poet who had enormous difficulty in shaking off his various influences,[15] and so we find in these two books echoes of his recent reading. Friends and teachers at Oxford had recommended the middle Yeats, Eliot, Hopkins, and Donne. Auden is said to have introduced Day Lewis to the poetry of Hardy and Frost.[16] And so, in the sequences of 1929 and 1931, an odd stylistic blend emerges. *Transitional poem* is often Yeatsian, but there are traces of an older lineage in the syntactic inversions to be found in many of the poems. There are also occasional attempts to develop conceited metaphors in the manner of Donne. In other poems we find balladic quatrains which provide faint echoes of Hardy. The subject-matter of the sequence is no less grounded in tradition than its manner. The poems are full of philosophical speculations as Day Lewis broaches the 'monstrous credibility / Of all antinomies'. As this phrase implies, despite the poet's aspirations to be 'ascetic and cerebral',[17] the dominant tone is undoubtedly Romantic. The place of poetry in relationship to nature, reason and love, provides the thematic material for many other poems in this largely unremarkable volume.

From *feathers to iron* continues in a similar vein. This sequence, however, has more thematic coherence, for here Day Lewis charts his wife's pregnancy from conception to parturition. As one might expect from such a project, much of the imagery is culled from nature and the seasons. But one also senses Day Lewis straining to impose the trappings of modernist imagery upon his essentially bucolic imagination. The results of this often sound naive, and teeter on the brink of absurdity. Nowhere is this more plangently illustrated than when the progress of his wife's labour is likened to the progress of a steam train:

Come out in the sun, for a man is born today!
Early this morning whistle in the cutting told
Train was arriving, hours overdue, delayed
By snow-drifts, engine-trouble, Act of God, who cares now?—
For here alights the distinguished passenger.
Take a whole holiday in honour of this! [18]

The tone, language and deliberate omission of connectives here are all reminiscent of Auden's early manner, particularly as it is manifested in *The orators*. The 'whole holiday' of the last line, signals Day Lewis's imaginative attachment to the public school ethos; an attachment which continually mars his work until the late 1930s. Such boyish enthusiasm may have its charm, but it is doubtful if Day Lewis's wife found the process of childbirth quite as breezey as the poet's lines suggest.

So far distant are many of the poems in the sequence from the recognisable realities of conception, pregnancy and childbirth that it is not merely symptomatic of the times to find that several reviewers found in *From feathers to iron* an implicitly revolutionary 'political allegory';[19] a feat which is now extremely difficult to emulate. According to Day Lewis the reviews came as a surprise to him, but perhaps such audience reaction prompted him to clarify matters by attempting to write in his next sequence, *The magnetic mountain*, what he later described as a 'violently revolutionary poem'.[20]

The magnetic mountain is, as Bernard Bergonzi has remarked, closely imitative of Auden 'for long stretches at a time'.[21] And it is the Auden of the 'Six odes' in *The orators* that Day Lewis here surpasses in naive schoolboy revolutionary enthusiasm. The direction of the revolution, and the means of attaining it, are as confused in Day Lewis's poems as they are in Auden's book. Crude applications of D. H. Lawrence's ideas about erotic love and true 'manhood' may be found in both works, together with an unhealthy longing for strong (implicitly dictatorial) leadership. But if the intellectual content of *The magnetic mountain* is sometimes disturbingly right-wing, the tone of the poems often allows the reader to adopt a less than serious attitude.

Wystan, Rex, all you that have not fled,
This is our world, this is where we have grown
Together in flesh and live; though each alone
Shall join the enclosed order of the dead,
Enter the silent brotherhood of bone.

All of you that have a cool head and safe hands
Awaken early, there is much to do;
Hedges to raze, channels to clear, a true
Reckoning to find. The other side commands
Eternity. We have an hour or two.[22]

Day Lewis's sequence is replete with this kind of facile Romantic utopianism. The world 'belongs' to a group of public-school chums who are going to save it for themselves in a spirit of 'play-up, play-up, and play the game'. The 'gung-ho' tones of Newbolt are to be heard without irony elsewhere in *The magnetic mountain*, particularly in the several references which reduce political struggle to the terms of a 'rugger' match. Such 'binary vision',[23] which sees everything in terms of 'us' against 'them', is a prominent feature of much First World War poetry. In the 1930s, (and particularly in some of the poetry of the Spanish Civil War) such bifurcated perspectives, which had their origins in the excoriating experiences of trench warfare, are reproduced in overtly political terms. But in Day Lewis's work, distanced as it is from action, 'binary vision' descends to simplistic melodramatic assertion. At the time he was writing this, Day Lewis was working at Cheltenham School, and as he says in his autobiography he had at this time 'never met a high-ranking industrialist or financier, a Cabinet-Minister or a Trades Union leader'.[24] On his own admission his vision of 'the enemy' was as romanticised as his idea of 'the workers'. The poem is like a pastiche of the Auden who wrote, 'Roar Gloucestershire do yourself proud' or 'Walk on air do we and how' from The orators. Its relationship to any serious political thought is entirely undermined by its air of meglomaniac conspiracy, and its trivialising satire, which reduces the forces of reaction to the status of comic-strip villains. There is no genuine indignation in the poem to give the critique of the ruling class any force. It is difficult not to believe that the 'righteous side' in the poem is something of an exclusive club: Wystan, Rex and the rest of the gang.

Several poems from The magnetic mountain were published in New signatures and New country. Like Auden's contributions to these anthologies, Day Lewis's show no traces of a Marxist position. On the few occasions when he assays a vision of the future, Day Lewis reminds us of the Fascistic overtones to be heard in The orators:

Born haters will blast through debris or granite,
Willing work on the permanent ways,
And natural lovers repair the race.
As needle to North, as wheel in wheel turning,
Men shall know their masters and women their need,
Mating and submitting, not dividing and defying,
Force shall fertilize, mass shall breed.[25]

However adolescent the tone of most poems in the sequence, it is hard to ignore the chauvinism in a passage like this. Day Lewis satirises the ruling class to which he belongs, but then articulates a position to the right not the left of their dominating ideology.

In 1934, the year following the publication of The magnetic mountain, Day Lewis published his book A hope for poetry. Far from being an attempt to develop a left-wing poetic, the book barely touches upon politics, but rather expresses Day Lewis's Romantic conservatism. Using a metaphor of the son's relationship to his father (Harold Bloom would like this) Day Lewis chooses Hopkins, Owen, and Eliot as the progenitors of the 'new' poetry which is being written by himself, Auden, and Spender. Hopkins and Owen are described as 'true revolutionary poets'[26] because they wrote innovative poems. This is a questionable assertion with respect to Owen, but the important point is that Day Lewis nowhere attempts to relate their work to politics. The same is true of his discussion of Eliot. All three poets are discussed in terms of their technique, and Owen is praised for his presumed virtues of 'pity and indignation'.

Day Lewis goes on to articulate his own views about poetry. The main criterion for good poetry is said to be 'intrinsic poetical meaning'.[27] Wordsworth's preface to the *Lyrical ballads* is quoted with approval, and Day Lewis goes on to argue that the 'savage torpor' detected in 'the people' by Wordsworth is a truth 'far more widely extended in our own day'.[28] Day Lewis continues to show his very conservative hand when he blithely remarks that 'the fact of universal elementary education is inimical to poetry'.[29] A Yeatsian preference for aristocrat and beggarman underwrites such a position. Further evidence of Day Lewis's Romanticism is not hard to find. 'Poetry', we are told, 'was born from magic', and the poet is gifted with marvellous powers: 'If the poet is not clairvoyant, he is nothing. And this clairvoyancy is particularly directed towards discovering the super-natural in nature and the superhuman in humanity. There can be no such thing as realist poetry'.[30] Day Lewis affirms Romanticism, and denies realism. The 'poet', in his view, has extraordinary powers, and is concerned with the extraordinary. The 'poet' is also, according to Day Lewis, a martyr. D.H. Lawrence speaks of the 'crucifixion into isolate individuality', thereby, as Frank Kermode has pointed out, articulating a position central to the Romantic tradition.[31] Day Lewis's 'crucifixion' is of a slightly different nature: '... there arises in him [the poet] a conflict between the old which his heart approves and the new which fructifies his imagination ... Standing at the end of an epoch, the poet's arms are stretched out to opposite poles, the old life and the new, that is his power and his crucifixion.'[32] If we choose to read this in psychological rather than political terms, Day Lewis's martyrdom is not far removed from Lawrence's. But Lawrence in his life and work was able to slough off much more of the 'old life' than was Day Lewis. Day Lewis's heart is with tradition, the old values, and his poetry and poetics continually return to them.

Having taught at Cheltenham School for five years, Day Lewis left in 1935 to become a full-time writer. At the same time he joined the Communist Party. The relationship between these events is not entirely transparent. In his autobiography Day Lewis manages to imply that he was joining the Communist Party out of 'conscience', and that his resignation from schoolmastering was idealistically related to this, and further that a contract from his publishers to write a novel merely 'encouraged' him to 'take the plunge'.[33] But it seems very doubtful indeed whether Day Lewis would have been able to afford to join the party if it hadn't been for his lucrative publisher's contract. As it was, he was able to maintain his relatively affluent lifestyle, whilst appeasing his conscience.

Joining the Communist Party is indicative, I think, of the depth of Day Lewis's ambivalence towards his own class. It was a case of what Raymond Williams calls 'negative identification';[34] that is, a superficial wish to identify with the working class, because of an intellectual rebellion against the bourgeoisie. Day Lewis has since written a very cogent account of his involvement with Communism. In his autobiography he speaks of the guilty conscience, the Romanticism, and the religiosity which motivated his political involvement.[35] He also stresses again his uneasiness with respect to his position in the 1930s: 'I never ceased to be aware of the forces in myself which kept pulling me towards the past, the status quo, the traditions and assumptions in which I had been brought up . . .'[36] That this is not merely a retrospective rationalisation may be evidenced by several poems in *A time to dance* (1935). The tone of the volume is more muted and subtle than that of *The magnetic mountain*. And in poems like 'The conflict', 'In me two worlds', and 'Johnny Head-in-Air', we find a precise articulation of the tensions in Day Lewis's position.

In 'The conflict' the poet juxtaposes his desire to escape on the 'wings of poesy', with his political perception that a choice is necessary in the world of action and event:

Singing I was at peace,
Above the clouds, outside the ring:
For sorrow finds a swift release in song
And pride its poise.

Yet living here,
As one between two massing powers I live
Whom neutrality cannot save
Nor occupation cheer.[37]

The poem continues, in an act of self-persuasion, to argue that 'only ghosts' live in 'No Mans Land', and that commitment to 'new desires' must be made. But as he says in, 'In me two worlds', 'the veteran longings of the heart' were too strong to make such commitment possible for the poet. The latter poem concludes with an image of ongoing internal conflict:

So heir and ancestor
Pursue the inveterate feud,
Making my senses' darkened fields
A theatre of war.[38]

If *A time to dance* shows a considerable advance upon *The magnetic mountain*, then Day Lewis's next volume, *Noah and the waters* (1936), must be taken to represent the nadir of his career in the 1930s. The volume is a poetic drama in which 'the waters of England' somewhat absurdly represent the forces of the revolutionary proletariat. Day Lewis casts himself in the role of Noah, torn between being drowned by the rising waters, and being carried by them to a new world. To use a Christian myth to figure a left-wing revolution is contradictory in itself. And, in this case, the implications of the allegory are deeply ambivalent. The Biblical flood destroys the old world, but then retreats to reveal the new. The implication in Day Lewis's poem is that the proletariat will destroy the old world, and then retreat. The upper-middle-class poet with the divided heart and conscience, figured by Noah, will inherit the new world! Day Lewis wisely and unsurprisingly deleted all but two choruses of this work from his *Collected poems* (1954).

By 1937 the fragility of Day Lewis's political 'commitment' was becoming apparent even to himself. He records feeling the conflict between social con-science and artistic conscience as increasingly irreconcilable.[39] In 1938 he left the Communist Party and published his final volume for the decade dedicated to that figurehead of liberalism, E.M. Forster. Appropriate to its title, the dominant tone of *Overtures to death* is elegiac and resigned. The message is that war is terrible but inescapable. All we can do is to mourn, and cling to liberal humanist values of individuality and love. Day Lewis says farewell to his brief flirtation with the left.

The only poems in *Overtures to death* which depart from a sense of disintegration, defeat and a tired reiteration of traditional values are two poems about the Spanish Civil War. 'The Nabara' is a long narrative poem which tells the story of a naval engagement with all the bloodthirsty heroics of *The boy's own paper*. The Republican Nabara takes on a blockading Fascist battleship, and the Republican crew fight to the death. The poem is all action and no politics until its final lines where Day Lewis wields that most fragile of abstract nouns, 'Freedom', in order to celebrate and justify the carnage. This closing rhetorical flourish is as artificial and unfeeling as Auden's talk about 'necessary murder'.

There can be little doubt that Day Lewis, like Auden, was anti-Fascist in the later 1930s. But this does not mean that either of them were pro-Marxist or Socialist. Despite the two and a half year involvement with the CP, it seems to me evident that Day Lewis could not detach himself sufficiently from his inherited values to commit himself intellectually and emotionally to the left without ambivalence. Even when he is writing about the heroics of the Republicans in the Nabara, or lauding the feats of English participants fighting Fascism in Spain, one can detect a Romantic conservatism directing the utterance. Here is the last stanza of 'The volunteer' which, with some irony given the idealism of the International Brigade, celebrates English combatants in Spain:

Here in a parched and stranger place
We fight for England free.
The good our father's won for her,
The land they hoped to see.[40]

That Day Lewis could unselfconsciously reproduce the sentimentality and chauvinistic patriotism for which Rupert Brooke has been so roundly castigated seems from the perspective of the present extraordinary. The impulse behind the poem is to reconcile an international left-wing movement with Day Lewis's patriotic and filial emotions towards the England of his class inheritance. It seeks to defuse the possibility of fighting for an international aspiration by making the volunteer fight for England rather than Spain. It was one of the last overtly political poems that Day Lewis was to write.

The last pages of *Overtures to death* are occupied with themes which prefigure Day Lewis' poems of the 1940s. The imagery is of country life, the sentiments Romantic and Georgian. As his career developed, Day Lewis's style settled into a quiet elegance, with Hardy the most obvious progenitor. There were no more left-wing pretensions.

Day Lewis's imitation of Auden in the early part of the decade shows both poets to share similar ideological conflicts. That Day Lewis's style progressively developed away from modernism with its radical Tory connotations towards a re-invigorated more liberal, Georgianism at the same time as he joined the Communist Party is signal, I think, of how deep his ambivalence was, and how difficult it was for him to equate his political beliefs with his poetry. His style became less self-consciously 'difficult', less cerebral, than Auden's, and this might have made it more accessible to a wider audience; but it spoke to that audience not of Socialism but the dilemma of a liberal conscience tied to liberal conservative traditions.

III

Stephen Spender's first commercial volume of poems was not published until 1933.[41] But Spender by this time was already implicated in the burgeoning mythology of a left-wing poetic renaissance, not only because of his friendship with Auden at Oxford but also because several of his poems had appeared in New signatures in 1932. As in Auden's and Day Lewis's contributions to that anthology, there are superficial signs of left-wing interest in the poems Spender printed there, but nothing that convinces one of either an informed intellectual understanding of Marxist Socialism, or an unalloyed commitment to the left. 'Oh young men oh young comrades', as its somewhat mawkish first line might suggest, is symptomatic:

Oh young men oh young comrades
it is too late now to stay in those houses
your fathers built where they built you to breed
money on money it is too late
to make or even to count what has been made
Count rather those fabulous possessions
which begin with your body and your fiery soul... [42]

Whilst at Oxford, Auden advised Spender to 'drop the Shelley stunt'.[43] This was easier said than done, so that what emerges in the lines above is a curious combination of Auden's hectoring, pedagogical tones, allied to the emotional afflatus of the High Romantics. Spender is addressing himself to the wealthy sons of industrial capitalists in the liberal tones of the rich who can afford to believe that money does not matter. What *does* 'count' to the poet is derived in part from D.H. Lawrence. Lawrence's insistence upon the crucial place of sexuality in the growth to fulfilment of an individual is hinted at by Spender. But as the poem proceeds, Spender concentrates upon a celebration of the body, rather than upon the idea of fulfilment. We hear of 'muscles extending like ranges', of counting one's 'eyes as jewels', and finally of one's 'valued sex'. All this is a prelude to the poet's final invocation:

Oh comrades, step beautifully from the solid wall
advance to rebuild and sleep with friend on hill
advance to rebel and remember what you have
no ghost ever had, immured in his hall.[44]

The upper-middle-class 'comrades' are going to sleep with their 'friends', and build a new world.

The path by which Spender had come to this emotional idealism will have a familiar ring to it. He was born into the upper reaches of the middle class in 1909. His father was a Liberal politician and journalist who was a friend of Lloyd George, whilst his uncle, one-time editor of the *Westminster gazette*, 'had interviewed kings, been the confidante of prime-ministers, and the patron of writers'. J.A. Spender counted Henry James, Robert Louis Stevenson and Oscar Wilde amongst his friends. So Stephen was born into a family with interests in both literature and politics; small wonder then, that in the 1930s he pursued both aspects of his inheritance.

Despite this relatively elevated patrilineal descent, Spender in his autobiography writes in a similar vein to Day Lewis of his class background. Noting how the First World War had 'knocked the ball-room floor from under middle-class English life', Spender goes on to record not a sense of privilege but one of economic and social insecurity: 'We lived in a style of austere comfort against a background of calamity. Little of our money seemed spent on enjoyment, but most on doctors and servants, on maintaining a standard of life.'[45] The class-consciousness implicit in this expression of not having quite enough affluence to support an accustomed and superior class position was exacerbated for Spender by his formal education. When he was young he spent some time at a preparatory school in Worthing. But when he was nine his mother died, and Stephen was brought home to attend a day-school in Hampstead so that he could be a companion to his father. Although his brother, Michael Spender, went to the same public school as Auden, Stephen went to University College School, and later, having already won a place at Oxford, attended classes at the Lycée Clemenceau in Nantes. When he arrived at Oxford he found, at first, that not to be a public school boy was something of a disadvantage, only made worse by his aesthetic interests which clashed with the athleticism of the public-school 'hearties'. He found Oxford to be 'dominated above all by the consciousness of class'. Noting the social ranking of the colleges, he goes on:

The strongest social tendency of the University was therefore to create a hierarchy, and this hierarchy reflected and supported, on the whole, the idea of the superiority of the students from the best public-schools over the others. Thus the University was very far from moving towards the idea of a classless society, and the giving of scholarships to grammar-school boys did not alter this, any more than did the existence of a University Labour club. In many cases the working-class students were simply the most obscure, most ground-down members of their colleges.[46]

Spender was, of course, not in the position of the impoverished working-class grammar school boys he describes here. He was a member of the 'middling' University College and had the £300 a year which, he says, was necessary in order not to be 'excluded from Oxford at Oxford'. His introduction to college life, however, was not entirely happy. He played the role of the 'mad Socialist poet', wearing a scarlet tie, and infuriating the 'hearties' to the point where they tried to break up his rooms. They also cut his tie into fragments, an action that Spender retrospectively felt was excusable, as a protest against the 'pose' in his political views: 'For probably most of the ex-public-school boys got to know – in the course of their games, hunting and pub-crawling – more about the workers than I, who found it impossible to overcome my shyness even to the extent of going alone into a pub . . . They felt unembarrassed with the workers because they were sure of their own social position. I was embarrassed because I felt guilty.'[47] It is not so much that Spender is not a public school boy that marks him out, but that he is not a 'hearty'. After all the literary 'gang' to which he was soon to be admitted was entirely made up of public school boys. Here we see Spender reacting against his own class and thus feeling differently towards 'the workers'. And, what is of most interest is Spender's implicit social insecurity, his admittance of ignorance of the working class, and the sense of guilt which must, at least in part, have derived from his liberal political inheritance.

Spender went down from Oxford in 1929 without taking his degree. His love of the Romantic poets, inculcated by his father from an early age, had been tempered somewhat by the influence of Auden. But as we have already seen the elevated tones, the overt emotionalism of the High Romantics were characteristics that Spender found difficult to modify. Nevertheless, Auden and Isherwood had contributed to Spender's determination to be a writer, and with his annual financial allowance secure, little stood in the way of his attempts.

Like Auden the first thing that Spender did on leaving Oxford was to make for Germany. Between 1930 and 1933 he spent six months of each year there, the remaining time being spent mainly in London.[48] It was in Hamburg in 1930 that Spender began a relationship with a young, working-class German named Walter, a relationship which Spender describes in his autobiography as one of 'mutual exploitation'.

At the time, such relationships were important in the development of Spender's emotional brand of politics: 'Through Walter, I imagined the helplessness, the moral weakness, the drift, of unemployment. I imagined, I suppose, that something which I was now beginning to call in my mind 'the revolution' would alter his lot, and I felt that as a member of a more fortunate social class I owed him a debt'.[49] The relationship with Walter, unsurprisingly, did not last. But we can see how short a step it is from this reminiscence to the sentimentality of 'Oh young men oh young comrades'. The poem entreats the 'young men' of the poet's own class to abandon the way of their fathers and to seek a rapprochement with the working class through sexuality. The poem, of course, ignores the exploitative nature of such sexual relations. And in the way the poem is addressed to a specific class it inadvertently tells us more about class-conscious divisions than it does about overcoming these.

If 'Oh young men oh young comrades' does not wholly convince as a statement of Marxist commitment, other of Spender's poems written in the late 1920s and early 1930s, that also appeared in New signatures are even less likely to be read as evidence of leftward leanings. 'I think continually of those who were truly great', for instance, is Spender's contribution to the Auden 'group's' concern with past heroes and new leaders. Spender's poem, however, is far more obviously nineteenth century in spirit than anything the others wrote; its conservatism is overt. The truly great are said to be those:

> ... Whose lovely ambition
> Was that their lips, still touched with fire,
> Should tell of the Spirit, clothed from head to foot in song.[50]

In a somewhat desperate attempt to be modern (if not modernist), similar sentiments in other poems are attached to machines. 'The express', like the famous 'Pylons' and 'The landscape near an aerodrome', unashamedly romanticises its subject matter. The locomotive, in 'The express', offers a 'first plain powerful manifesto', and continues to be seen as an image of elated power, where 'speed' is said to 'throw up' strange shapes 'like trajectories from guns'. This is reminiscent of Italian Futurism with all its attendant Fascistic overtones.

But in 'The funeral' we find Spender trying to fly the red flag, and tellingly it is the worst of the poems he published in New signatures. Any writer who wishes to express an as yet unrealised alternative to the status quo must struggle to avoid being utopian. Spender is clearly embattled with this problem here, so much so that it is hard now to believe that the poem was written without irony. But so it was. A 'worker's' funeral is imagined, taking place in a Communist 'World State' where 'They', the 'workers', are apparently immune from grief, and celebrate with laughter their dead comrade's ability to make 'driving belts'. 'They' continue their festivities for the rest of the poem, as Spender argues that in the perfected society, personal mourning will be erased and collective emotion rule:

> They think how one life hums, revolves and toils,
> One cog in a golden singing hive:
> Like spark from fire, its task happily achieved,
> It falls away quietly.

> No more are they haunted by the individual grief
> Nor the crocodile tears of European genius,
> The decline of a culture
> Mourned by scholars who dream of the ghosts of Greek boys.[51]

In its implications, this unfortunately tends towards the Fascistic. It reduces human life to machinery, denies the working class any individual feeling, and suggests that the proletariat are going to become mindless automata after the revolution. And where is the poet in relation to all of this? Are 'we' (as opposed to 'they') all supposed to be the liberal homosexuals mentioned at the end of the poem? The use of 'they' all through the poem ironically distances the poet and audience from the utterance. Again a sense of class difference is rendered rather than class unity. It seems possible that Spender is trying to implicate himself in the final lines. But the last stanza only compounds the problems of the poem by implying that homosexuality is part of a decadent bourgeois culture which will disappear when the virile *machismo* of the workers takes over. As in 'Oh young men oh young comrades' one feels Spender's personal psychosexual dilemmas informing the utterance.

All of the poems we have looked at so far appeared in *Poems* (1933), and for the most part they reflect the tenor of the volume. But there are two other major themes in the book which we have not yet broached: love and 'pity'. Here the poet shows his liberal hand as against the more extreme implications of 'The funeral'. Some of the love poems are personal like, 'Your body is stars whose million glitter here' or 'Never being, but always at the edge of Being', which closes with the line, 'I claim fulfilment in the fact of loving'.[52] Others, however, develop the implications of 'Oh young men oh young comrades', and speak of love as a political panacea. In 'After they have tired of the brilliance of the cities', for instance, we hear of the 'palpable and obvious love of man for man', which will, with interesting Biblical connotations, give rise to a 'beautiful generation that will spring from our sides', miraculously without female participation.[53]

But the 'palpable and obvious' love between men does not hinder Spender from registering the distance between people of different classes. And it is here that 'pity', learnt from Wilfred Owen, enters Spender's poetry. But Spender's 'pity' for the working class too often tends to result in self-pity. In poems like 'My parents kept me from children who were rough', and 'Moving through the silent crowd', the ostensible focus is the working class, but the poem's real subject is the poet's own feelings. The 'children who were rough', and 'wore torn clothes', are imaged as virile and frightening. They are described making fun of the poet's lisp, slinging mud, and being generally disagreeable. The poet 'looked the other way', and 'longed to forgive them, but they never smiled'.[54] Spender sounds sorry for himself as he expresses his class-consciousness. He seems to be accusing his parents of sheltering him within their own class. But if the poet had had any sensitivity towards left-wing thought, he could not have put himself in the extraordinary position of wanting 'to forgive' the working classes.

We have seen already how distant Spender felt from the 'workers' whilst he was at Oxford. His homosexual encounters with working-class men in Germany like Walter seem to have rendered his sense of class-consciousness more acute, rather than allaying it. The kind of condescension, and distance from the realities of working-class life, apparent in the foregoing poem are also apparent in Spender's poem about the unemployed. 'Moving through the silent crowd', Spender goes on to portray a caricature of men who 'idle in the road', and 'turn their empty pockets out' with the 'cynical gestures of the poor'. Having presented this less than convincing cartoon-like image, the poet goes on to register his reaction to what he has supposedly seen.

Now they've no work, like better men
Who sit at desks and take much pay
They sleep long nights and rise at ten
To watch the hours that drain away.

I'm jealous of the weeping hours
They stare through with such hungry eyes
I'm haunted by these images,
I'm haunted by their emptiness.[55]

The word 'better' here is, I think, intended to be ironic. But the movement of Spender's poem militates against the irony having effect. For if the unemployed really are 'empty' shells of men, if they are so cynical and defeated, then their condition tends to validate the adjective 'better'. The final lines of the poem register the poet's wish to suffer because he feels guilty, and then proceeds to an articulation of self-pity in which the unemployed become mere 'images' of 'emptiness'. It is salutary, having read a poem like this, to recall the marchers of the Jarrow Crusade, who hardly correspond to the spiritless, ennervated, cynical wraiths of Spender's imagination. He tries to depict the working class but renders them lifeless precisely because he simply does not know enough about working-class life to depict it with any feeling or conviction.

To be fair, this is something that Spender was increasingly willing to acknowledge as the decade went on. Just a few months after the publication of *Poems* (1933) he was writing in his essay 'Poetry and revolution'[56] that the bourgeois artist is unable to join the proletariat because his imagination is, and always will remain, bourgeois. Despite the title of the essay with its advertisement of Spender as 'revolution-ary', the contents are, as we might by now expect, rather less than apocalyptic. Spender defends himself against an imaginary Communist by justifying his position specifically as an artist. The implication is that any other member of the middle class might be able to 'go over' to the proletariat, but the artist cannot because his creative powers have their origin in the bourgeois world. The position is Romantic; the artist is a special case because of his superior insight. This view also underpins Spender's attitude to party politics. Writing poetry, he says, is one of the 'least revolutionary activities'. The artist should not be 'led into practical politics'. But this does not mean that the bourgeois poet is merely writing 'propaganda' for a middle-class view of the world. The artist, because of his special gift, portrays 'the truth' about the past and present, and thereby indirectly aids the revolution.

Given the kind of life Spender was leading at this time, it is not suprising that he was unwilling to give up notions of individualism. Once his book was published he began in London to 'lead a literary-social life of luncheons, teas, and week-ends at country houses'. This was hardly likely to increase his commitment to Marxism or his empathy with the working class. The members of the Bloomsbury group, and the circle that Lady Ottoline Morell had drawn around her, were passionately devoted to the idea of the aristocratic individual.

Here Spender describes the privileged 'world' he was increasingly becoming a part of:

Thus I began to enter this civilized world of people who lived in country houses, pleasantly modernized, ... They had libraries and good food and wine. They discussed few topics outside literature, and they gossiped endlessly and entertainingly about their friends. In my mind these houses in the south and south west of England, belonging to people who knew one another and who maintained approximately the same standards of living well, talking well, and believing passionately in their own kind of individualism, were connected by drives along roads which often went between hedges.[57]

This was the literary-political world of his inheritance, and Spender unsurprisingly clung tenaciously to it, whilst at the same time engaging in the difficult task of reconciling it with Marxism. Spender did not waver from this pursuit throughout the decade. His critical writings are all intent upon arguing that the Romantic, individualist artist is really a servant of Communism, and therefore should be left alone to get on with writing. As he says in his book-length study, *The destructive element*, which deals with the writings of Henry James, Yeats, Eliot and D.H. Lawrence, he is 'on the side of the greatest possible degree of freedom' and insists that to write 'as one cares and about what one wishes' is not to be a traitor to the Socialist cause.[58]

The artist, then, according to Spender, is serving Socialism whatever he writes down as long as he adopts a liberal notion of 'freedom'. Such a view clearly depends upon the idea that by telling 'the truth' one criticises the past and present, thereby helping the revolutionary to see his or her activity in its correct perspective. But if the vision of history portrayed in a work of art is that of a liberal, bourgeois, intellectual, it does not necessarily reveal the 'truths' that a Socialist might see in the past. If one thinks of Spender's own poems like, 'I think continually of those who were truly great', or 'Beethoven's death mask', one perceives an idea of history predicated not upon the economic relations of classes to the means of production, but on crude notions of the biography of great men. The only way in which such poems may serve Socialism, it seems to me, is negatively; they demonstrate everything that Marxism is not. The poems in and of themselves do not contribute to a Socialist understanding of history.

Spender never reveals himself to be at all interested in a Marxist view of history. Nowhere is this clearer than in his attitudes towards language. Rather than perceiving language to be part of the 'super-structure' predicated upon the economic base, and thus subject to change, he espouses Eliot's conservative view that language is the repository of somehow 'pure' meanings, which have to be preserved by poetry against corruption.[59]

Spender's attitudes to art and the artist were consistent throughout the 1930s. He maintained an adamant defence of his own position, and would not be pressurised away from his liberalism. As he admits in his autobiography, he could not shed his liberal notions of 'freedom' and 'truth' even when he was manoeuvred into joining the Communist Party for a few weeks in the winter of 1936-7.[60] On the grounds of Spender's anti-Fascist position with respect to the Spanish Civil War, Harry Pollitt, the chairman of the CPGB, persuaded Spender to join the party, with the proviso that Spender should be allowed to state his position publicly in the pages of the *Daily worker*. Spender's article duly appeared and was roundly criticised by several members of the party because of its liberalism.

The *Daily worker*, however, was responsible for sending Spender to Spain as a reporter, but his membership of the CP soon lapsed. He paid no fees, and attended no meetings of the Hampstead cell to which he was supposed to be attached. Later, on more than one occasion, Spender was to remark that his affiliation with the Communist Party, no less than his interest in leftist politics generally, was motivated by a sense of personal and social guilt.[61] After his first visit, Spender went again to Spain in the summer of 1937 to attend a writers' conference in Madrid. This was held in support of the Republican cause, but in Spender's account the meeting only acted to display the distance between wordy intellectualisation and the bloody proceedings of the war. He came back to England harbouring 'a deep dissatisfaction' with what he had encountered in Spain.[62]

The poetry Spender wrote between 1933 and 1939 follows a similar pattern to that found in the progress of Auden's and Day Lewis's work. As we have seen, both the last-named poets published their most extreme work in the early part of the decade, and then reverted to a liberal conservatism. So too does Spender. His volume *The still centre*, published in 1939, contains most of the shorter poems written in the last five years of the decade, and here we find as the decade progresses, an increasing obsession with abstract and metaphysical investigations of the poet's selfhood.

There are, however, some poems in the book which broach more public matters, notably the poems about the Spanish Civil War, and those which attempt to express attitudes to social issues: 'Easter

Monday', 'An elementary school classroom in a slum', and 'A footnote (from Marx's chapter The working day)'. As with his poem about unemployment that I considered earlier, these poems do attempt to portray social realities in a way that Auden and Day Lewis rarely venture. But they all betray Spender's class prejudices and how far distant he is from any sympathetic understanding of classes other than his own. In his portrait of an elementary school classroom, for instance, we find what might be called a negative romanticisation of the working class. The children are portrayed as ugly, cunning and potentially criminal. They have no redeeming features. A boy is described with 'rat's eyes', and all the children are said to live in 'cramped holes'. It neither occurs to Spender that criminality and cunning may not be the only response to poverty, nor that a working-class home may be cramped but not necessarily a 'hole'. Most damagingly there is a complete lack of self-indictment or indictment of the gross inequalities which create such poverty under capitalism. The final stanza is an invocation to 'governor, teacher, inspector, visitor', who are called upon in a spirit of Victorian philanthropy to 'break the town / And show the children to the fields'. Spender's conservative and nostalgic hope is that the children will be tamed into Romantic, bourgeois idealism through contact with nature.

As we might by now expect, Spender's 'Footnote (from Marx's chapter The working day)', shows little advance upon this position. The footnote in question refers to the Fourth Report of the Children's Employment Commission (1865),[63] and deals with the 'degree of culture' exhibited by working children at that time. It makes sobering reading, and Spender cleverly incorporates the words of the children verbatim into the opening stanzas of his poem, creating an appropriate folk-ballad effect:

'Heard say that four times four is eight,'
'And the king is the man what has all the gold'
'Our king is a queen and her son's a princess
And they live in a palace called London, I'm told.'[64]

Spender goes on in the following stanzas to provide the context for this. He maintains his balladic stanza effectively, but then abandons it in favour of a lyrical commentary in his own voice. The children, victims of vicious nineteenth century work practices, are referred to by Spender as 'the birds of a songless age / Young like the youngest Gods'. Instead of the negative romanticisation of the working class, we are here treated to the positive pole. Instead of leaving the audience with a powerfully dramatic rendition of the plight of child labour in the nineteenth century, Spender imposes his conservative imagination to transform the realities by a sentimental 'spiritual' consolation:

In the sunset above these towns
Often I watch you lean upon the clouds
Momently drawn back like a curtain
Revealing a serene, waiting eye
Above a tragic, ignorant age.

There is inadvertent irony here: little could validate the concluding line so much as the complacent self-indulgence of the four lines which precede it.

But this perhaps is to be over-censorious. Spender always maintained that he was obliged to write from a bourgeois perspective, and so he does. A poem like 'A Footnote (from Marx's chapter *The working day*)', however, does highlight how vulnerable his theoretical arguments about the artist recording historical 'truths' are. For here he takes historical 'truth', and then imposes upon it a 'consolatory' vision which implicitly denies and denigrates the suffering and the material realities upon which that 'truth' rests.

Spender's poems about the Spanish Civil War are, for the most part, less gauche than the last three poems we have looked at. But they do not show any traces of political commitment to the Republican cause. On the contrary, if Spender had not recorded in his autobiography and elsewhere his support for the Republicans, it would be very difficult from these poems alone to infer that such was the case. Rather, in their Owenesque concentration upon 'pity' and 'suffering' they tend to imply a pacifist position which, in the context of the Spanish Civil War, is close to an endorsement of the British government's policy of non-intervention.

After his brief membership of the Communist Party, and his second visit to Spain, Spender remarks of his poetry: 'I reacted from the attempt to achieve Communist self-righteousness towards an extreme pre-occupation with the problems of self'.[65] Such a preoccupation is clearly in evidence in poems like 'Variations on my life I and II', 'Darkness and light', and the ambitiously titled, 'The human situation', written between 1937 and 1939. But it should not be thought that this was a sudden change of direction, and that prior to his leaving the Communist Party all of his work was publicly oriented. Spender translated and published Rilke's 'Orpheus, Eurydice' in 1934, and wrote poems throughout the decade which were, though much less fine than Rilke, attempting to follow the German poet in expressing a personal metaphysical vision.The tendency to turn inwards was an aspect of Spender's ambivalence for much of the decade. He has spoken of his sense of the public world 'intruding' upon the private during the 1930s, and this verb seems to me significant. The liberal individualist was unwillingly forced to consider the public world because of his conscience.

Stylistically Spender's work is further removed from the Auden-esque than that of Day Lewis. There are, however, tonal echoes of Auden's pedagogical manner in some poems, and Spender occasionally uses ellipsis by severing connectives in the same way as the early Auden. But it is easier to see Spender's ideological ambivalence manifested in stylistic variations between poems, rather than rendered within single poems. The contrast between his 'social' poems and his 'metaphysical' poems is illustrative of this. On the one hand one has a heightened, lyrical, yet relatively straightforward speech, on the other a convoluted abstraction. The High Romantic and Georgian inheritance may be observed in one, and a variety of modernism derived not only from Eliot but also from the Post-Symbolist Rilke in the other. And the tendency towards Futurism in the imagery of some of the earlier poems should not be forgotten here. A poem like 'The express' combines a lyrical impulse with images of machinery in a way which suggests the tension between liberal tradition, and radical (in this case radically right-wing) thinking.

As in Day Lewis's case the ambivalence in Spender's position is often easier to perceive than in the case of Auden. This is, I think, indicative not only of less talent as writers, but also of a greater degree of ambivalence in their position. Auden wrote in a letter to a friend during the 1930s that he would not, and could not join the Communist Party because he was, and always would remain, a bourgeois. Spender, as we have seen, continually acknowledged and defended his position as a bourgeois artist, but was still tempted into a brief association with the CP. But in his poetry the liberal Edwardian values he was so steeped in continually reassert themselves against all other pressures.

IV

In *A hope for poetry*, C. Day Lewis mentions 'superficial signs' of a 'boom in poetry' which, he says, 'has been connected in some quarters' with the names of Auden, Spender and himself. Although one of MacNeice's poems is quoted elsewhere in Day Lewis's book, by 1934 MacNeice had not quite become a full member of the 'Auden gang'. The simple explanation for this may be that having published his first book of poems in 1929, MacNeice did not publish another until 1935.[66] And, since much of the work contained in the earlier volume might justly be deemed juvenilia, it is not entirely surprising that in 1934 MacNeice's publicity did not rival that which Auden, Day Lewis and Spender had attracted. But there are, I think, other reasons why MacNeice was not incorporated fully into the Auden mythology until relatively late in the decade. Unlike other members of the 'group', MacNeice's work did not appear in either *New signatures* or *New country*. Furthermore, in the first half of the decade, he made explicit statements which indicated his scepticism towards Communism. He also, in 1935, displayed a less than approbatory attitude to some aspects of his contemporaries' work. In a book entitled, *The arts today*, MacNeice contributed a chapter on poetry, in which he remarked upon the 'myths of themselves' to be found in the poetry of Auden, Spender, and Day Lewis: '... these poets make myths of themselves and of each other. This personal obsession can be collated with their joint Communist outlook via the concept of comradeship. . . Comradeship is the Communist substitute for bourgeois romance; in its extreme form (cp. also fascism and youth cults in general) it leads to an idealisation of homosexuality'.[67] MacNeice endorses the idea that Auden *et al.* were Communists, but not without exerting a critique which points to the relationship between their supposed beliefs and their personal life. If MacNeice was prepared to so distance himself from the self-mythologisers, how was it that he became involved with the Auden group at all? Apart from the fact that MacNeice met Auden and Spender at Oxford, his literary association with them may be traced to several sources, not least the pages of Geoffrey Grigson's magazine, *New verse*. And it was with Auden that MacNeice went to Iceland in 1936. The two poets then collaborated in the writing of *Letters from Iceland* which had been commissioned as a travel book, but in fact tells one relatively little about Iceland, but rather a great deal about the authors' state of mind with respect to the developing political crises in Europe. Also in 1936, a third edition of Day Lewis' *A hope for poetry* was printed with a postscript in which MacNeice's *Poems* (1935) are referred to at some length. Here Day Lewis attempts to place MacNeice's work in relation to what he calls the 'New country generation', and the emergent 'new generation' of 'pure poetry' represented by Barker, Thomas and Gascoyne. Although Day Lewis perceives in MacNeice's work a reaction away from 'recent preoccupations' with 'social justice', MacNeice is still claimed for the 'New country' generation because he has little in common with the 'pure' work of the next 'generation'.[68]

MacNeice himself assented to this view when, in 1938, he published his book *Modern poetry: A personal essay*, which, as we shall see is his most crucial contribution to the Auden mythology. Here MacNeice aligns himself with the *New country* poets and specifically with the work of Auden, Day Lewis and Spender. Whereas in 1935 MacNeice had been criticising the self-mythologisers, by 1938 he was prepared to endorse their myths fully. But before looking more closely at this change of direction, it is first salutary to look at MacNeice's biography to establish what he had in common with the others.

Like Day Lewis, MacNeice was born in Ireland, the son of a clergyman. And, by strange coincidence, like both Day Lewis and Spender, MacNeice lost his mother whilst still very young. His education was begun at home, and his father began to teach him Latin at the age of nine. The following year, MacNeice was sent to England to Sherborne school (the same school that Day Lewis went to) where he remained until he was fourteen when he won a scholarship to Marlborough.

Despite this entrance to one of the most famous of English public schools, it was some time before MacNeice gained any sense that his social position was secure. In his autobiography he describes his isolation as a child, and, like Auden, Day Lewis and Spender, his sense of being caught uncomfortably between two classes: 'The Lower Classes were dour and hostile, they would never believe what you said. Not that the Gentry were much better; even then I was conscious that to be the son of a clergyman was to be something the Gentry only half accepted and that in a patronising way'.[69] At Sherborne MacNeice records feeling 'superior to the town boys', but when he moved to Marlborough found that all conversation was 'infected' with 'social snobbery', and that he was now on the receiving end of this unpleasantness. Confidence, however, grew with age so that by the time he was preparing to leave Marlborough to take up his place at Oxford, MacNeice and his friend Anthony Blunt felt themselves to be 'the cream of the world', and life was 'one big party'.[70]

MacNeice describes his values at this time as being purely 'aesthetic'. Certainly his education would do little to discourage such an attitude.

MacNeice had been encouraged by various masters in his enthusiasm for English poetry, and he was an apt pupil of Classics. At Oxford he continued in the same vein: 'I continued my classical education which had already come to condition my whole outlook. This traditional English form of education is rooted in that same class-system which conduces to an ethics of self-interest; it thus came about that when I was nineteen I joined to a dislike of science a disbelief in altruism. Skimming the cream off the milk; skimming the cream off the cream; you begin to forget there are cows.'[71] Although there is a gentle hint of self-recrimination in this retrospective analysis of his Oxonian self, MacNeice, as we shall see, never fully threw over the influence of his education. Certainly during his career at Oxford, by his own testimony, no progress at all was made in this direction. He records, like Spender and Day Lewis, the social hierarchies of Oxford and notes the division between 'hearties' and 'aesthetes'. He also mentions that in Oxford, 'homosexuality and "intelligence", heterosexuality and brawn, were almost inexorably paired.'[72] Since MacNeice was neither brawny nor homosexual he found himself, to some extent at least, on the outer, but nevertheless enjoyed the company of a select few friends: John Hilton, Graham Shepard, and Adrian Green-Armytage. MacNeice seems to have known Auden and Spender at Oxford without being particularly well-aquainted. It is possible that MacNeice's hetero-sexuality was at least at this stage something of a barrier.

What is clear is that he mixed with people from the same class. His stated attitude to grammar-school boys at Oxford was one of aggressive superiority. Attending lectures and tutorials is described by MacNeice as 'a game for the "monsters",' 'i.e. the grammar-school boys, those distorted little creatures with black teeth who held their forks by the middle and were set on making a career. I used to sit wedged between these monsters at dinner, listening superciliously as they discussed Noel Coward and Bernard Shaw; in my opinion no one intelligent would mention such writers'.[73] With such attitudes intact, MacNeice graduated from Oxford, got married, and gained a job as lecturer in Classics at the University of Birmingham. He worked in Birmingham from 1930 to 1935, and it was here that MacNeice wrote the majority of poems included in Poems (1935). It might be supposed that exposure to the industrial Midlands might modify MacNeice's snobbery somewhat. But if it did, it was a slow process. He writes of living in some style with his new bride in 'a converted stables on the south, the genteel, side of Birmingham'.[74] He also remarks that although the slump was on the way, he and his wife 'were not the keepers of the badgered employees or the badgering unemployed, of the slaves of the assembly-belts, the fodder of the mills'.[75] He could at this stage 'accept a clean-cut working man', but he could not accept the 'hybrids' that he was obliged to teach. They were too intent on 'finding a berth in the lower middle or the middle middle classes' to meet with MacNeice's approval.[76] Later he remarks that Birmingham 'reconciled' him to 'ordinary people'. But of course, the very designation of these people as 'ordinary' marks MacNeice's superior distance from them. He, by implication, is not 'ordinary'.

Unsuprisingly then, Poems (1935) shows MacNeice to be fully aware of his situation as an upper-middle-class, Anglo-Irish poet, living in an English urban and suburban society on the verge of economic collapse, devoid of religious or moral scruples. His response to these circumstances differs from that of Auden, Spender and Day Lewis in several respects. The most crucial distinction is that in these poems of the early 1930s, MacNeice does not take upon himself an overtly pedagogical role. He entirely distrusts dogmatic systems of thought, and offers no redemptive vision. His tones are less strident, more contemplative than those of his three contemporaries. There is little inflation and no flippancy in MacNeice's work, and he entirely eschews naive enthusiasm or public-school oratory. He is also more openly and self-consciously engaged with the aesthetic problems of the Romantic–Symbolist tradition than were Auden, Spender and Day Lewis. The movement of his poetry is away from Romantic transcendentalism, away from the Romantic image of integration (though there is a nostalgic regret for its loss) and towards the local, particular and sometimes demotic. In political terms MacNeice wavers between conservatism and an anarchistic celebration of flux. However gloomy his vision might sometimes be, MacNeice nevertheless often manages to celebrate the here and now, showing a degree of acceptance absent in the early work of his associates. In the concluding stanza of the last poem in Poems (1935) MacNeice writes: 'For nothing is more proud than humbly to accept'.[77]

MacNeice then, does not seem to be as self-divided as Auden and friends. In a poem called 'Valediction' MacNeice says goodbye to the Ireland in which he was raised. Although the impetus of the poem derives from a wish to leave Ireland, MacNeice concludes by accepting his past and who he is in relation to that past. For some reason, possibly his heterosexuality, possibly his Irishness, possibly his slightly more elevated and therefore more secure class position, MacNeice did not react against his own class with the same animus and intensity to be found in the work of his English contemporaries. MacNeice's vision is deeply individualistic, but he is not ashamed of this, and so I think his poems are less tortured than many of those written by the Auden group. MacNeice always avoids the expression of personal neuroses through eloquent obliquities.

His poem, 'To a Communist', is a confident, knowing dismissal of the millenial vision. There is no guilt here:

Your thoughts make shape like snow; in one night only
The gawky earth grows breasts.
Snow's unity engrosses
Particular pettiness of stones and grasses.
But before you proclaim the millenium, my dear,
Consult the barometer –
The poise is perfect but maintained
For one day only. [78]

The very camp 'my dear' indicates that MacNeice has in mind the *kameradeschaft* which drew Auden and Spender to Berlin in the early 1930s, and to which they and Day Lewis gave expression in some of their work. There is also the cunning implication, carried by the image of a snowy earth-mother, that upper-middle-class 'Communists' create a security-blanket from their beliefs in order to compensate for their loss of a mother-figure. As in his prose account quoted earlier, MacNeice recognises in the 'Communism' of his contemporaries a manifestation of personal need and neurosis, rather than one of hard-headed intellectual commitment.

'To a Communist' introduces us to concerns which govern many of *Poems* (1935). The tensions between particular and general, between permanence and flux, find echoes in several other poems. In 'Wolves', 'Train to Dublin', 'Cuckoo', 'Snow', 'August', and 'Nature morte', we find similar attitudes to those expressed in 'To a Communist', but in these poems the concern is predominantly aesthetic, rather than overtly political. MacNeice shows himself to be acutely aware of his Romantic and Symbolist inheritance as he explores the status of the Romantic image of integration within the modern suburban world.

'Nature morte', for instance, begins at a suburban table, but ends with a meditation upon poets who look to 'the pretentious word' in order to 'stabilise' the world. But this pursuit, MacNeice regretfully avers, is impossible, even a still life by Chardin exudes the 'appalling unrest of the soul'.[79] MacNeice expresses this sense that permanence is impossible, flux is all elswehere. In 'August' he speaks of man's impulse to impose frames upon time in order to fix it, and demonstrates such an inclination by describing a man mowing a lawn: 'a still-bound fête / Suspending every noise, of insect and machine'.[80] But such stasis, achieved through the artifice of the image, is described later in the poem as 'a dilletante's lie'. MacNeice concludes: 'We being ghosts cannot catch hold of things'; we, like things, are insubstantial spectres because we too are chameleon, always changing with time.

But in poems like 'Snow' and 'Train to Dublin', the unrest MacNeice perceives is neither quite so 'appalling' as in 'Nature morte', nor so ennervating as it is in 'August'. In 'Snow' MacNeice shows a positive relish as he speaks of the 'incorrigibly plural', and of 'the drunkenness of things being various'.[81] And in 'Train to Dublin', having established that our thoughts are as difficult to grasp and hold as the steam from a locomotive, MacNeice proceeds to proffer a celebration of transient life, of the 'incidental things which pass', through images 'given' in a way not unlike the list offered in Rupert Brooke's poem, 'The great lover'. Characteristically, however, MacNeice concludes not in unalloyed praise like Brooke, but draws back to qualify his position:

I would like to give you more but I cannot hold
This stuff within my hands and the train goes on;
I know that there are further syntheses to which,
As you have perhaps, people at last attain
And find that they are rich and breathing gold.[82]

MacNeice does not preclude the possibility of further syntheses, but clearly he places himself in a situation where he is not 'rich and breathing gold'. Rather, he is steeped in the mutability of life; a fact which is variously celebrated and lamented.

The resistance to the notion of some final integration in the political sphere, expressed in 'To a Communist' is extended to other areas of experience. MacNeice rejects the Romantic image of integration as he rejects all dogma. The political implications of the poems we have looked at so far tends towards the anarchistic, but on occasion we also hear the voice of a reactionary fatalism. In 'Turf stacks', for instance, MacNeice gives voice to a Yeatsian nostalgia for the rural peasantry of Ireland, whose life is contrasted to that of the English industrial middle class. The peasantry are said to be aided by their environment in avoiding the 'ideas', the 'shuddering, insidious shock of the theory vendors', who tilt their 'aggregate beast against our crumbling Troy'. MacNeice typically has no answer to this perceived disintegration; he can offer no alternative 'theory'. Recognising that a return to Yeats's preferred society of 'Aristocrat and beggarman' is not possible, MacNeice can only propose the extremes of Romantic escape, or harsh scepticism:

For we are obsolete who like the lesser things
Who play in corners with looking glass and beads;
It is better we should go quickly, go into Asia,
Or any other tunnel where the world recedes,
Or turn blind wantons like the gulls who scream
And rip the edge off any ideal or dream.[83]

We detect here the tones of the beleaguered individualist who wishes to be left alone to celebrate the 'lesser things', and to 'play' with beads and looking glass (presumably a figure for the poet or aesthete) however narcissistic this may be. We also notice the sense of inevitable disintegration: Troy is crumbling, MacNeice argues, and people like himself are obsolete.

There is a point of contact here between Auden, Spender, Day Lewis and MacNeice. All of them express in one way or another the sense that the upper-middle class are about to be destroyed. The difference between MacNeice and the other three poets is tonal. Whereas Auden can speak of 'death of the old gang' with apparent nonchalance, and Day Lewis can summon his public-school chums to join a utopian revolution, MacNeice's attitude is consistently elegaic. Nowhere does he see positive potential in either the cultural or political disintegration he observes around him. As my earlier quotations from his autobiography imply, his attachment to received values is more positive, less ambivalent than in the work of his colleagues. Any celebration in his work is either of raw vitality, or of incidental beauty amidst the ruins.

This may be observed clearly in 'Birmingham', a poem which explores the contemporary cultural situation. Here in the long seven and eight stress lines with their 'sprung' rhythm one may detect the influence of Hopkins. And in the subtlety with which MacNeice juxtaposes the hectic triviality of modern suburban life with the heroes and gods of older cultures, one might perceive Eliot's heir. But modified by Georgianism, the tone becomes all MacNeice's. The poem entirely lacks Eliot's sobriety, or Hopkins's reverence. Through vital language MacNeice conveys not disgust or nihilism, but a nice ambivalence:

In these houses men as in a dream pursue the Platonic Forms
With wireless and cairn terriers and gadgets approximating to the fickle norms
And endeavour to find God and score one over the neighbour
By climbing tentatively upward on jerry-built beauty and sweated labour.
The lunch hour: the shops empty, shopgirls' faces relax
Diaphanous as green glass, empty as old almanacs
As incoherent with ticketed gewgaws tiered behind their heads
As the Burne-Jones windows in St. Philip's broken by crawling leads... [84]

Although it could be argued that this is as aristocratically condescending in its attitude to the working and lower-middle classes as anything
in the writings of Auden, there are, I think, differences of approach
between the two poets. First of all MacNeice figures here as elsewhere
the physical realities of lower-middle to middle-middle-class suburban
and urban existence. This is something that Auden rarely does.
Secondly, in MacNeice's poem there is undoubtedly a sense of lament
for the conditions in which people subsist in the city and its suburbs.
But it is the culture that has broken down, not the people who live
within it. Part of MacNeice surely applauds the men and women he
describes, whose impulse to find meaning and coherence is frustrated
by circumstance; whose beauty like that of the Burne-Jones window,
is marred by a trivialising social context, and by neglect. These are the
'ordinary' people he finds reassuring.

Nevertheless it is entirely significant that MacNeice's description of
Birmingham hardly touches upon the experience of the working class
except to mention 'sleep-stupid faces' entering factory gates. And it is
entirely symptomatic of this distance that MacNeice's portrayal of the
shopgirls hinges upon an aesthetic response. As in the case of Eliot, one
feels the force of MacNeice's nostalgia for a legendary past which had
a culture replete with religious and aesthetic meaning. The sense of the
imminent demise of all that he has held dear also informs MacNeice's
next major collection of verse which was published in America in
1937, and in England the following year with the title *The earth compels*.
There are fewer good poems in this than in his previous volume, many
of them being spoiled by a sentimental yearning for an unknown
beloved to arrive and save the deteriorating situation. The book
advances many themes we have already encountered, but now the
elegaic note has been intensified, the prophecies of doom become
more certain, in key with European political developments.

In 1938, MacNeice said that 'on paper and in the soul' his sympathies were to the left, but in his 'heart and guts' he lamented the

'passing of class'.[85] This may not be an admirable sentiment, but it does have the virtue of plain speaking. And in *The earth compels*, it is his 'heart and guts' that are expressed with equal clarity. In poems like 'The sunlight on the garden' and 'Only let it form', a lament for what MacNeice takes to be the impending demise of his own class is tellingly articulated:

The sunlight on the garden
Hardens and grows cold,
We cannot cage the minute
Within its nets of gold,
When all is told
We cannot beg for pardon.

Our freedom as free lances
Advances towards its end;
The earth compels, upon it
Sonnets and birds descend;
And soon, my friend,
We shall have no time for dances.[86]

It is important to notice here that the change of which MacNeice speaks is akin to that Heraclitan sense of flux expressed in his earlier work; it is natural change, imaged by the seasons. There is no revolutionary Marxist idea underlying the utterance. But there is that sense of guilt for individual privilege which 'cannot beg for pardon'. The poem continues to acknowledge, 'We are dying, Egypt, dying / And not expecting pardon', but closes on a note of gratitude for the privilege of having basked in 'the sunlight on the garden'.

Apart from love-poems, and elegies for a dying way of life, there are attempts at more broadly based cultural criticism. 'An eclogue from Iceland' is an extended meditation upon the political, moral, and aesthetic problems in European culture. The point of view is liberal humanist as MacNeice, through his persona of 'Grettir', asserts that in the face of disintegration, a gesture, however small, must be made to assert 'human values' and express a 'hatred of hatred'.[87] Such direct statement of perspective is not to be found elsewhere in the book, but it does I think, accurately reflect MacNeice's only hopeful stance. In his famous, romping ballad, 'Bagpipe music', the voice is tersely ironical, and if it were not for the energetic rhythms, one might be tempted to deem it nihilist in its attitudes.

Here all aspects of society are pilloried. A vision is communicated of a bankrupt civilisation in which the upper classes are mindlessly decadent, and the lower classes ape this behaviour, seeking cheap thrills, consumer articles, and creature comforts. In different stanzas 'all we want' is variously equated with 'a Dunlop tyre', 'A mother's help', and a 'packet of fags'. The poem concludes like this:

It's no go my honey love, it's no go my poppet;
Work your hands from day to day, the winds will blow the profit.
The glass is falling hour by hour, the glass will fall forever,
But if you break the bloody glass you won't hold up the weather. [88]

Despite the anarchistic implications of much in the poem, the final stanza communicates a conservative, fatalistic resignation to the status quo which has been said to be 'no go' all through the poem. Violent gestures, the breaking of the barometer, MacNeice argues, will achieve nothing. Man and society are implicitly involved in force-fields beyond their control.

In 1938, the year of the Munich crisis, MacNeice published his contribution to the decade's critical ruminations in the form of his book, Modern poetry: a personal essay. This volume is extremely important both with respect to MacNeice himself, and to the literary-historical myth of the 1930s. Walter Allen, in his introduction to the 1968 edition, expresses the idea that the book 'may well have been in part the expression of a moment of conversion to positive commitment'.[89] But this argument is predicated upon the notion that Auden, Spender and Day Lewis were 'socially committed'; a premise which, as I hope I have demonstrated, is very questionable indeed. What we may say with certainty is that just as Auden, Spender and Day Lewis were retreating into increasingly conservative positions due to the impending outbreak of war, ironically MacNeice attempted to move in the opposite political direction from conservatism to a more liberal position. Having for eight years resisted all threats to his position as an individualist, MacNeice in 1938 sought to align himself with the poets of New signatures and New country via the opening chapter of Modern poetry. It is here that MacNeice accepts the myth that the Auden group represent the left, and seeks to identify himself with that political affiliation by association with them.

But when we read the book what we find is neither commitment to Marxism, nor a commitment to the left, but a somewhat muddled commitment to liberalism. MacNeice says that he is in favour of 'impure poetry' and wishes to 'readjust the ratio between various conflicting extremisms'. Yet he privileges the idea of the 'poet' and 'poetic truth', and is happy to extol what he calls the 'practical idealism' of Auden *et al.* The relationship beween 'impure' poetry and 'practical idealism' remains unexplored.

Auden, Spender and Day Lewis figure largely in the book as representatives of a contemporary poetry which is claimed to be superior to every conceivable progenitor. The aesthetes of the 1890s, Eliot, Yeats, Hopkins, Housman, Kipling and the Georgians are all tried and found wanting. MacNeice's argument suggests that they lacked the idealism to take sides: 'The poets of *New signatures*, unlike Yeats and Eliot, are emotionally partisan ... The whole poetry... of Auden, Spender and Day Lewis implies that they have desires and hatreds of their own, and further that they think some things ought to be desired and others hated . . .'[90] These statements seem to me paradigmatic of MacNeice's problems. It is surely an extraordinarily idiosyncratic reading which robs Yeats and Eliot of 'emotional partisanship'. Their emotional attachment to right-wing values is rarely concealed in their work. It is also telling that MacNeice does not, or can not, articulate what things they are that Auden, Spender and Day Lewis think 'ought to be desired and hated'. But MacNeice does, perhaps inadvertently, point towards the real orientation of the *New signatures* poets when he remarks later that 'original sin' is cardinal for them. A concept more at odds with Marxist thought than 'original sin' would be difficult to imagine.

That MacNeice, in *Modern poetry*, is torn between joining the Auden mythology and maintaining the individualism which had hitherto sustained him, is evidenced by the book's subtitle: *A personal essay.* And several chapters of the book are devoted to MacNeice's personal 'casebook', charting his development as a poet from childhood through public school to Oxford. There follows a further chapter on the 'personal factor' in poetry, before successive essays on 'Imagery', 'Rhythm and rhyme', and 'Diction', where the work of Auden, Spender and Day Lewis is compared and contrasted in technical terms with their immediate progenitors. The direction of MacNeice's argument here is that the *New signatures* poets are more 'vulgar' and down-to-earth than their predecessors. But he then goes on to deal with the difficulties of this argument in a chapter entitled 'Obscurity', wherein he admits that much of Auden's and Spender's writing is obscure and esoteric, because they had inherited a tradition from Eliot. There is little attempt made to square these propositions with those relating to the *New signatures* poets in his opening chapter.

MacNeice then wants to align himself with the poets who are distinct from preceding generations, and who are supposed to be committed. But his book shrugs off the most pertinent issues of how they are different, and to what exactly they are committed. The best that can be said of Modern poetry is that it avoids extremes and shows some democratising impulses. What it most certainly does not accomplish is any advance towards a left-wing poetic, or towards political allegiance to the left.

Walter Allen cogently remarks that Modern poetry was published when MacNeice was half-way through writing his long, last poem of the decade, Autumn journal, and that the two works are 'expressions of one single impulse; Modern Poetry provides the critical rationale of the poem'.[91] This, I think, is true. I believe that Autumn journal shares with Modern poetry the manifest tensions of MacNeice's position in 1938. It was the Munich crisis which galvanised MacNeice and threatened to lead him away from individualism in the direction of 'solidarity': 'Nineteen thirty-eight was like my dream of the skeleton house. The alarm came in the autumn. Perched on the very joists I scrambled down quickly, began shrieking for solidarity.'[92] Like many others, MacNeice saw the necessity of combating Fascism, but this does not mean that he committed himself to the left. Both Modern poetry and Autumn journal are an intensified expression of the concerns which dogged MacNeice throughout the decade.

There is hardly enough space here to do Autumn journal justice. The poem is a record of MacNeice's thoughts and feelings immediately before, during and after the Munich crisis. Written in twenty-four cantos, and rhyming two lines in every four, MacNeice creates a relaxed voice which can encompass quotidian experience and description, as well as his reflections upon the political situation at home and abroad. The poems are impressive in so far as they provide a panorama of public and private experience. If they have a fault, it is their aleatory nature; each canto is only loosely related to the next, and the movement of subject-matter in some individual cantos occasionally seems arbitrary. But these reservations may, to some extent, be excused because of the ambitious nature of the enterprise. It is after all an experiment in form, and MacNeice's poems have the virtues and vices of a journal, wherein the author is talking to himself as well as to his audience.

Essentially the poem is an expression of MacNeice's perplexities; no settled point of view emerges. Many of the cantos do not deal specifically with political matters. There are, for instance, three love-poems; Canto IV seems to me one of the loveliest celebrations of a woman written this century. Much space is also given to a review of

MacNeice's classical education. Both school and university careers are discussed, the ethics of self-interest dying hard. Here, as elsewhere, Plato and Aristotle figure large in MacNeice's philosophising. It is typical of him, and of *Autumn Journal* as a whole, that his attitude to their thought cannot be definitively pinned down. Although in Cantos II and XIII MacNeice says goodbye to Plato, it seems that Plato was unwilling to leave. For in Canto XVII we hear that 'Plato was right to define the bodily pleasures / As the pouring water into a hungry sieve'. Elsewhere Aristotle is applauded, but in Canto IX MacNeice dismisses the 'humanist in his Jacobean panels' discussing the thought of ancient Greece. He implies that it is close to an irrelevance in the present times: 'It was all so unimaginably different / And all so long ago'.

Just as MacNeice's attempts to say goodbye to Plato strike one as an act of self-persuasion, so too with his attitude to politics in the poem. He continually implies that the time of laissez-faire is over, and speaks of the need for the exercise of will in action. But nowhere does it become clear precisely what action should be taken, and to what end. Paradigmatic of MacNeice's position are the following lines from Canto V:

And the individual, powerless, has to exert the
    Powers of will and choice
And choose between enormous evils, either
    Of which depends on somebody else's voice.[93]

This is close to the ironic awareness of *Catch 22*. The powerless individual exerts power to choose between evils neither of which he either wants or likes. MacNeice's resigned scepticism lurks behind the utterance as it does every time he attempts to imagine a better future.

In Canto III, MacNeice registers his awareness of the deficiencies of capitalism. It is 'an utterly lost and daft / System'. But he openly admits his difficulty in imagining anything better; he too has 'the slave-owner's mind':

            … habit makes me
    Think victory for one implies another's defeat
That freedom means the power to order, and that in order
    To preserve the values dear to the elite
The elite must remain a few. It is so hard to imagine
    A world where the many would have their chance without
A fall in the standard of intellectual living
    And nothing left that the highbrow cared about.
Which fears must be suppressed.[94]

MacNeice, however, finds these fears extremely difficult to suppress, and this is, I think, why he could not commit himself to the left. A few lines later, this is made even clearer as the poet again attempts self-persuasion. Talking of his own past history which is 'Matter for the analyst', he goes on:

> But the final cure is not in his past-dissecting fingers
>   But in a future of action, the will and fist
> Of those who abjure the luxury of self-pity
>   And prefer to risk a movement without being sure
> If movement would be better or worse in a hundred
>   Years or a thousand when their heart is pure.[95]

Implicitly MacNeice is precisely one of those who cannot decide whether 'movement' is worth the risk. And the 'will and fist' with their Fascistic overtones are clearly unpalatable to his liberal conscience. There is no sense in these lines that MacNeice thinks it might be worthwhile fighting for a better future; he has no unequivocal faith that such a future is possible.

Nevertheless MacNeice himself described the poem as 'both a panorama and an expression of faith'. Where then does the faith reside? In order to answer this question we encounter again ideas familiar from his earlier work. MacNeice is critical of the past, sceptical towards the future. His hope and faith then are placed in metaphysics rather than politics. And here we encounter two distinct attitudes which are not reconciled in his work. On the one hand there is an affirmation of life for life's sake; an acceptance of flux, violence, pain, occasional beauty: the whole gamut of experience. On the other hand there is the hope of the Romantic integration of antinomies. In Cantos II and XXI, we find oblivion and Nirvana rejected in favour of life for life's sake, whereas in Canto XXIII MacNeice turns back to a Romantic religiosity for solace:

> May God, if there is one, send
> As much courage again and greater vision
>   And resolve the antinomies in which we live . . .[96]

Autumn journal concludes with a similar statement:

> To-night we sleep
> On the banks of Rubicon — the die is cast;
>   There will be time to audit
> The accounts later, there will be sunlight later
>   And the equation will come out at last.[97]   (Canto XXIV)

The resolution of antinomies, the future solution of the equation, are offered as palliatives in the face of impending disaster. MacNeice reverts to the ideas and values he has inherited, despite the prickings of conscience.

Autumn journal was published in 1939. Together with *Modern poetry* it secured MacNeice's place in the mythology of 'MacSpaunday' because here he gave direct expression to concerns that Auden, Day Lewis and Spender essayed earlier in the decade. The difference between MacNeice and the others is that he expressed the conflict between the past and a possible future in a far more open way. There is little evasion in his work, and little pretense at believing in revolution. His individualism is always openly alluded to. Stylistically his poems do not exhibit the sometimes violent tension between modernism and Georgianism to be found in the work of his contemporaries. One might detect the influence of Hopkins, Yeats and Eliot in his work tempered by the more vernacular Georgians. And in *Autumn journal* the definite article is sometimes wielded in an Audenesque way. But using the combination of a lyrical, sometimes decorative surface, with very plain statement, MacNeice achieves a singular voice. MacNeice was his own man, and his own poet. Recently Margot Heinemann published an article in which she says of MacNeice that he came to 'a strongly felt . . . socialist commitment'.[98] However much one might like him to have held such beliefs, there is no evidence whatsoever to support this contention. MacNeice was a conservative, liberal, individualist like the rest of the 'Auden gang'. He differs from them only because he was not frightened of saying so.

Notes

1 A. Prochaska, *Young writers of the Thirties*, London, 1976.
2 R. Carter, ed., *Thirties poets: 'the Auden group': a casebook*, London, 1984.
3 C. Day Lewis was educated at 'Wilkie's', which was a private prep school in London, and later at Sherborne. MacNeice attended Sherborne and Marlborough.
4 Spender attended University College School, London.
5 C. Day Lewis, *The buried day*, London, 1960, pp. 216-17.
6 Ibid., pp. 17-19.
7 Ibid., p. 29.
8 Ibid., p. 67.
9 Ibid., p. 108.
10 Ibid., p. 117.
11 Ibid., p. 80.
12 Ibid., p. 131.
13 Ibid., pp. 158-9.

14 Ibid., p. 159.

15 G.S. Fraser, *The modern writer and his world* (1953), revd. ed. London, 1964, pp. 300-1.

16 See Day Lewis, *The buried day*, pp. 164-5 and 170, and Sean Day Lewis, *C. Day Lewis: An English literary life*, London, 1980, p. 42.

17 Day Lewis, *The buried day*, p. 197.

18 C. Day Lewis, *Collected poems, 1954* (1954), London, 1970, p. 18.

19 C. Day Lewis, *A hope for poetry* (1934), revd. ed., Oxford, 1936, p. 38.

20 Day Lewis, *The buried day*, p. 204.

21 B. Bergonzi, *Reading the thirties: texts and contexts*, London, 1978, p. 39.

22 Day Lewis, *Collected poems*, p. 109.

23 P. Fussell coins this phrase and applies it to poetry of the First World War in his book *The Great War and modern memory*, London, 1975, pp. 75-113.

24 Day Lewis, *The buried day*, p. 210.

25 Day Lewis, *Collected poems*, p. 112.

26 Day Lewis, *A hope for poetry*, pp. 12 and 17.

27 Day Lewis, *Collected poems*, p. 28.

28 Ibid., pp. 34-5.

29 Ibid., p. 31.

30 Ibid., pp. 29-30 and 75.

31 F. Kermode, *Romantic image*, London (1957), 1971, p. 18.

32 Day Lewis, *A hope for poetry*, pp. 47-8.

33 Day Lewis, *The buried day*, p. 206.

34 R. Williams, *Culture and society, 1780-1950* (1958), Harmondsworth, 1979, pp. 178-80, 264.

35 Day Lewis, *The buried day*, pp. 209-10.

36 Ibid., p. 212.

37 Day Lewis, *Collected poems*, pp. 127-8.

38 Ibid., p. 130.

39 Day Lewis, *The buried day*, p. 222.

40 Day Lewis, *Collected poems*, p. 191.

41 S. Spender, *Poems*, London, 1933. Spender printed both his own first volume, *Nine experiments*, and Auden's *Poems*, privately on a hand-press. Subsequently, in 1930, Basil Blackwell printed a non-commercial limited edition of Spender's *Twenty poems*. See *EA*, p. 431; Stephen Spender, *World within world*, London, 1951, p. 116, pp. 144-5; Prochaska, *Young writers of the thirties*, p. 7.

42 S. Spender, *Collected poems, 1928-1953*, London, 1955, p. 46.

43 Spender, *World within world*, p. 62.

44 Spender, *Collected poems*, p. 46.

45 Spender, *World within world*, pp. 2-3.

46 Ibid., p. 35.

47 Ibid., p. 34.

48 Spender also visited several other countries between 1930 and 1933: Spain, Italy, Austria and Yugoslavia. He continued to travel extensively during the rest of the decade. See L. Bartlett, ed., *Stephen Spender: letters to Christopher*, Santa Barbara, 1980.

49 Spender, *World within world*, p. 118.

50 Spender, *Collected poems*, p. 47.

51 Ibid., p. 53.

52 Ibid., p. 29.

53 Ibid., pp. 49-50.

54 Ibid., p. 30.

55 Ibid., p. 36.

56 S. Spender, 'Poetry and revolution', *New country*, ed. M. Roberts, London, 1933, pp. 62-71.

57   Spender, *World within world*, pp. 142-4.
58   S. Spender, *The destructive element: a study of modern writers and beliefs*, London, 1935, p. 235.
59   Spender, 'Poetry and revolution', *New Country*, p. 69.
60   Spender, *World within world*, p. 210.
61   R. Crossman ed., *The god that failed*, London, 1952, p. 276; *World within world*, p. 137.
62   Spender, *World within world*, p. 247.
63   K. Marx, *Capital* (1887), trans. S. Moore and E. Aveling, Moscow, 1954, pp. 247-8.
64   S. Spender, *The still centre*, London, 1939, pp. 43-4.
65   Spender, *World within world*, p. 254.
66   L. MacNeice, *Blind fireworks*, London, 1929; *Poems*, London, 1935.
67   L. MacNeice, 'Poetry To-Day', *The arts to-day*, ed. G. Grigson, London, 1935, pp. 56-7.
68   Day Lewis, *A hope for poetry*, (1934), revd ed., Oxford, 1936, pp. 79-83.
69   L. MacNeice, *The strings are false*, London, 1965, p. 58.
70   Ibid., p. 100.
71   Ibid., p. 102.
72   Ibid., p. 103.
73   Ibid., p. 104.
74   Ibid., p. 130.
75   Ibid.
76   Ibid., p. 131.
77   L. MacNeice, *Poems*, London, 1935, p. 64.
78   L. MacNeice, *Collected poems*, ed. E.R. Dodds, London, 1966, p. 22.
79   Ibid., p. 21.
80   Ibid., p. 23.
81   Ibid., p. 30.
82   Ibid., p. 28.
83   Ibid., p. 18.
84   Ibid., pp. 17-18.
85   L. MacNeice, *I crossed the Minch*, London, 1938, p. 125.
86   MacNeice, *Collected poems*, p. 84.
87   Ibid., p. 47.
88   Ibid., p. 96.
89   W. Allen, Introduction to L. MacNeice, *Modern poetry: a personal essay*, (1938), Oxford, 1968, p. x.
90   MacNeice, *Modern poetry*, p. 25.
91   Allen, *Modern poetry*, pp. vi-viii.
92   MacNeice, *The strings are false*, p. 174.
93   MacNeice, *Collected poems*, p. 109.
94   Ibid., pp. 105-6.
95   Ibid.
96   Ibid., p. 149.
97   Ibid., p. 153.
98   M. Heinemann, 'Three left-wing poets', *Culture and crisis in Britain in the 1930s*, eds. J. Clark, M. Heinemann, D. Margolies and C. Snee, London, 1979, p. 110.

5

Geoffrey Grigson's New verse

Having re-read the poetry of 'MacSpaunday', we are left with one major bulwark of the literary-historical mythology of the 1930s to demolish, and this concerns Grigson's New Verse. This magazine has a central place in the mythology. It is widely considered to be the 'best' poetry magazine of its time. It is associated with Auden, with the left, and with a particular 'objectivist' poetic. Grigson himself encouraged an identification between his magazine and Auden by asserting in the last issue (May 1939) that 'New Verse came into existence because of Auden'.[1] This retrospective claim may have as much to do with Grigson's exploiting a chance to ensure the place of his magazine within history as it has with the more complex facts of the matter. But the perpetuation of Grigson's own publicity is easily demonstrable. As early as 1943, Denys Val Baker in a survey of Little reviews 1914-30, speaks of New verse 'fostering' the development of a wide and important range of poets, 'including in addition to Auden, Day Lewis and Spender such new writers as Christopher Isherwood, Kenneth Allott, Louis MacNeice, Charles Madge, Julian Bell, William Empson, William Plomer, Geoffrey Grigson'.[2] The Auden 'group' are centrally placed in his appraisal. That no creative writings at all by Isherwood, Plomer or Bell were published in New verse, and that Day Lewis and Spender published relatively few there, does not seem to have impinged upon Baker's consideration. This casual approach to the facts of the matter is also evident when he goes on to ascribe to the 'whole New verse group' an adherence to Grigson's 'objectivism'.

More recent critics have followed Baker's lead. Julian Symons, A.T. Tolley, Ian Hamilton, Alvin Sullivan and Samuel Hynes all subscribe to a mythical perspective as this selection of quotations amply testifies: 'New verse set a standard rather than a style, yet there was a certain poetic style, based on careful observation and deliberately elegant choice of epithet ... a style labelled by its opponents "bourgeois objectivisim" ... "New Verse came into existence because of Auden" ... and in a very real sense Auden's devices of style and habits of feeling are the 'thirties or a large part of the 'thirties' (Symons);[3] 'Undoubtedly the most

important periodical in the history of poetry in the nineteen-thirties
was New Verse . . . [Grigson] had a very decided notion of what poetry
should be, and even more decided notions of what it should not be'
(Tolley);[4] Above all there was Auden. It was the presence of Auden
and the glimmerings of a new wave in poetry which his presence
seemed to be encouraging that provided the chief impulse behind the
founding of New Verse' (Hamilton);[5] 'New Verse was political, left-wing
and propagandist from its beginnings, because the writers whom
Grigson admired and wanted to publish were political' (Hynes);[6]
MacNeice and Auden produced the model poems for which New Verse
would be known, a style that one critic has called "British Objectivism"...' (Sullivan).[7] If New verse is to be considered the most important
periodical for the history of poetry in the 1930s, it is crucial that it
should be so for accurate reasons. Here I wish to demonstrate that New
verse was not dominated by Auden, that it was neither propagandist nor
left-wing, that it published a wide range of poets writing in different
styles and, that Grigson's 'theorising', his so-called 'objectivism',
constitutes nothing more than his inevitably subjective, personal taste
for the contemporary. To this end it seems best to begin at the
beginning with the magazine's inception, concentrating particularly
upon the beliefs and values that Grigson brought to the editing of the
magazine.

Grigson came from the same class and educational background as
'MacSpaunday'. He was born in 1905 and, like C. Day Lewis and Louis
MacNeice, was the son of a clergyman, the vicar of Pelynt in Cornwall.
But Grigson's lot was seemingly harder than that of these contemporaries. He was the seventh son of an ageing father, and was brought
up in an atmosphere of faded grandeur, with cooks, maids and
governesses gradually disappearing, to leave his mother with the
housework and with the difficult task of keeping up appearances.
Grigson's education was also affected by the family's declining
fortunes. He attended less prestigious schools than did his brothers –
minor, and by his account rather shabby, prep and public schools –
in Plymouth and on the south coast.

That this left a mark on Grigson is made clear in his autobiography,
which is tellingly entitled The crest on the silver. The book dwells upon
the family lineage, and is permeated with nostalgia for a lost tradition
and regret for present impecunity. At Oxford Grigson could not afford
to go to the college of his choice, and had to endure one of the least
fashionable colleges, St Edmund Hall. Grigson acerbically points out

that this was populated largely by 'aliens from the industrial North and Midlands', and also refers to his fellow collegians in sneeringly dismissive terms as 'white mice'.[8] The snobbery and social bitterness implicit in such dismissals is made overt when Grigson remarks that at Oxford he 'envied those who had money and assurance', and that on leaving Oxford he 'envied . . . those eldest sons who inherited a settled and ancient house and its surrounding lands'.[9]

Grigson's enthusiasms are rural and have an air of feudalism about them. He is an aristocrat manqué, an attitude imbibed during childhood. Speaking of Yeats's admiration for a society of aristocrats and beggarmen, and of his concomitant contempt for the lower-middle classes, Grigson goes on: 'From the lower-middle-class I was more or less separate in my childhood. Aristocrats were as remote from our Parish. But the poor were the Yeatsian poor, not the proletarian poor... but a poor possessing even so late some remnants within them of that peasant past and those peasant virtues which Yeats quite properly respected.'[10]

Grigson regrets the lack of aristocrats, but clearly celebrates the 'peasantry' who are viewed as implicitly superior to the 'proletarian poor'. With such attitudes seemingly intact, Grigson graduated from Oxford and under the necessity of earning a living, secured a job through Oxford 'connections' with the London office of the Yorkshire post. From there he moved to the London morning post and it was whilst working as literary editor on this paper that Grigson planned New verse 'with some innocence at tea-time'.[11] The part Auden played in Grigson's motivations is not entirely clear. As an undergraduate Grigson had not met Auden and not 'awoken' to his poems, but had been aggressively 'for Eliot': 'Those who were against Eliot . . . were aspirants to that lower-middle-class of the mind which gives its tone to literary-journalism and the writing of novels'.[12]

By 1932 Grigson had 'discovered' Auden's early work but this understandably did not modify a belief in the aristocratic individuality of the poet. In his opening editorial for New verse Grigson wrote of the 'masses, aristocratic and bourgeois as much as proletarian', who 'vulgarise all the arts' and who have 'captured the instruments of access to the public'. His magazine 'is going to combat this by becoming one of the few grave and entertaining quarterlies and monthlies which strive obstinately to continue'. It is implicitly admitted that the magazine is going to be an expression of the editor's taste:

It favours only its time, belonging to no literary or politico-literary cabal, cherishing bombs only for masqueraders and for the everlasting 'critical' rearguard of nastiness, now represented so ably and variously by the *Best Poems of the Year*, the Book Society and all the gang of big-shot reviewers. NEW VERSE does not regard itself as a verse supplement to such periodicals as the *Criterion* and *Scrutiny*. There is no 'poetic' and therefore no supplementary experience; poetry by its words (to borrow a metaphor of Eliot's) and so by itself drives roots down to draw from all human experience. If the poem is only one organism in the creation of which those experiences are collected, concentrated, transmitted, it is the chief organism; and one (incidentally) in such an ulcerous period as our own which can serve magnificently.[13]

Grigson here is anxious to carve a niche for himself and his magazine. He and it are going to have nothing to do with the 'masses' of any class and their supposed 'vulgarity'. A position of aristocratic individuality like that proposed by the older modernists, Eliot, Lawrence and Wyndham Lewis is asserted. It hardly needs to be said that this tends politically towards a radical Tory position rather than to the left. But we are assured that *New verse* is to have no dealings with politico-literary cabals, with literary journalism, much less with the academy as represented by the *Criterion* and *Scrutiny*. Furthermore, the magazine is to have 'no poetic'. These negative delineations do not leave Grigson with much secure ground to stand upon, and it is telling that when he moves from negative to positive definition, he also moves into contradiction. Poetry, we are told, serves to collect, concentrate and transmit *all* human experience. The inclusiveness of this is in direct conflict with the exclusiveness of Grigson's earlier remarks; the experience of the 'masses', he implies, is too vulgar to be part of all human experience.

There is nothing in this opening editorial to lead one to suppose that Grigson's ambitions were left-wing, propagandist or objectivist. And there is nothing to indicate the influence of Auden in the founding of the magazine. But the astringently combative tone, the anti-literary-establishment attitude, suggest that Wyndham Lewis's example in *Blast* and *The enemy* was more influential in Grigson's endeavour than Auden's writings were. Grigson was a friend of Lewis in the 1930s, and in the former's autobiography Grigson implies that Lewis provided a model with respect to literary politics. Describing the impression Lewis made upon him, Grigson writes: 'The man was pure stimulus to anyone in his twenties . . . Here in a London of selling I knew a man not for sale combative, fearless and independent, but combative in the support of a consistent notion of life and art'.[14] What Grigson took this consistent notion of 'life and art' to be is not certain.

Grigson approvingly attributed to Lewis a belief in art as 'a constant stronghold of the purest human consciousness' (whatever that may mean) and was influenced by the older writer's aristocratic view of the arts. Speaking of changing his job from the Yorkshire post to the London morning post Grigson writes: 'And I was a socialist shifting from Toryism to dogmatic Toryism. Still between them de Toqueville, Ortega y Gasset and Wyndham Lewis had made me sceptical enough of a democratic left in the arts or a democratic middle in the arts which would do for the mass of all parties. The arts are aristocratic or not arts at all but propaganda for an average view of things.'[15]

The unmerciful campaign against Edith Sitwell (the 'Old Jane') which Grigson conducted in the pages of New verse is also reminiscent of Lewis, whose paranoiac ragings against Bloomsbury, against publishers, against anybody and everybody who had the temerity to disagree with him, reached their apotheosis in the 1930s. When asked in an interview if Lewis had encouraged his anti-Sitwell attitude Grigson replied, 'Anti-Sitwellian, anti-aesthetic, anti-society-art attitudes, yes'.[16] But how does this relate to Grigson's claim that he was a socialist? It should not be forgotten that in 1930 Lewis published his study, Hitler, which approved of 'National Socialism'. Despite the attentions of kind apologists who have pointed out that Lewis 'misunderstood' Hitler, and stress that he recanted the position outlined in the book, there can be no question that Lewis's politics in the 1930s were radically right-wing. Although it would be going too far to suggest that Grigson was pro-Nazi, we can be forgiven for asking exactly what kind of a 'Socialist' he was, since he could so admire and share in Lewis's literary values.

In 1970, asked to define his political position in the 1930s, Grigson described himself thus: 'A natural supporter of the under-doggishness in myself and others. Or a natural opponent of the agreed and settled average. Or a natural private socialist'.[17] It is evident that Grigson attempted to occupy an uncomfortable and indistinct middle ground between his own warring impulses. A supporter of the 'underdog' he is against the 'lower-middle-class of the mind and the settled average'. He is against the aristocratic Sitwells, but a supporter of the notion that art is aristocratic; against aestheticism, but for art as 'the expression of the purest human consciousness'. Grigson wants to be both underdog and aristocrat, both socialist and high Tory, both aesthete and anti-aesthete. But such ambivalence is difficult to sustain even-handedly in practice, and what emerges from the editorial policy of New verse is an aristocracy of one, Grigson himself, the rebel intellectual. Paradoxically and perhaps unwittingly he attaches himself to the tradition of conservative Romantic isolation. And he brought to New verse no integrated political and literary standards, other than a belief in himself and in the sanctity of art above politics. In this he showed himself to be more the Tory aesthete than the left-wing Socialist.

Having articulated his policy (or lack of one) in the opening editorial, Grigson found it necessary to reiterate his position and that of his magazine several times. Clearly there were those in his audience who wanted New verse to have a well-defined political position, just as subsequent critics have looked for and found such definite ground in the magazine. Grigson continually stressed that no such convenience was to be offered by New verse. In the second issue he 'warns' his readers that New verse 'has no politics', and reminds them that 'individualism is required'. He concludes his editorial: 'If there must be attitudes, a reasoned attitude of toryism is welcome no less than a communist attitude. This is not two-faced, since poetry is round and faces all ways.'[18] To say that the magazine has no politics is disingenuous. Clearly Grigson wished to avoid commitment. He, like his definition of poetry, faces all ways, or at least faces in different directions at different times. His insistence upon individuality, however, is a constant to which he returned in issue 12 for December 1934. Again his purpose is to disavow politics: 'NEW VERSE is neither True Blue nor Red, nor liberal nor white ... believing that the extent of a political situation is strict and near and mean compared with the immense far-off limit of every rich individuality'.[19]

Despite this overt disclaimer, still it was assumed by some that New verse had left-wing pretensions. But by 1936 the truth, or part of the truth, was beginning to dawn upon those committed to the left. An article in International literature noted that strong tendencies were drawing some poets away from the People's Front and that New verse had now 'lost every semblance of a genuine left-wing journal'. The point is, and Grigson was quick to make it, that New verse had never been committed to the left, much less to the People's Front. Grigson printed the accusations from International literature , and his reply to them, in the December 1936 issue of New verse. Again he states that 'New verse was never left-wing or right-wing'; he maintains that 'all virtuous intellect' need not be 'exclusively Communist, or Catholic or reactionary'. Typically Grigson's riposte finishes by asserting the importance of individuality, and significantly sneering at C. Day Lewis's recently published 'mob-sucking' novel![20]

It was not until 1938, two issues before the magazine's demise, that Grigson showed signs of retreating from his 'apolitical' stance, and his policy of having 'no poetic'. Issue 31 was a special double 'Commitments' number in which, as Sullivan has remarked, Grigson 'announced the end of political isolation ... almost ludicrously late'.[21] Like MacNeice's increased political concern in the later 1930s, Grigson's manoeuvre was almost certainly prompted by the imminent dangers posed by Nazi Germany, rather than through an increased commitment to the left. The substance of Grigson's own essay attempting to define his political and poetic commitment certainly bears this out, for it is anti-Hitler but certainly not pro-Socialist or Communist.

Significantly the essay is titled 'Lonely, but not lonely enough',[22] pointing again to that sense of, and reverence for, isolated individuality which lies at the core of Grigson's attitudes. But Grigson develops the theme of loneliness only towards the end of the essay. The bulk of his argument is concerned to persuade his audience that 'what we can see of objects is the beginning of sanity'. To 'desert' the 'world of objects' is, we are told, 'to become the mouth under the moustache on the last night of Nuremberg'. Here then is the basis of the 'objectivism' attributed to the magazine by subsequent critics. But Grigson's attempt to articulate a theoretical position is very sketchy, and expresses conflict rather than coherence. His argument is vulnerable because he fails in his essay to either establish what he means by the word 'object' or to show how a desertion of 'objects' leads to Nazism. He asserts that a writer may be judged by what he can 'see of objects' and what he 'uses of objects', but then confuses 'objects' with 'images' when he says: 'Desert the image for the general phrase or for the purely private image – at the worst you become Hitler or Chamberlain, at best Mr. Ezra Pound in his black shirt'.

It is difficult to imagine the kind of poem that Grigson has in mind here. It is even more hazardous attempting to explicate the political dimensions of his argument. Apparently Grigson is advocating a poetry which relies upon public images or objects, and which eschews abstractions or 'the general phrase'. But of course the questions are begged as to what distinguishes a public from a private image, and what separates the general from the particular phrase. Compounding these difficulties is the implicit idea that politicians like Hitler and Chamberlain, no less than poets like Ezra Pound, rely upon private images and general phrases. Contrary to Grigson's argument, it would seem to me axiomatic that the rhetoric of politicians of any persuasion is dependent for success upon public images. And the swipe at Pound tells us more about Grigson's wish to distance himself from the American's poetics and politics than it does about the nature of Pound's poetry.

This introduces another important point. For it might be assumed by some that Grigson's 'objectivism' derives from the objectivist poetics of American writers like Louis Zukofsky, who edited *An objectivist anthology* in 1932, or William Carlos Williams, some of whose books were published by the Objectivist Press in the 1930s. In fact there is little evidence to suggest that Grigson was interested in either of these writers. Judging by a scathing review of Williams's *Collected poems 1921-31* that Grigson wrote and published in *New verse* in 1934, Grigson had little but contempt for that physician's literary work.[23] Furthermore, both Williams and Zukofsky were self-consciously developing Pound's Imagist ideas, and both of them were interested not only in clarity of focus upon an object through the poetic image, but also in the idea of the poem as 'object'. This latter notion is one that Grigson specifically rejects when he goes on in his essay to struggle with the relationship between ideas and objects: 'The use of ideas (as against being used by ideas) depends upon this fidelity to objects and objects include language but not "poetry". I object to "poetry" or the "poet" or the "artist".' It is tempting to suggest that 'I object' is the basis of Grigson's 'objectivism'. For as this quotation further demonstrates, it is well nigh impossible to illuminate exactly what Grigson is advocating. The distinction between using and being used by ideas is rather unhelpful without further qualification, and once we are told that 'objects include language', it becomes quite clear that any poem whatsoever might be deemed 'objectivist'. Grigson's essay follows the pattern of his earlier editorials: he is much more adroit in defining his position negatively than in articulating any positive convictions.

It is not then suprising to find Grigson concluding his essay by attempting to distinguish between his own position and that of 'Socialist Realism'. Having implicitly defined his beliefs as oppositional to Conservatism (Neville Chamberlain), Nazism (Hitler), and Fascism (Pound's black shirt), Grigson goes on to separate himself from the left. He accuses Socialist Realists of evading 'their inconveniences' and using their 'ill-defined theory and their politics to cover up their deficiencies'. This 'fanaticism', he says, will not do: 'What we need now is not the fanatic but the critical moralist; and the one loneliness which is justified is Rilke's loneliness surrounded by everything thorough, exact, without slovenliness, impressionable and honest'. Grigson politically feels obliged to oppose Fascism but aesthetically he is drawn to the post-symbolist modernism, the Romantic loneliness of Rilke. For a man professedly disinterested in 'poetry and the poet' this was a curious example to uphold, since Rilke was the type of the Poet with a capital P, who courted loneliness in order to preserve his idiosyncratic metaphysical vision. Grigson's own 'ill-defined theory' (if his ideas may be graced with that term) is an attempt to reconcile the irreconcileable and inevitably collapses.

To discuss Grigson's short essay in such detail leaves me open to the accusation of breaking a butterfly upon a wheel. But given the perpetuation of the idea that Grigson was an 'objectivist', it seemed to me entirely necessary to demonstrate the paucity of meaning behind such a label. Grigson, of course, was not alone in 1938 in holding a rather confused and contradictory position. And given the dilemmas writers were faced with at that time (particularly upper-middle-class writers with a bad conscience) this cannot be suprising. What is of crucial interest, however, is the way in which confusion and contradiction have been resolved into certainties by subsequent commentators who have refused to scrutinise in detail where Grigson stood, preferring rather to perpetuate myths about both him and his magazine.

The only other statement of principles from Grigson in the 1930s appeared in 1939 as the preface to an anthology of poems from New verse. Grigson here edges uneasily and perhaps unknowingly closer to Rilke's mid-career position, when the European poet spoke of learning to 'be severe and see'[24] and of finding 'equivalents among the visible for the inwardly seen'.[25] But Grigson's essay suffers from the same inconsistency, the same irresolution as 'Lonely, but not lonely enough'.[26] There is a great deal of mellifluous pontificating about Rupert Brooke, Auden, MacNeice and Spender. Auden and MacNeice are praised for being closer to the spirit of 'Augustanism' than the Romanticism of Wordsworth. But then we are told that 'an imaginative poet of the best kind' is one who sees 'objects as themselves and as symbols all at once', and who is 'more than ever careful to convey the inner by the outer shape of things'. This is plainly much closer to the Wordsworthian tradition, to which Rilke may be readily attached, than it is to the principles or practice of the Augustans. Towards the end of his introduction, however, Grigson abandons 'theorising' in favour of a frank admission concerning the editorial policy governing the anthology. He says that he has chosen poems 'for the sake of the poems, and not for the sake of anything else, or any abstraction...'. Although Grigson concludes his preface by asserting that he judges every poem written now by 'the degree to which it takes notice, for ends not purely individual, of the universe of objects and events', it is my contention that the editorial policy of New verse was identical to that of the New verse anthology. The poems were chosen not on any theoretical principle but on the grounds of Grigson's taste, which was strongly allied to the tradition of Romantic individualism. The two essays of 1938 and 1939 not only post-date the first thirty issues of New verse, but also show 'objectivism' to be a chimera. Grigson was being forthright in his opening editorial when he said that he and his magazine had 'no poetic'.

It might be assumed that some exact standards of editorship might be inferred from Grigson's famously vitriolic reviewing. But this is not so. His criticisms are almost wholly destructive; he found it easier to demolish than to be constructive. Grigson has since expressed regret for the tone of his reviewing in New verse,[27] and there is scarcely need here to reproduce his self-delighting dismissals of various poets including George Barker, A.J.M. Smith, Rayner Heppenstall and (most surprisingly) Wallace Stevens, since Ian Hamilton has already provided such a service.[28] But before going on to look at the poetry Grigson published in New verse, it is worth quoting from one review which, I think, demonstrates that Grigson's judgement of poetry was not always free from ideological bias. Writing of Hugh MacDiarmid's volume Second hymn to Lenin, Grigson says the poems have 'just a little virtue', and remarks that they contain 'neat sentiment'. A grudging acknowledgement is made that 'great authors have been read and respected'. All this is the faint praise preceding damnation: 'But the poems read only a little better than the ballads hawked round by the unemployed. They are very similar. They have the same sincerity, and they have the same roughness, which is pathetic and moving in the street, but dull and ridiculous in a Scottish highbrow.'[29] Grigson here dismisses the possibility that ballads which are 'sincere', 'rough' and 'moving' can have anything to do with the art of the highbrow. And yet Grigson himself chose to publish two anonymous nineteenth-century folk ballads in his magazine. Perhaps it was not ballads he objected to, so much as poetry being written and 'hawked around' by the unemployed. However this may be, Grigson's judgement of MacDiarmid is surely perverse. It would be difficult to choose a poet less given to 'neat sentiment', and MacDiarmid's work rarely sounds simply like folk poetry. It was MacDiarmid's genius to create a rough-hewn style which combines intellectual vigour with striking, familiar imagery; a style imbued with passion which never succumbs to the facile or over decorative. But Grigson turns MacDiarmid's virtues into vices. The Scots poet was too feelingly committed to the left for Grigson's taste. And it was surely by mutual consent of poet and editor that no poems by MacDiarmid appeared in New verse.

But which poets did Grigson publish and do they conform to the prevailing view of the magazine and of the decade? Did Auden's poetry dominate the magazine as it is said to have done? Is there a house style evident in the poetry published in New verse, and what relationship, if any, did this have to the Audenesque or to the hazy tenets of 'objectivism'? Was the poetry left-wing and propagandist from the start as Hynes has stated?

The facts of the matter are that the eight poets most represented in New Verse were Grigson himself, Auden, MacNeice, Bernard Spencer, Kenneth Allott, Norman Cameron, Kathleen Raine and David Gascoyne. All these published between seventeen and twenty-two poems each in the magazine. Contrary to the statement Grigson made in 1939, that New verse had published more poems by Auden than by anybody else, Grigson himself was the poet most represented. Alvin Sullivan noticing this fact is quick to reassure us that after Grigson, Auden was the poet who appeared most frequently in New verse.[30] But this too is misleading, for the eighteen poems that appeared under Auden's name compare with twenty-one by Bernard Spencer, twenty by Cameron, nineteen by Kathleen Raine and eighteen each from MacNeice and David Gascoyne. It is only if one includes three of Auden's very early poems (they might justly be described as juvenilia) quoted in an article by Christopher Isherwood in the 'Auden' double number of New verse[31] that Auden's contributions become second in number only to Grigson's.

It was not then Auden's poetry which dominated New verse, but rather his publicity. Grigson constantly promoted Auden's poetry and particularly in the double number where twenty-two other poets contributed their comments, reminiscences of, and tributes to Auden. Most of what was published here contributes to the Auden mythology. Spender purported to chart Auden's progress, 'From Oxford to Communism',[32] an understandably difficult pursuit since Auden never reached the latter destination. Other writers like MacNeice and Grigson praised Auden's anti-establishment position, reserving specific commendation for his daring to write about prep and public schools. MacNeice also remarked enthusiastically that Auden 'was always taking sides'.[33] Typically, he forbore to deal with the problem of exactly which sides these were. Edgell Rickword injected a note of perspicacity when he remarked that Auden expressed 'the feeling of insecurity that affects a section of the middle-classes', and went on to notice the 'essence of Nazi demagogy' in certain lines from *The Orators*. Rickword also bemoaned the 'emotionally irresponsible' in Auden's poem 'Spain', and asserted that Auden and Isherwood were evading political issues in their verse dramas. He concludes rhetorically that Auden 'is too good a poet to fall back into the simple exploration of individuality'.[34] Rickword had evidently already perceived such a tendency manifesting itself in Auden's work. But Rickword's view has not prevailed against the myth-makers.

And it is not only Auden's poetry that the myth distorts. His poetry is said to dominate *New verse* because of his influence upon other poets who published there. It is argued that the Audenesque corresponds to Grigson's 'objectivism' and that not only Spender, Day Lewis and MacNeice were acolytes of Auden, but also that such poets as Bernard Spencer and Kenneth Allott are mere representatives of a collective idiom derived from Auden. The contributions of poets who do not fit into this scheme are either ignored, or twisted ingeniously to fit the convenient jig-saw. In Samuel Hynes's book, of the eight poets most represented in *New verse*, only Auden and MacNeice receive extensive treatment. One of Spencer's poems is quoted as a 'symptom' of the times, and the poetry of Raine, Cameron, Allott and Grigson is ignored. Although David Gascoyne's involvement with Surrealism is touched upon, only one of his poems is dealt with, and this is said to be made up of 'second-hand 'thirties properties . . . all familiar to a reader of the early work of Auden, Spender and Day Lewis'.[35]

Alvin Sullivan, in his study of *New verse*, though he does not ignore the leading poets in the magazine, does manage to make them all into 'objectivists'. Speaking of Auden, MacNeice and Spender he says: 'The qualities exemplified by these poets were the ones stressed in the preface to his [Grigson's] anthology: the avoidance of poetic inflation or too much vagueness and subjectivity of illustration, the use of terms and images commonly understood and above all the observation of natural facts and forms'.[36] Other poets are implicitly equated with the same poetic. Sullivan says of Bernard Spencer, for instance, that he wrote a poem 'characteristic not only of New verse but of most poems written in the Thirties'.[37] Norman Cameron is dragged within the objectivist fold by quoting a review in which Grigson cited Cameron's work as an example of 'pure poetry'. Most telling, perhaps, is Sullivan's treatment of Gascoyne and Raine: 'When one considers how antipathetic their style was to Grigson's taste, the only explanation for their inclusion seems clearly to lie in their belief that objects contained and revealed the highest values and that the poet's task was a rigid adherence to physical details'.[38] This remark entirely obscures the metaphysical direction of Raine's work, and the theory and practice of Surrealism as propounded by Gascoyne, in order to bring both poets into line with Grigson's assumed preferences.

Sullivan is not the only critic to have minimised the role played by Surrealism in New verse in order to give the poetry within its pages an appearance of homogeneity. Ian Hamilton speaks of New verse's 'brief and barely rewarding flirtation with Surrealism' and furthermore says that this 'surrealist fad' did not 'last long'.[39] He notes that both George Barker and Dylan Thomas received hospitality in New verse , but goes on to say that 'neither had ever seemed to fit comfortably in its clinical pages; they both seemed to have issued from that corner of now forgotten, now presumably-regretted interest in the Surrealists'.[40]

If we decide neither to 'forget' nor 'regret', but turn back to the pages of New verse, an entirely different picture emerges. Grigson first published poems with a Surrealist orientation in the fifth issue of the magazine. And he continued to publish such poems until issue 29 – five issues from the magazine's demise. Another telling statistic is that Gascoyne, Barker and Thomas, three poets associated (however fairly or unfairly) with Surrealism in the 1930s, and whose work is often placed in the shadow cast by the Audenesque, between them published more poems in New verse than Auden, Day Lewis, and Spender put together. Furthermore, between issues 24 and 29 of New verse Grigson published eight poems by Philip O'Connor who has more claim to be considered a genuine Surrealist than either Barker or Thomas. The opening lines of O'Connor's 'Blue bugs in liquid silk' adequately demonstrates the flavour of his writing:

blue bugs in liquid silk
talk with correlation particularly like
two women in white bandages
a birdcage swings from the spleen of ceiling frowning her
        soul in large wastes

and a purple sound purrs in basket-house
putting rubies on with red arms [41]

The irrational extravagances evident here are surely incompatible with
Grigson's presumed preference for public and objective images. And
not only did Grigson print poems like this, but he also gave space in
issues 10, 20, and 21 of his magazine, to three essays about Surrealism;
two attempting to explain it, and one by Auden expressing 'Honest
doubts' about it. But Auden's arguments were apparently not enough
to deter Grigson, for in issue 23 he published several pieces of
anonymous Surrealist prose which he had purchased from a London
bookshop. All this, I think, bespeaks the myth of a house style or
homogeneity in New verse. It points again to the possibility that Grigson
could not make up his mind about Surrealism, and that he was editing
by instinct rather than principle.

In his autobiography, Grigson says that it is rather more than he 'can
bear to look now in old numbers of New verse'. But he goes on to reassure
himself and his audience that 'At least there was some degree of sanity
and direction about New Verse, at least (or so I think) there was no
wangling and no compromise, and none of that dotty inclusiveness,
that mental masturbation which has come to be the character of "little
magazines" during the war and since'.[42] It should by now be clear that
I cannot agree with Grigson's generous summary of his own
achievement, or with the implications it has for literary history. The
importance of New verse seems to me to lie in its relative heterogeneity
rather than in its 'standards', 'principles', or homogeneity. The 1930s
was a time when various styles co-existed. Surrealism plainly represents one extreme. But it is as I shall argue later, an extreme which
ideologically tends towards the right rather than the left. The one
genuine, major, British left-wing poet of the 1930s, Hugh MacDiarmid,
did not appear within the pages of New verse. This is where Grigson drew
his line. His tastes were catholic as long as the ideological implications
of a poem were not too left-wing. His magazine reflects the dominance
of liberal and conservative ideology throughout the 1930s.

Notes

1   G. Grigson, New verse, New Series No. 2, May 1939, p. 49.
2   D.V. Baker, Little reviews, 1914-39, London, 1943, pp. 31-32.
3   J. Symons, The thirties: a dream revolved, revd. ed., London, 1975, pp. 73, 142.
4   A.T. Tolley, The poetry of the thirties, London, 1975, p. 203.
5   I. Hamilton, The little magazines, London, 1976, p. 82.
6   S. Hynes, The Auden generation, London, 1976, p. 116.
7   A. Sullivan, 'New verse', British literary magazines, vol. IV, the modern age, New York, 1986, p. 292.
8   G. Grigson, The crest on the silver, London, 1950, p. 91.
9   Ibid., pp. 95 and 131.
10 Ibid., pp. 49-50.
11 Ibid., p. 162.
12 Ibid., pp. 116-17.
13 G. Grigson, 'Why', New Verse, No. 1, Jan. 1933, pp. 1-2.
14 Grigson, The crest on the silver, p. 165.
15 Ibid., p. 172.
16 'A conversation with Geoffrey Grigson', The review, No. 22, June 1970, p. 16.
17 Ibid., p. 22.
18 G. Grigson, Editorial, New verse, No. 2, March 1933, pp. 1-2.
19 G. Grigson, Editorial, New verse, No. 12, Dec. 1934, p. 2.
20 G. Grigson, 'New verse goes Trotskyite', New verse, No. 23, Dec. 1936, p. 24. The 'mob-sucking' novel referred to was Day Lewis's, The friendly tree, London, 1936.
21 Sullivan, British literary magazines, vol. IV, p. 295.
22 G. Grigson, 'Lonely, but not lonely enough', New verse, Nos. 31-2, autumn-winter 1938, pp. 16-17.
23 G. Grigson, New verse, No. 8, April 1934, pp. 18-19.
24. R.M. Rilke, Poem 34, The book of hours, Das Stunden-Buch, Book I, Of the monastic life, Sämtliche Werke, Vol. I, Berlin, 1955, p. 274.
25 R.M. Rilke, The notebooks of Malte Laurids Brigge, 1910, trans. H.D. Herter-Norton, New York, 1949, p. 4.
26 G. Grigson, Preface to the First Edition, New verse, an anthology, (1939), 2nd ed., London, 1947, pp. 15-24.
27 Grigson, The crest on the silver, p. 162.
28. Hamilton, The little magazines, pp. 88-94.
29 G. Grigson, New verse, No. 19, Feb.–March 1936, p. 19.
30 Sullivan, British literary magazines, vol. IV, p. 292.
31 C. Isherwood, 'Some notes on Auden's early poetry', New verse, Nos. 26-7, Nov. 1937, pp. 4-9.
32 S. Spender, 'From Oxford to Communism', New verse, Nos. 26-7, Nov. 1937, pp. 9-10.
33 L. MacNeice, 'Letter to W.H. Auden', New verse, Nos. 26-7, Nov. 1937, pp. 11-13.
34 E. Rickword, 'Auden and politics', New verse, Nos. 26-7, Nov. 1937, pp. 21-2.
35 Hynes, The Auden generation, p. 388.
36 A. Sullivan, Geoffrey Grigson's New verse, Ph.D. Thesis, St. Louis University, 1972, p. 44.
37 Ibid., p. 56.
38. Ibid., p. 46.
39 Hamilton, The little magazines, p. 86.
40 Ibid., p. 90.
41 P. O'Connor, 'Blue bugs in liquid silk', New verse, No. 25, May 1937, p. 12.
42 Grigson, The crest on the silver, p. 163.

6

An Oxbridge clique?

I

In 1938 the poet D.S. Savage accused Geoffrey Grigson of cultivating an 'Oxbridge clique' within the pages of New verse.[1] In his riposte Grigson remarked, 'I should like Mr. Savage to tell me what good non-bourgeois poet is ringing the doorbell of New verse without getting an answer'. In other words Grigson believed there were no working-class poets who were any 'good'. Also, Grigson's implicit definition of 'middle-class' here is like that of Samuel Hynes; anyone who does not attend the universities of Oxford or Cambridge does not belong.[2] And, although Grigson's editorial policy was more catholic than his exchange with Savage might suggest, it is true that seven out of the eight most published poets in the magazine were educated at Oxbridge. I have already offered a reading of Auden's and MacNeice's work; here I want to look at the poetry of Grigson himself, of Bernard Spencer, Norman Cameron, Kathleen Raine and Kenneth Allott.

All five of these poets were born within the fourteen-year span by which Hynes defines his 'Auden Generation', yet none of them is dealt with in his study. Several questions arise from this circumstance which need to be addressed. Is it the case that the work of these poets merely represents a pale imitation of the Audenesque, and therefore may be comfortably ignored in a literary history of the period? Or is it simply that these five poets did not write enough 'good' poems to be included in the 1930s pantheon? And what was their ideological position? If the 'Auden gang' were not committed to the left, where do these five poets stand, and do they share a collective idiom derived from shared concerns?

What I wish to show is that here we encounter five individual voices, distinct from the Audenesque, which nevertheless share ideological positions which eschew the left, and which often go beyond liberalism in their conservative orientation. On the question of quality and quantity it should be made clear that although some work to be discussed here is vulnerable to criticism on a technical as well as ideological basis, the level of craftsmanship displayed by poets like Spencer, Cameron and Allott stand up well compared with that of say, Spender and Day Lewis.

In this chapter then, the distortions of the literary-historical myth of the decade should become ever clearer. And we will begin to see the difference that class as well as educational background makes to poetics and ideology. For although Kathleen Raine attended Cambridge, and Allott was a postgraduate at Oxford, neither of them belong so securely to the public-school-educated upper-middle classes as do Spencer, Grigson and Cameron. The difference this makes to their writing will be discussed in due course. For now let's turn to Bernard Spencer who, of the five poets to be discussed here, is closest to Auden and friends.

II

Bernard Spencer was born in Madras into a collateral branch of the Spencer-Churchill family in 1909.[3] His father, Sir Charles Spencer, was a Judge in the imperial service. Bernard, however, was to remember little of imperial India, since he was sent back to England at the age of eighteen months, and, in his own words, 'farmed-out' to the families of rectors and vicars.[4] We have already seen how various sons of clergymen felt insecure about their class background, caught as they were between the gentry and the lower-middle class. Bernard Spencer provides no exception: This is how he recalls his childhood: 'As belonging to a country clergyman's household, my brother, my sister and myself were regarded as solidly too good for the company of village children, and by the gentry as not good by and large for the company of theirs. Consequently we made our own amusements...'[5] So Spencer, like many of the other poets we have considered so far, had a highly developed sense of class-consciousness. And the educational journey appropriate to his class, through prep schools to Marlborough, and from there to Oxford was, as we have seen already, unlikely to diminish such consciousness.

Whilst at Oxford Spencer published his first poems, and enjoyed the company of Stephen Spender, Louis MacNeice, Richard Goodman and Isaiah Berlin. On leaving Oxford, he had no settled career in view, and between 1932 and 1940 made a living in a variety of occupations including prep school master, advertising copywriter and film scriptwriter. The similarities between Spencer's background, education, and experience in the 1930s and that of the Auden 'group' are quite clear. And given his acquaintance with Spender and MacNeice, it comes as little surprise to hear Spencer himself speaking retrospectively of the 'strangling influences' at work during the decade.[6] Critics have taken Spencer at his own word, and reduced his work of the 1930s to a mere adjunct to that of 'MacSpaunday'. Alvarez speaks of Spencer writing 'regulation political poems'[7] in the 1930s, and Bowen of his contributing to 'the collective text of the decade'.[8]

It is undoubtedly true that Spencer wrote his finest poems in the 1940s and 1950s, but his 1930s work should not be subsumed under such easy categorisations. For his voice has none of the pedagogical pretensions of the Audenesque and few of its stylistic mannerisms. Spencer's work is cool and meditative. It has a less difficult, dazzling surface, and is less vatic than Auden's work; it is more cerebral, less sentimental than say, Spender's. If Spencer's 1930s poetry resembles anybody else's work, it is that of his fellow-pupil at Marlborough, Louis MacNeice. They share a painterly eye, and strive to communicate their images and ideas through a relatively straightforward syntax. Spencer also shares with MacNeice a very open attitude to his political position; his liberalism is overt and unabashed. Nevertheless Spencer distinguishes himself from MacNeice in having a quieter, more glacial utterance that did not waver under the political pressures of the second half of the decade.

Spencer did not publish his first volume of poems until 1946.[9] Most of his poems written in the 1930s found a place in *New verse* and those that did not appeared in anthologies in the course of the decade. It should not, however, be thought that this kept him from an audience. We should recall that *New verse* had a regular readership of a thousand; the same number who bought Auden's first volume of poems between 1930 and 1933.

'Allotments April' is a poem which has been singled out as representative not only of Spencer, but also of many poems written in the 1930s. The poem, first published in 1936, takes up that traditional theme of English poetry from Chaucer onwards: the advent of spring. Spencer juxtaposes his own sensual and aesthetic enjoyment of the season's onset with the religious and artistic past, and with the threatening violence of the public world. In the opening stanza he poses the question: 'In what sense am I joining in / Such a hallooing, rousing April day'. The rest of the poem seeks to answer this conundrum. Any religious 'festival joy' is gone, and 'the love-songs, the medieval grace / The fluting lyrics' have 'stopped singing'. But still Spencer finds aural and visual perceptions which compensate for these and other losses. He hears the 'rough voices of boys' and sees 'red fires / Of flower pots'. These, he says, 'make a pause' in the wireless news of 'pacts, persecutions / And imprisonments, and deaths.' The public world thus intrudes implacably upon the private, neatly validating the sense of 'pause' Spencer feels.

The next stanza continues to consider the public world closer to home. The nearby town is surveyed as the poet ponders, 'The worry about money, the eyeless work / Of those who do not believe, real poverty / The sour doorways of the poor...' April, he says, does not 'deny or conceal' any of this. Rather, it adds,

What more I am; excites the deep glands
And warms my animal bones as I go walking
Past the allotments and the singing water-meadows
Where hooves of cattle have plodded and cratered, and
Watch today go up like a single breath
Holding in its applause at masts of height
Two elms and their balanced attitude like dancers,
                    their arms like dancers.[10]

There is no attempt made here to conceal the distance between the upper-middle-class poet, and 'the sour doorways of the poor'. Furthermore, there is an almost disarming honesty in the self-congratulation of the phrase, 'What more I am'. This phrase, and what follows from it, the return to a celebration of the animal and aesthetically aware individual, is an answer to the question initially posed. The meditation provoked by April has allowed the poet to see the contrast between himself as an individual and the lives of others which are shattered by public circumstances. Spencer is able to join in the 'hallooing day' through his privileged seeing and saying which is predicated upon his superior class position. He, like April, does not deny or conceal negativities in the world of men, but inspired by the season, Spencer admits of hope through aesthetic perceptions of nature. He rejoices in an attitude balanced like the 'arms' of the elm trees.

The broad subject-matter of the poem with its combination of public and private concerns may be typical of some 1930s poetry, but the manner of the poem is all Spencer's. His overt celebration of nature, reminiscent of Edward Thomas, owes a greater debt to the Georgian than other poets have done so far. And his use of an image of balanced integration accepts a Romantic position more unequivocally than we have seen hitherto. There is no hint of any kind of radicalism here at all.

This is not, however, true of all Spencer's poems of the 1930s. In 'A thousand killed', for instance, which was published in *New verse* in 1936, we find Spencer in the opening stanza making what appears to be a straightforward declaration of political allegiance. He speaks of being 'thrilled', like a man hearing good news at the elections, when he reads of the 'scrounging imperial paw' being 'bitten' to the tune of 'a thousand killed'. But in the second and final stanza, Spencer ironically exposes his own position. War is not, he says, like an election; elections are 'paid for with cheques and toys', whereas war is bought with 'the lives, burned-off, / Of young men and boys'.[11] The poem is salutary in so far as it exposes the distance between reading about a war and the grim actualities of its procedure. But the plangent final lines also act to eradicate the notion that one might be partisan, and glad that the imperialists have suffered a defeat. The poem is pacifist and quietist in its implications.

Three further poems, all published in 1937, give equally clear expression to Spencer's political position. 'A cold night' has the poet cosy in domestic comfort by his fireside, troubled only by his consciousness of the embattled and oppressed in England and Europe. But thoughts of the public world are apparently only a momentary distraction:

I turn back to my fire. Which I must.
I am not God or a crazed woman.
And one needs time too to sit in peace
Opposite one's girl, with food, fire, light,

And do the work one's own blood heats,
Or talk, and forget about the winter
– This season, this century – and not be always
Opening one's doors on the pitiful streets

Of Europe, not always think of winter, winter,
             like a hammering rhyme,
For then everything is drowned by the rising wind,
             everything is done against Time.[12]

The ironic form of the poem, with the ostensibly shortlived workings of conscience re-asserting themselves in the passionate finale, tempers what might otherwise be thought of as a plea for absolute political quietism. The conflict in the poem is clearly between the private life of the individual, and the perception of public evils which might prompt political action or commitment. Implicit in the poem is the idea that whatever the political situation might be, the individual should have the freedom to choose domestic comfort, to shut the door upon the public world.

In 'Cage', as the title might suggest, 'freedom' is the principle concern. The poet contemplates a canary measuring its 'prison'. This leads him to meditate upon the individual's relationship to the state:

The dead laws of a stiffening State
Shoot up forests of oppressive iron;
The shouting of each military saviour
Bolts bars of iron;
Money, houses, shudder into iron.
Within that fence I am whatever I am.
And I carry my inherited wish to be free,
And my inherited wish to be tied forever,
As natural to me as my body.[13]

Spencer apparently accepts the 'dead laws of a stiffening State', and the necessity of some limitation to personal freedom. But he also asserts his individuality within the 'fence', and accepts his own 'naturally' paradoxical attitude to liberation and oppression. The poet goes on to say that sometimes he 'lunges to left', and sometimes to 'right', but finds in both only 'mist's pretence'. He concludes that much of his life will be spent 'exploring' his 'fence'. The poem seeks to divorce the private life from the public; it implies that however Fascistic a state may be, the individual still has a certain autonomy. Spencer has no faith in radical solutions to political problems. He accepts a middle road which upholds the paramount importance of the individual.

Spencer's poems concentrate upon himself. Far from reacting against his liberal inheritance, with its belief in the individual, and in the sanctity of the domestic, he openly celebrates it. And one feels that any political concern he might have stems from a wish to preserve these threatened values. Nowhere is this clearer than in a love poem, 'Part of plenty' which returns us to the conservative Spencer who sat by his fire in 'A cold night'. Here we have a striking hymn to marital domestic harmony, which locates a supreme richness in essentially quotidian experience. This is less typical of Spencer's 1930s work than other poems we have considered. But again it demonstrates Spencer's plain-speaking, his Georgian inheritance, and his values. It is clear that Spencer was anything but a revolutionary. He clearly wished to be left alone to indulge in his domestic and aesthetic pursuits. And his lack of radicalism, his acceptance of inherited values, are clearly reflected in his style wherein there are few traces of modernism. His language is elegant, his syntax conventional, and his metaphors anything but startling. His work is further testimony to the vulnerability of the idea that 1930s poetry was dominated by an Audenesque style, and left-wing politics.

If this is true of Spencer's work, it is even more so with that of Geoffrey Grigson, whose first volume of poems was published in 1939.[14] Given Grigson's theorising about 'objectivism', we might expect to encounter some relationship between precept and practice here. But when we turn to his poetry we find a far more private voice than his writings about 'objectivism' might lead us to expect. Grigson's poetry may throw light upon his tastes, but does not conform to his stated preference for public images. He is primarily a poet who sees and describes 'things' in nature. This Georgian allegiance, however, is modified by following Auden's early predilection for attenuated rhythms, and a cold precision which distrusts emotion. An over-fondness for the definite article, for self-consciously surprising adjectives, and for occasional imperative opening lines, also remind one of Auden's less attractive mannerisms. But these Audenesque traits are integrated into a style which lacks the tension to be found in Auden's work. Grigson's inherited values are rarely questioned. Signal of this is that he seldom engages with the urban and suburban world with their attendant social and political problems. There is little in any of Grigson's poems to suggest that he found anything to be complained of in England's situation, and it was only in the closing years of the decade, as the situation in Europe deteriorated, that Grigson exhibited in his poems some small concern with public events.

This lack of conflict in Grigson's work is manifested stylistically in an avoidance of metaphor. He believes that to name things in nature is enough to give them suggestive resonance. Grigson also distinguishes himself from the Audenesque by eschewing a proliferation of abstract nouns. But he solves this problem only to create another, and one that is equally, if not more, damaging. For too often his poems consist of a list of images, sometimes connected by the clumsiest of syntactic manoeuvres, which leave the reader with little more than description. Anticipating just such censure, Grigson writes in the preface to his Collected poems:

... I shall risk another reminder – that, for example, such a remark as 'A White Stone', by itself or extended into a poem isn't necessarily either *description* or *nature verse*. Images (so I think) should retract into themselves, and shouldn't be extended too much into explanation – a white stone *because it is hard, heavy, white, conspicuous, dead, lonely, cold, different, indifferent,* et cetera et cetera. It has always struck me as disappointing that so elementary and obvious a possibility of verse frequently goes unnoticed.[15]

Grigson inadvertently illustrates the problem implicit in his poems here. His 'elementary possibility' for verse is open to equally elementary objection. For to say 'a white stone' most surely *is* mere description without a further context to supply the richness of suggestion Grigson would have it impart. How hard, heavy, conspicuous, or different a white stone is depends upon its size, its geological formation and its geographical location. Whether it is perceived through personification to be lonely, cold and indifferent is entirely dependent upon the 'eye beholding'; a white stone on a pebble beach in summer does not necessarily have any of these qualities.

Many of the poems Grigson published during the 1930s suffer because the images used do not sufficiently resonate for an audience. The flatness of such documentary titles as: 'Several observations', 'Five occupations', 'Three landscapes', or 'Around Cadbury Castle in June' is equalled by a use of image which is both private and less than exciting. The last-named poem serves admirably to demonstrate how Grigson's use of image tends towards the solipsistic, rather than looking outward to an audience, or to the world of event and action. The poem comprises a single sentence split into seven unrhymed quatrains, the whole welded together by the sometimes repeated participles, 'Walking', 'watching', 'recalling'. Grigson begins likes this:

Walking around Cadbury Castle
on a late day in June,
admiring elder flowers and yellow
stones and emery mole hills

And blue Glastonbury we
enjoy so little and will not
admire so soon. Startling
flies from a round dung ...[16]

The elision of the first-person pronoun, and the inclusion of the rhetorical second person, does not prevent this from remaining completely self-involved. Objects and places are named but not

evoked. That the poet admires elder flowers is clearly important to
him, but of marginal interest to a reader who is so little informed as
to what makes the observed phenomena 'admirable'. Why 'we' enjoy
Glastonbury 'so little' is impossible of answer, and since the poet is
already admiring the place, the phrase 'and will not enjoy so soon',
is equally mystifying.

As the poem continues we move ever further from enlightenment.
The sun goes down, and the poet considers that it would, 'watch as
soon / say earwigs or grey-heads of grass or clerks'; a juxtaposition
which only just escapes a sneer. Then the poet 'recalls Rubens', 'the
husband and wife quarrelling', and moves via another disparate
recollection to the following conclusion:

Recalling cockerel malice of a   The rotten lung, the preference
fresh-faced writer,   for dogs, the strange geology
the shifty liberal, and   that directs the stream, evil
the short moustache,   I share, good I do not do.

This is surely very private in its import. 'Geology', 'bad lungs', and
a 'preference for dogs' have, I submit, little to do with good or evil,
with the political implications of the penultimate stanza, much less
with Cadbury Castle. The self accusation of the final lines carries little
emotional weight. We are left with the implication that Grigson
dislikes 'liberals' and Fascists (the 'short moustache' is presumably a
metonym for Hitler) and with an ostensible expression of guilt which
is so complacent as to render it meaningless.

In other poems, written towards the end of the decade, the word
'Europe' is wielded in much the same way that 'Glastonbury' is used
in the foregoing poem. 'Europe' is meant to denote the world of public
events intruding upon Grigson's private enjoyments. But again it is a
case of naming rather than evoking situations. 'And forgetful of
Europe' is a description of the poet's pleasurable vacations in Mlini
with his beloved. He shows himself here to be capable of more
sensuous description than in 'Around Cadbury Castle', but it is
description largely for its own sake. The point of the poem is tellingly
encapsulated in the final lines where the poet speaks of a walk home
on a warm night after an evening playing bridge. Four lines are
expended detailing the bridge scores and the financial losses incurred
at cards, before 'forgetful of Europe', the couple stop to notice 'the
lights of the fish-spearers' and the 'moon over the cypresses'.[17] The
detail expended upon the bridge game is in obvious contrast to the

unwillingness to describe why it is best to be forgetful of Europe. The end result is to give the impression that playing bridge is rather more important to Grigson than Europe; privacy is celebrated in a private poem.

'Meeting by the Gjulika Meadow' is a more convincing poem on a similar theme. Here we are again located on vacation in Eastern Europe where Grigson describes meeting and sharing a campfire with a 'Slovene'.[18] The poem is nicely dramatic and evokes the pleasures of casual intimacy in a strange place. The two men 'talk under the thunder' about 'Europe', and although they also converse of other matters, they cannot escape 'Europe'. The poem closes with ambivalent images of nature: the 'sneering thunder' and 'scent of magenta and cyclamens'. Because thunder has already been associated with 'Europe', these final images suggest metaphoric resonances; the thunder points towards impending disasters in Europe, whilst the cyclamens by contrast are associated with the accord possible between two men of different nationalities. This poem then, works in a way that many of Grigson's do not, but even so the reader has to supply the context of 'Europe' whereas the private experience is evoked more fully. In this it remains characteristic of Grigson's work. There is never any sense in his poetry that he could or should engage in social and political matters.

In the same number of New verse that Grigson reviewed Hugh MacDiarmid's Second hymn to Lenin, he also wrote a review of Norman Cameron's first book, The winter house and other poems (1935). Grigson's remarks about the two poets are nicely contrasting; MacDiarmid is damned with faint praise, whereas Cameron's work is described as 'a genuine pure poetry'.[19] Given these remarks, and given what I have said about Grigson's own poetry, it is not surprising to find in Cameron another political quietist or fatalist.

Cameron was an exact contemporary of Grigson, born in Scotland in 1905. He was educated at Fettes public school in Edinburgh, and subsequently at Oxford where he was a contemporary of Auden et al. Cameron's poetry was well represented in the Oxford poetry anthology of 1927, edited by Auden and Day Lewis. On leaving Oxford, Cameron lived near his friend Robert Graves in Hammersmith for a time before taking up an appointment as an Education Officer in southern Nigeria.[20] Here, from 1929 to 1932, he lived 'like a gent', attended by three servants in what he described as a 'middle-class paradise'.[21] Needless to say, it was only paradisal for the white colonists. Eventually

Cameron tired of his job, and left Nigeria to join Graves in Majorca with the idea of devoting himself to letters. But as Graves records, Cameron 'needed to have a routine job on the side, and a London pub round the corner', in order to fulfil his 'natural part'.[22] So after a corrosive row with Laura Riding, Cameron returned to London where he became an advertising copywriter for J. Walter Thompson, a job he both enjoyed and did very well. One of his claims to fame is that he invented the idea of 'night starvation', which became the basis for the advertising of Horlicks for many years! Cameron continued in this job until 1939, when he began his participation in 'hush-hush political warfare'.[23]

As the details of his career might imply, Cameron was anything but a radical. Yet it remains a tribute to his artistic integrity that he owes nothing stylistically to either Auden or Day Lewis, and that he wrote only sporadically when, as James Reeves has remarked, he had something to say.[24] There are only sixty poems in Cameron's Collected poems, and of these eighteen were published in New verse. Robert Graves, as well as Reeves, has acted as an advocate for Cameron's less than well-known work,[25] and it is not difficult to see why this should be so. For if Cameron's work may be said to resemble any of his immediate forebears, it resembles that of Graves.

Urbane, witty, epigrammatic, written in traditional metres and in a language which, though clear, is not afraid of occasional archaism, Cameron's poetry has a lineage which may be traced via Graves back to the Elizabethans. There is a fondness for clear argument and counter-argument in the poems, and as a corollary, rhetorical questions and syllogistic constructions abound. Cameron's major thematic concerns have been admirably summarised by James Reeves thus: 'The sensual man at war with a Calvinistic upbringing; the ambitious man aware of the wickedness of ambition; self-waste, self-love, self-hate; the difficulty of upholding a decent morality against one's own, one's friends' failings'.[26] As the description implies, Cameron's poetry is largely self-involved, and particularly concerned with metaphysical guilt, moral paradox, the nature of good and evil. His conversion to Roman Catholicism some two years before he died cannot be a surprise to those acquainted with his poetry. Although this self-involvement rarely confronts political issues directly, this does not mean that it is wholly private, or wholly 'apolitical'. One of Cameron's finest poems, 'Summer's slave', demonstrates how the appropriate development of metaphor may transform private origins into public utterance:

What have you now to answer, summer's slave,
To autumn's cold call of emancipation,
What, beside gooseflesh? Indeed, summer's slave
Can never be the citizen of winter.
It would be wiser, then, to keep your livery.
Follow your master in his sulky exile
Off to some feudal, decorative coast;
An easy life, obtaining sustenance
From gossip and report of winter's doings,
Knowing the body politic of winter
Is well established without help from you.[27]

Doubtless Reeves would perceive here that clash between Calvinism and sensuality which he speaks of when summarising Cameron's thematic interests. But the language in which the conflict is cast begs for an overtly political reading. When the poem is considered in terms of a conflict between the socially irresponsible, reactionary, sensualist and the progressive, nonconformist, socially minded ethos, we perceive that Cameron is a political quietist. The poem maintains a delicate balancing act poised between two paradoxes. One can either be a slave to pleasure with all that this implies of loss of community values, or one may join the 'body politic of winter', with its less than attractive connotations of cold self-abnegation. Neither option is very attractive.

Many of Cameron's poems are poised in the same manner. In 'Public house confidence', for instance, Cameron adopts a knowing persona who exploits class differences to his own advantage. By appearing in 'designing rooms and laboratory' dressed in overalls the persona fools both 'workmen' and the 'in-between and smart commission men'. The former thinks the persona is from 'the other end', and the latter that he 'has some pull with the boss':

So, playing off the spanner against the pen,
I never let the rumour get across
Of how I am no use at all to either,
And draw the pay of both for doing neither.[28]

The poem portrays the cynical individualist who sees the absurdity of class distinctions, but has no hope in political solutions, and merely uses his ingenuity for personal gain. And, although Cameron distances himself from his utterance through the adoption of a persona, there is nothing in the poem to indicate that he does not share an equally resigned attitude.

This kind of acceptance of how things are is often evident in Cameron's work. Implicit throughout his writing career (even before his conversion) is a quasi-religious belief in the inevitable co-existence of good and evil within the world which no political change could alter. This conservatism is also evident in his style. There is no question that in terms of craftsmanship his poems are more finished, more polished than some more prolific practitioners. Nevertheless, despite this 'passionate exactitude',[29] the reliance upon elegant language, and traditional forms, often leaves an air of complacency about his writing. It would, in my view, be more appropriate to speak of Cameron as a purveyor of 'neat sentiment', rather than Hugh MacDiarmid. And, as to being a 'pure poet', this is clearly not the case; Cameron's work is inevitably shot through with ideological implications, and in this case they are of a very conservative kind.

III

Spencer, Grigson and Cameron then, though they share a similar class and educational background to MacSpaunday, do not react as strongly against their inheritance; they share conservative positions, and their respective styles demonstrate this, with few traces of modernism being evident in their work.

Now we turn to Kathleen Raine and Kenneth Allott, both of whom attended Oxbridge, yet were not educated at public schools; their origins are somewhat less elevated than all the poets we have discussed so far. And, although the work of Raine and Allott is very dissimilar, they share distinctive attitudes to poetry and poetics, which differentiate them from other Oxbridge-educated poets. I do not think this is a coincidence. Coming from a less affluent background, divorced from the ruling class, makes them less prone to the social guilt which lies behind so much Audenesque writing. And unlike Spencer, Grigson and Cameron they cannot rest secure with their inherited values. There is struggle in the work of Raine and Allott for they too react against their background. But this does not lead towards any sentimental flirtation with the working class. Rather it inspires a wish to escape from humble origins into the 'aristocracy' of art. Their poetry and poetics are more extreme than that of the other poets we have looked at so far, as they explore the problems of self within a society which they regard as disintegrating to a point beyond rational hope.

Kathleen Raine attained her place at Girton College, Cambridge the hard way. Brought up in lower-middle-class, suburban Ilford, she attended state primary and elementary schools before winning a place at a secondary school. She describes her elementary school as a 'red-brick prison', but was happier with her 'excellent' secondary school.[30] Raine's access to Cambridge was made possible by a small college exhibition and a Major County Scholarship. None of this financial aid would have been forthcoming, however, without the help of Raine's father, who taught her the necessary Latin she needed to pass the Cambridge entrance exams.

Raine's father was a schoolteacher in the state system. His father, and his father's father, had been Durham coalminers. Unsurprisingly given such a background, Kathleen's father was a Methodist and a Socialist whose radical politics were an extension of his Christianity. He preached both creeds with 'a missionary zeal' to the inhabitants of Ilford, a place that his daughter came to hate as much as, if not more than, her father's politics. Raine's four volumes of autobiography bear consistent witness to her harsh, intense and lasting reaction to her class and familial background.

The seeds of this reaction were sown in a childhood that encapsulated two worlds, one rural and idyllic, the other suburban and, according to Raine, horrific. The rural interludes to London life came when the young Kathleen visited her mother's cousin who lived in a village called Bavington in Northumberland. Here Raine found a symbol of everything Ilford was not. Rural peace, beauty, and tranquility fostered in Raine a nostalgic feudalism which was pitted against the supposedly democratising impulses represented by the surburban lower-middle classes of Ilford. Ilford epitomised and epitomises for Raine both material and spiritual ugliness. Describing the transformation of rural Essex into suburban Ilford after the First World War, she speaks of the 'beautiful world' being usurped by 'the meaningless and vulgar'. The unfortunate surburbanites are described as 'nameless nomads' and 'timid swarms' who are 'too frightened to raise their voices' and 'doubted their right to exist'. This new way of life, she goes on, had 'neither the realism nor the poetry of the feudal world'.[31] Raine admits that she knew little of her fellow sufferers in 'Hades', but she clearly felt enough to denigrate, despise and condemn them. The literacy that she inherited from her father's profession, together with her rural experiences provided all the ammunition she needed. As she repeatedly insists in her autobiographies, her one thought was to 'escape'.[32] Unsurprisingly, this 'escape' did not lead her towards the working class. On the contrary she asserts that she 'didn't know' the working-class world,[33] and her only memory of her grandfather's and great-uncle's houses is 'the crude raw stench of the poverty'.[34] For Raine 'poverty', material deprivation, inequality all amount to 'ugliness'. Her route away from all this was via the 'beauty' of art and science.[35] Her entrance to Cambridge provided an opportunity to 'free' herself; it was an escape that has been rigorously cultivated ever since. She describes herself at Cambridge as a 'young barbarian of talent', and carefully places herself in terms of class:

There is a great difference between the situation of the poor students of my generation, who really were admitted – albeit to an extent more limited than we ourselves realised – into a higher social class, with a tradition and a culture different from, and superior to, our own, and the present situation of such students ... who, being now in the majority, create their own standards. In my student days we were the exceptions; and we were able to learn, to assimilate something from those – still in the majority – who inherited the old culture of England's educated classes ... in those days revolution was the last thing we wished for.[36]

But this transition into a 'higher' cultural and social position was not quite as smooth as this passage implies. Elsewhere Raine notes that most of the undergraduates were members of the upper and upper-middle classes who were 'merely continuing to live within a world which was already theirs'.[37] These young women from Cheltenham and St Leonards Ladies' Colleges were 'beautiful and well-groomed' moving with 'ease and assurance' through the world. Raine admired them from afar, but they knew as she knew that there was little resemblance betweeen them.[38]

Nevertheless, Cambridge remained for Raine an entrée into a tradition and a culture which she presumed to 'belong' to a higher social class than that of her origin. It enabled her to escape the 'underworld' of Ilford and to set her sights upon the 'aristocracy' of art. Raine's life in the 1930s continued this pattern of struggle against her inherited background. She had two serious relationships with Cambridge contemporaries, which by her own admission were part of her escape from Ilford, enabling her to live in Cambridge and London for much of the decade and to remain in touch with literary intellectuals.

Raine's autobiography demonstrates that she sees her life and work not only in terms of Christianity, but also as a defence of a minority 'culture' against the majority whom she is pleased to designate 'barbarians'. This extreme and uncompromising elitism is only implicit in Raine's poetry of the 1930s, which expresses a Christian mystical tradition in opposition to her father's more pragmatic Methodism, and a political disengagement contrary to her father's active Socialism. She reacted against what she perceived as the material and spiritual ugliness of her background into a disembodied a-social world of 'beauty' and the 'spirit'. Raine writes: '... the desire to escape from one's class, manner, speech, habits, ignorance and idiom, place and time, drives us out of the human world into the tolerant company of plants and stone and water'.[39]

Accordingly her poems are dominated by images either taken from nature or of an abstract metaphysical kind, and her vision of the 'poet' is religious rather than social. 'Invocation' is a poem which demonstrates this, and also shows Raine's willingness to express feelings directly without irony. Here she deals with poetic inspiration. The 'Poem' is invoked as a spirit that 'hovers' in the 'upper air', and which the poet is desperate to incarnate in words. Raine's muse is a 'God'. And so great is her desire for Him to visit, that she is apparently willing to undergo all kinds of unlikely, not to say unwholesome, tortures, 'if only the lips will speak':

Let my body sweat
let snakes torment my breast
my eyes be blind, ears deaf, hands distraught
mouth parched, uterus cut out,
belly slashed, back lashed
tongue slivered into thongs of leather
rain stones inserted in my breasts,
head severed ...[40]

Thankfully this is Raine writing at her worst. But in its Expressionist extravagance the poem plangently illustrates how Raine differs from other poets we have looked at, and shows the extremity of her commitment to the Romantic notion that extreme suffering is necessary to the creation of art.

Many of Raine's poems of the 1930s aim for a more glacial utterance than we have seen in 'Invocation'. The mellifluous use of elemental imagery evident in the latter poem, is tempered elsewhere by metaphysical argument. 'This planetary blood' provides a good example and is concerned with the idea of religious suffering:

This planetary blood
streams crucifixion
in the space of bounded life's
attraction and repulsion

widening on the rude
improvisation that the senses build
staking extremities
to mark the victories ...[41]

Raine finds 'victories' in 'extremities'. All of the other poets we have
considered have been anxious to avoid extremity. In Raine's case, she
attributes the 'true victories' (and thus the extremities) to Christ. Their
fulfilment lies beyond our world, but by emulating Christ's suffering
we may work towards crucifixion and victory. Raine attempts to
circumvent the political implications of her victorious extremes by
concentrating upon her Romantic Christian vision. But it is clear that
the implications of Raine's Christianity tend to be right-wing.

Other of Raine's early poems, 'Nature's no syllogism', 'Nature
unseen', 'Every morning I wake', as well as 'This planetary blood', are
concerned with the relationship of the sensual world to a higher
transcendental reality. The poet urges the argument, akin to Christian
Neo-Platonism, that the senses merely 'improvise'; the 'truth' lies
above and beyond material reality.

But this is not to say that Raine was absolutely unaffected by the
political troubles of the 1930s. Although she accurately describes the
kind of poetry that Auden and Spender wrote as 'alien' to her,[42] she
did on occasion attempt to grapple with public events in her work. But
when she does so it is implicitly to deny the efficacy of political
struggle in contrast to the validity of the individual's spiritual battle.
'Fata Morgana' is a long three-part poem which takes the Spanish Civil
War as an implicit point of reference. The title of the poem is
interesting as it casts the poet in the Arthurian role of the enchantress
Morgana le Fay, who is seen in various versions of the legend as both
a healer and a hostile figure. Here, though the relationship of title to
poem is never entirely transparent, we are pointed towards the poet's
ambitious view of herself and her art; towards her desire to be
spiritually healed and a healer through the magical intercession of
poetic utterance.

None of the three parts of this poem are entirely achieved. All the
sections are autobiographical, and register the poet's sense of
separation from the Civil War in Spain:

But I who have no words, nor heart, nor name
Can still suppose how it would feel to march
Guided by stars along the roads of Spain
Because of what I learn but cannot teach.

Can words invent gorillas, sweats and murders?
Can breath of breezes set us free?
Or the great tempest of invading soldiers
Redeem us from our own captivity?[43]

The irresolution in these closing stanzas of part one is maintained throughout the poem; so too is the oscillation between the writer's individual struggle to become a poet and her imaginative involvement with Spain. The second part of the poem deals with the former aspect. Raine wishes to exorcise her past which, she says, has been 'wasted in pursuit of ends' that were 'not her own'. She wishes to reach the 'holy wells' where she will gain 'force to move'; presumably the power to move people through poetry. In the first seven stanzas of the third and final section of the poem, Raine reverts to her dream of marching through Spain. It is neither made explicit that she is speaking of the Civil War, nor, as a corollary, which side she is on in that conflict. What is plain is that the poet feels that warfare is the harbinger of little but despair. The only lame hope articulated is that the 'face of things might change'. The last stanza of the poem takes us out of Raine's dream world, and back into her present. 'It is remarkable', the poet concludes,

to wake and spend another day
With all the people we can only touch
With tales of long ago and far away.

These lines refer us back to the title of the poem. One can only reach people, Raine suggests, with 'old tales' rather than contemporary issues. The effect of this is to relegate the Spanish Civil War to another old story. It is implied that war is a constant throughout history, and that writings about war are part of a social reality divorced from that 'higher' reality to which Raine aspires; she is more interested in what she takes to be the 'holy wells', the imaginative truths of poetry.

Despite the Romanticism of Raine's work, and that her Tory ideology is more impassioned and thoroughgoing than Grigson's, it is not difficult to see how she found in him a congenial editor for her work. She aspired to, and joined, the 'Oxford clique'. The case of Kenneth Allott is more complex, and it must be conceded immediately that his work is difficult to characterise. Some aspects of his poetry

correspond with the Audenesque, whilst other traits prefigure elements shared by other poets to be dealt with in subsequent chapters.
But this in itself is of interest not least because, like his work, his
background and education are not easy to categorise.

Allott was born in Glamorgan in 1912. His father was a doctor who
served with the RAMC in the First World War, and who was the son
of a Church of England clergyman.[44] This upper-middle-class and
establishment background is typical of most of the poets we have
looked at so far. But shortly after the war, Allott's father left home,
leaving his sons in the care of their mother. Allott was initially sent to
state elementary and grammar schools. But this was not the end of his
educational peregrinations. His mother was a Roman Catholic, and in
1924 his father agreed to send his sons to a Jesuit preparatory school,
St Johns, from which Allott progressed in 1925 to Beaumont College,
a Catholic public school. Allott was only there for a year before his
mother died, and he was given over to the care of his aunts who sent
him to St Cuthberts Catholic Grammar School in Newcastle-upon-
Tyne. Although at this stage Catholic grammar schools were not state
funded, as the poet's brother D.N.G. Allott attests, St Cuthberts 'was
in fact poorer in resources, staff, and buildings than the local state
schools at that time'. Kenneth Allott continued to live with his aunts
and attend St Cuthberts until he won a scholarship to Durham
University where he gained a First Class degree and Teaching
Certificate, before going to Oxford in 1935 to take his B.Litt. Between
1937 and 1939, whilst earning his keep in a variety of journalistic
pursuits, he helped Grigson to edit *New verse*. He published his first
volume of poems in 1938.[45]

These biographical details show that although Allott shared something
of the upper-middle-class, public-school and Oxbridge tradition, he
also shares in experiences with middle-middle and lower-middle-class
poets whom we will be discussing later on. Hitherto, because of the
Auden mythology, on the few occasions when Allott's poetry has been
discussed, it has been in terms of the Audenesque. And it is true that
his manifest concern with social and political issues, and his use of
some stylistic traits to be found in Auden's work (particularly the use
of the definite article and odd adjectives) to some extent justifies this.
But crucial to my argument are the differences in style and attitude to
be found in Allott's work. Early in the decade, for instance, Allott
experiments with a style which has affiliations with Surrealism, and
owes very little to Auden. Syntax, metre, and the spatial disposition of

words on the page, are all unconventional, and work to produce an effect of controlled irrationality:

journeyman to axis
reader of papyri
voice in the lift shaft
wine meniscus
thinlegged child
lover of cambric
loser of sixpence
expecting the second feature
expecting the second coming
expecting the last post
expecting to be late
with a smile
       showing incipient caries
with a word
       in the Oxford English Dictionary
with a tear
       probably glycerine
for the dead travel fast.[46]

This differs from much Surrealist poetry in so far as it does not exploit bizarre juxtapositions of sexual, excremental, and alimentary imagery. Each image and phrase (apart from the last one) has a correlative not in the depths of the subconscious but in the outside world. What the poem does share with Surrealism, however, is that there is no logical connection between the images. The poem works by provoking associations which plunge us into a nightmare world where the conventionally significant and insignificant are juxtaposed in an extravagantly random fashion, implicitly communicating the poet's sense of absurdity. The poem resists belief systems, destabilises our sense of order and time, and denies the possibility of emotional sincerity. It is a poem which expresses a far more radical sense of disintegration than anything we have encountered so far.

Other early poems like 'Signs' and 'Valediction' are similarly experimental, but Allott soon modified his style imposing a more conventional syntax and metre upon his work. Nevertheless many poems retain an atmosphere of nightmare and dislocation, where incantatory lists of sometimes disparate images retain a Surrealist flavour. The following lines from 'Azrael' provide a good example. Here Allott is describing aspects of the Angel of Death:

The sheen of treacherous sand, the salmon lights
The moth in the silk of conscience, the savage future
The judge's smile, the knuckle of rock in the straits
The monsters moving round the silent crater
Their hearts against their ribs, shadows on stilts
Fire-damp and fever, these are his signature.[47]

There is a grim intensity in the way Allott juxtaposes rational and irrational 'signatures' of death. Death attacks from within (the 'moth in the silk of conscience') and from without (the 'judge's smile'). Society, and the individual's psyche, are seen to partake of a general doom.

Allott distinguishes himself from the Audenesque because he can find no positive principle to cling to. He is clearly in radical opposition to society, but can find no hope in either past or future. His only marginal affirmation is that of the fragile, anarchic individualist. Yet he does not express his vision uniformly through the studied irrationality of Surrealist techniques. In 'Aunt Sally speaks' which was written in the latter half of the decade, he asks the rhetorical question, 'How shall we live', where 'we' are, 'Neither the whimsical mob', nor those whose 'better times / Are only a Pierrot's disguise'. He goes on to identify himself and his audience as those who can neither believe in the future, nor accept the 'habit' of tradition, who find the 'preacher's word' inadequate, and refuse the temptation of narcotics or neurosis. He concludes:

What shall we do with our hardened arteries
Under the zeppelin shade of catastrophe,
But emulate the gloss and selfishness of china
    Till the clocks fly away?[48]

Allott gives plain utterance to his dilemma here. He has no political idealism; he uses a characteristically bourgeois locution to dismiss the working class as the 'whimsical mob', and is too sceptical to believe in conservatism. He cannot identify with any class successfully, and he has no faith in past, present or future, so his only recourse is to take up a position of right-wing anarchism which is oppositional to society, but affirmative only of self. And, as the title of the poem and its final image make clear, Allott does not adopt this position in a spirit of hope. For clearly the threat of war is seen as potentially destructive of the frail 'china' individualist.

This lack of hope, and sense of impotency in the face of society's dilemmas, is not only attested to by Allott's poetry. In his contribution to the 'Commitments' number of New verse, Allott seeks to articulate the limitations of his role as a poet. He says that he dislikes contemporary English society, but goes on to disavow 'second, or third or fourth hand' experience: 'It is hysterical to pretend to have the same feelings about social evils, slums, malnutrition, bad working conditions, as one has about the immediate disagreeable experiences which happen every day'.[49] One admires the honesty of this, but it is difficult not to deplore the implicit complacency. Allott's distance from the problems he recognises is made painfully clear. Allott's view of the poet, and the poet's role is, however, in consonance with this sense of separation:

... a poet is a human being with five senses and two legs, a little morals and a number of prejudices, and his poems – however fixed by imagery, allusion, and rhythm in his own times – can and should be concerned over and above contemporary events and forms of society (or better through them) with the permanent instincts and the remarkably stable wishes and needs of human beings which are the expression of instincts ... I do not know much about society because I cannot do much to make or mar any society. I know a little more about poetry because sometimes I write it.[50]

In his prose no less than poetry Allott is anxious to turn away from abstract conceptions to images which embody feelings. Elegy and lamentation are, in Allott's view, the business of the poet. He can find no place for joy or celebration. The poet, 'he suspects', can say 'very little', but value is located in the 'force, feeling and penetration', with which the poet expresses the eternal sadnesses that exist whatever the condition of society.

Despite the sense of powerlessness which Allott articulates, and despite the emphasis upon feelings that 'transcend' social immediacy, Allott never retreats as far from social and political issues as does Raine. 'Men walk upright' is one of his finest poems of the 1930s, for here he ranges over the whole of society, expressing bluntly his feelings of anger and frustration, in the face of public pressures. The poem is important too, for it expresses an anti-Romantic tendency, which we will have cause to discuss further in the next chapter. 'Men walk upright' begins with a note of determined scepticism announcing 'The end of expectancy', the end of romantic legend and of hope. The rest of the poem elaborates upon this by articulating a contrast between the life of the different classes in England. Allott notes that his 'freedom' (and that of his audience) is predicated upon the lives of the poor, but can see no solution to this situation. There is something of an

Audenesque sense of guilt in this, but Allott distinguishes himself by being able to describe the lives of poor people without descending to sentimentality, and without surrendering the honesty of his individualism. There is no pretence that he is going to do anything about the social conditions he describes, or that he has any answers to them. He writes of the 'haggling to save a halfpenny', the 'fecund red-elbowed women', and their 'humourless menfolk', before continuing like this:

These will never hold aces or travel farther
Than a tram will take them. And their summum bonum,
The threepenny double which comes up by a head,
   Unlimited bitter.

It is the freedom of light, the right to go walking
Well fed in drawing-rooms and gardens which has refined
Us if only to an impotence of anger. Think.
   You too are an animal.

Although we might detect some condescension in the first stanza quoted, we also find here Allott writing at his best. For the juxtaposition of 'head' with 'unlimited bitter' neatly encapsulates the irony of 'summum bonum'. The implication is that the only chance for the working class to indulge in a few beers is to win on the races; the head of the horse leads by association to the head on the beer. But this progression, Allott suggests, leads only to bitterness. He goes on to acknowledge and arraign the upper-middle-class anger of the drawing room, but this does not lead to hope, rather to hoplessness, 'The end of romantic expectancy'. The poem concludes with Allott identifying with those whom he is addressing:

… I am like you.
The blackbirds sing and I see no end of agony,
   The pink and the white blossom

Spangles the chestnuts, the theatres pour into the streets
The unimaginative. And the earth renews
In Europe its solar gaiety, and the earth moves on
   To no destination.[51]

This is very unlike Bernard Spencer's vision of spring in 'Allotments April'. The 'Oxford clique' shared conservative positions, but it may be clearly perceived that Raine and Allott are more uncomfortable conservatives than Spencer, Grigson or Cameron, and their discomfort, I submit, is at least in part due to their different class and educational background. Raine escapes her inherited background by seeking solace in Christian mysticism and aestheticism. Allott, having renounced his inherited Catholicism at the age of fifteen, expresses a tougher vision in which a pervading sense of nightmare, disintegration, and hoplessness is given impassioned expression. Spencer could fall back upon his inheritance to find positive values. Allott, as the lines above clearly indicate finds no solace at all. The round of the seasons is seen as an image of futility.

Notes

1 A. Sullivan, 'New verse', British literary magazines, vol. IV, The modern age, New York, p. 295.
2 S. Hynes, The Auden generation: literature and politics in the 1930s, London, 1976.
3. For biographical details here and elsewhere, I am indebted to R. Bowen, ed. 'Introduction', Bernard Spencer: collected poems, Oxford, 1981, pp. xiii-xxxi.
4 B. Spencer,'Notes' for a public lecture delivered at the University of Madrid in 1962. Typescript MS, Modern Literature Archive, The University of Reading Library.
5 Ibid.
6 P. Orr, ed., 'Bernard Spencer', The poet speaks, London, 1966, p. 234.
7 A. Alvarez, 'Autumn collections', Observer weekend review, 26 Sept. 1965, p. 25.
8 R. Bowen, 'Native and exile: the poetry of Bernard Spencer', Malahat review, Jan. 1979, pp. 5-27.
9 B. Spencer, Aegean islands and other poems, London, 1946.
10 B. Spencer, Collected poems, ed. R. Bowen, Oxford, 1981, pp.1-2.
11 Ibid., p. 14.
12 Ibid., p. 10.
13 Ibid., p. 12.
14 G. Grigson, Several observations, London, 1939.
15 G. Grigson, Preface to Collected poems, 1924-1962, London, 1963, p. 7.
16 Grigson, Collected poems, 1924-1962, p. 24.
17 Ibid., p. 26.
18 Ibid., p. 29. (See also G. Grigson, The crest on the silver, London, 1950, p. 170.)
19 G. Grigson, 'Elements of verse', New verse, No. 19, Feb.-March, 1936, p. 17.
20 R. Graves, Introduction to The collected poems of Norman Cameron, 1905-1953 (1957), London, 1967, p. 10.
21 Letter of Norman Cameron to Robert Graves quoted in The collected poems, p. 11.
22 R. Graves, Introduction to The collected poems, pp. 20-1.
23. Ibid., p. 21.
24 J. Reeves, Commitment to poetry, London, 1969, p. 281.
25. R.Graves, Introduction to The collected poems, pp. 9-24.
26 Reeves, Commitment to poetry, p. 282.
27 Cameron, The collected poems, p. 41.
28 Ibid., p. 35.
29 R. Graves, Introduction to The collected poems, p. 21.
30 K. Raine, Farewell happy fields, London, 1973, pp. 87-8, 162.
31 Ibid., pp. 98-103.
32 Ibid., p. 109.
33 Ibid., p. 157.

34 Ibid., pp. 62-3.
35 Ibid., pp.116-17.
36 K. Raine, *The land unknown*, London, 1975, pp. 13-14.
37 Ibid., p. 25.
38 Ibid.
39 K. Raine, *Faces of day and night*, London, 1972, p. 50. It is important to note that this fragment of autobiography was written in the early 1940s. The attitudes, and some of the incidents recalled in the later autobiographies, are present in this volume, which suggests that Raine's perception of her class background and reaction to it, has changed little over time.
40 K. Raine, *Collected poems*, London, 1954, p. 4.
41 Ibid., p. 3.
42 Raine, *The land unknown*, pp. 109-10.
43 *New verse*, No. 25, May 1937, pp. 7-9.
44 For information regarding Allott's upbringing and education I am indebted to a letter from D.N.G. Allott of 9 April, 1986.
45 K. Allott, *Poems*, London, 1938.
46 *New verse*, No. 19, Feb.-March 1936, p. 4.
47 K. Allott, *Collected poems*, London, 1975, p. 37.
48 Ibid., p. 50.
49 K. Allott, 'Several things', *New verse*, Nos. 31-2, autumn 1938, pp. 4-7.
50 Ibid.
51 Allott, *Collected poems*, pp. 15-19.

7

Twentieth century verse and the poetry of Julian Symons, Derek Savage and Ruthven Todd

I

Kenneth Allott's poetry involves a complex stylistic variety, in which we are able to discern elements of the Audenesque, of Surrealism and of impassioned plain speaking. It is not surprising then to find that his poetry appears regularly in more than one of the little magazines of the 1930s. Of the Oxbridge writers dealt with in preceding chapters, who contributed so much to New verse, Allott is the only one who appeared in Twentieth century verse. This was no coincidence. In the following discussion of Twentieth century verse, and three of its major contributors, Julian Symons, D.S. Savage and Ruthven Todd, we will be able to see how Allott's work bridges the divide between the public-school, Oxbridge-educated poets, and those who do not fully share in this upper-middle-class inheritance.

Twentieth century verse was founded by Julian Symons in 1937. The magazine ran for eighteen numbers, published twice quarterly until July 1939. Unlike New verse it has found no secure place in the literary historical myth of the decade. The poets Symons published have either been consigned to oblivion or are associated with other more illustrious movements and magazines. Symons himself, assessing his own achievements in various memoirs of the 1930s, has trodden a thin line between self-deprecation and self-applause. On the one hand he remarks that 'Twentieth Century Verse never did more than palely reflect New Verse's virtues', and that both magazines were based in 'the world of rational intelligence and close observation'.[1] But on the other hand he congratulates himself, quite rightly in my view, for making a contribution to the decade by encouraging such poets as George Woodcock, Ruthven Todd and Kenneth Allott who, he says, 'owed the smallest possible debt to Auden or Thomas'. In such self-judgements it is possible to see why the magazine has been largely ignored by literary historians; it is either regarded as merely supplementary to Grigson's so-called 'objectivist' achievements in *New verse* or deemed irrelevant because the poets who most frequently appeared there do not fit comfortably into the notions of homogeneity governing the myth of the 'Auden generation'.

Symons has been a consistent admirer of Grigson and *New verse*. 'No other editor of the 'thirties', Symons asserts, 'was so sharply intelligent as Grigson.'[2] Such praise is not difficult to understand given that the editors shared much in common during the 1930s. Both insisted upon the importance of individuality to poetry, both were friends and admirers of Wyndham Lewis, both had aspirations towards the avoidance of any political commitment. But there are also important differences between the two editors which are, in the broadest sense of the word, political.

Symons came from a less elevated class-background than Grigson. He was born in 1912. His father was a 'Polish or Russian Jew' who changed his name for unknown reasons and married an English woman who had some French and Spanish ancestry.[3] Before Julian's birth, this colourful pair had run various second-hand clothing stores that had failed, and by the time of his early childhood they had embarked upon another similar business venture with the crucial difference that this time they were successful. The 1914-18 War apparently was influential in turning the business tide for the Symons family, so that in 1918 they were able to move from Battersea into a larger house in Clapham. The poet's father prospered briefly, expanding his activities to second-hand general dealing, and eventually purchasing an auction room. At one stage the family had a motor-car with a chauffeur and owned four racehorses! But as Symons ruefully recalls in his autobiography, this prosperity did not last, and within a couple of years racehorses, cars and auction rooms disappeared. His father then tried his hand as an hotel-manager in Brighton and as a bookmaker before unsuccessfully trying to run another auction-room in Soho.

Amidst this mixed entrepreneurial activity, Symons underwent a similarly mixed education. In Brighton he attended a school for 'backward' children because he had a speech defect. On returning to London he went to an elementary school until he was fourteen. When he left he attended a commercial college where he learnt the shorthand and typing which subsequently enabled him to secure a job as a secretary with the Victoria Lighting and Dynamo Company at 27s 6d a week. It was in the succeeding few years, with his formal education over, that Symons undertook his own literary self-education. In the early 1930s he was reading Joyce, Pound and Wyndham Lewis, and came to feel in doing so that his poor education was not necessarily disadvantageous: 'To be as little educated as I was, to have left school at fourteen, may have compensations. It gave me a desperate desire to learn quickly what literature was about. Ignorance meant that I encountered great novels and poems with a shock of surprise ... everything I was able to appreciate came upon me with the force of a revelation.'[4]

This reading, however, was proceeding against a less than scholarly background. After work at the Lighting Company Symons would play table-tennis or billiards at the local Temperance Hall before eating a pie and beans supper at a café. There were also regular poker nights. His friends at this time included a lorry-driver, a milkman and a bookmaker's clerk, a point that Symons is anxious to make;[5] his lived experience was entirely different from that of the upper-middle-class poets: 'I have always felt at ease with unintellectual working-class people, always been uneasy in the presence of typical Eton and Winchester, Oxford and Cambridge, products. A deplorably slapdash generalisation I know, yet one conveying an essential truth about my lifelong desire ... not to be bound by an accent, a style, a code of manners, a way of eating food or wearing clothes.'[6] On the one hand he wishes not to be bound by class, but on the other his reaction to Oxbridge 'products' is surely predicated upon the insecurities of his class position.

The anarchic individualistic implications of not being bound by particular rules and conventions had its corollary in Symons's literary activities. He 'vaguely aspired' to 'bohemianism' in contrast to Geoffrey Grigson whom Symons describes as 'bourgeois and respectable'. Grigson is said to dress in 'clothes sedately smart' and to have 'no taste for literary bohemianism'.[7] The implicit equation made here between class difference and differences in literary attitudes also informs Symons's approach to the inception of his magazine, Twentieth century verse. In recalling his motivations for this venture, Symons admits that he and his friends were motivated by the desire to see their work in print, and that of poets from a similar background: '... there was a real difference of attitude then between poets who had been to a university, like Auden, Spender, MacNeice, Day Lewis, Empson, Lehmann, and those who hadn't like Thomas, Barker, Ruthven, Roy Fuller and the three of us. There was a whole range of subjects from which we were cut off and about which most of them wrote, but also they seemed to have a common tone as of friends talking to each other in a way that excluded strangers.[8]

To understand the differences of attitude between various poets which Symons mentions here, is crucial to a proper understanding of the literary history of the decade. And it is precisely such differences which previous accounts have expunged. Symons and his friends were not interested in schoolboy revolution or in any complacent conservatism. But this does not mean that Symons was further to the left than Grigson. On the contrary, in his opening editorial, it could be argued that Symon's position leans more adamantly and anarchistically to the right than Grigson does in New verse. The principles Symons outlines are unreluctantly attached to the tradition of art for art's sake. It is, he says, inevitable that 'a new magazine of verse should be published for a civilised minority'. He goes on to further define his position saying that he is not interested in making money, and that he does not believe poetry is a 'tributary' of 'politics, or music, or machinery'. The chief aim of the paper is 'to print the work of young poets who for one reason or another the cut of their jacket, or the colour of their tie, do not get much of a hearing elsewhere'.[9] It is important to notice that Symons uses metonyms for class (the 'cut of their jacket') and politics (the 'colour of their tie') to describe his contributors. That he does so after denying any connection between poetry and politics constitutes not only an irony but also a disabling weakness in his argument.

This opening editorial must have drawn some adverse comment, for Symons felt obliged to defend his position in the second issue of his magazine. Here he denied that he wished 'to cultivate poetry in an atmosphere as rarefied as possible', reiterated that his magazine was not being run as 'an advertising campaign for any literary clique or party', and asserted that poetry 'need not be concerned with politics... to discuss in detail poetry and politics is to tread worn and we believe barren ground'. He also conceded that the 'criterion of a good poem' was the 'editor's personal and humanly fallible taste'.[10]

Like Grigson, but in a slightly more exaggerated way, Symons maintains the stance of the individualist aesthete. His taste, however, was not entirely unaffected by both politics and literary politics. Symons was intent upon steering a delicate course which would distinguish his endeavours, and those of his friends, from the contributors to *New verse*, *Left review*, and the supposedly Surrealist *Contemporary poetry and prose*. Interestingly, the third issue of *Twentieth century verse* was initially advertised as a special Surrealist number, but the editor changed his mind and his tactics. Instead of the promised Surrealist number, Symons printed an editorial entitled 'Against Surrealism', which constituted a comprehensive attack upon the aesthetic of that movement. The Surrealists, Symons argued, in placing a high valuation upon automatic writing eschewed all standards of craftmanship and form. Thus it was, he bluntly concluded, that 'every crackpot' could 'write a poem that may be called Surrealist'.[11] Symons also objected to the supposed affiliation of the Surrealists with the left, and furthermore he suspected them because they could be seen as a 'movement'. He clung tenaciously to the belief that 'art finally is made by individuals and not by groups'.[12]

It is through the problematic and finally frail argument that 'form' somehow precedes 'content' that Symons has subsequently sought to define his attitude to poetry in the 1930s. Writing retrospectively of his magazine, he says that as he saw it in the 1930s, there was too much attention paid to content, too little to form. It was necessary, he argues, to stress that 'poems are made with words not primarily out of *feelings* about Spain or Munich'.[13] Symons goes on to talk about what kind of words he preferred: 'Georgian language, world/furled/hurled poems' were totally unacceptable. In practice, however, Symons's editorial decisions did not fully match his ideals. As he retrospectively admits, 'shape, intelligence and coherence' were rare attributes, and in practice he published verse that had 'little more to recommend it than a stimulating flash of imagery, a touch of wit, a reasonably fresh use of language'.[14]

Symons's poetics then had little originality. Personal taste, individualism, 'shape', and a dislike of Georgian language formed his conservative orientation. But as the 1930s progressed towards the Munich crisis, Symons became increasingly radical in his right-wing views. This was signalled by his devoting a double number of *Twentieth century verse* solely to that self-styled 'great professional outcast of the pen', Wyndham Lewis. Symons contributed a challenging editorial in which large claims were made for Lewis in a language which curiously makes 'the enemy' sound like a latter-day Matthew Arnold. Symons speaks of the desirability of looking at the 'contemporary scene with an alert scepticism', and 'testing with some concrete touchstones the miscellaneous wares offered by poets as much as Prime Ministers'.[15]

In Symon's opinion 'No man alive' knows 'better than Lewis the necessity of these touchstones', and furthermore no other figure in the literary world had 'anything like his breadth of vision'. Symons concluded that Lewis was 'the most valuable and interesting writer of our time'.

But to speak of touchstones is one thing; to articulate what these might be is quite another. And it is equally pertinent to ask just how 'concrete' the touchstones were that allowed Lewis to publish his guarded approval of Nazism in *Hitler* (1931), and then to write a recantation in *The Hitler cult* (1937). In his own typically combative contribution to the number of *Twentieth century verse* dedicated to his work, Lewis provided few clues in answer to this puzzle. Anticipating his critics, he denied that he was a counter-revolutionary, asserted that he was the type of the 'pure revolutionary', and went on to say that art 'was of no use to politics' since it 'functioned in the abstract' and 'spoke only with God'.[16] This combination of a vague religious aestheticism with an equally vague idea of being a 'pure revolutionary' is a somewhat secularised version of Raine's Romantic religiosity. Lewis sees himself in political opposition to the establishment, but has no positive principles to assert other than the importance of individuality as it is manifested in art. Symons, it seems, was entirely sympathetic to this point of view.

Symons's public devotions to Lewis were an act of some courage in a decade in which 'the enemy' had largely been ignored. Predictably, there were some subscribers for whom Symons had gone too far, and who felt that the magazine had become ideologically suspect. Symons was unrepentant, and in subsequent issues defended his championship of Lewis in the most vociferous manner. And, as the international political situation worsened, there was on Symons's part an increasing tendency to ape Lewis's rhetorical bluster. In a review published early in 1939, Symons wrote: '… the detached viewpoint today is too near the mud-brained Liberal–Labour viewpoint in poetry as well as politics. Better the B.U. *Quarterly* than the *New Statesman*; no readers at all than plain readers'.[17] Symons here seems to have forgotten that throughout his magazine's life he had advocated precisely the viewpoint which detached art from politics. And, whilst one would hesitate to suggest that Symons genuinely preferred the Quarterly published by the British Union of Fascists to the *New statesman*, there is no question that remarks as extreme as this place him further to the right than Grigson.

But political events were fast overtaking Symons and *Twentieth century verse*, and clearly they were shaking the editor's beliefs. The last issue of the magazine, which appeared in July 1939, was ironically devoted to that 'well-trodden ground' that Symons had disdained to tread in the second issue: poetry and politics. Although the title of this symposium was 'The poet and the public', inevitably a high degree of political content was unavoidable. This was by no means homogeneous. Roy Fuller and Desmond Hawkins, in their respective essays,[18] maintained a liberal position by not relinquishing their interest in bourgeois art-forms, but asserting a democratic attitude towards an audience. George Barker, on the other hand, took the unequivocal view in his 'Note on narrative poetry', that 'Poetry is poison to the people',[19] and apparently saw no reason why it should be otherwise. One of the most interesting contributions came from the editor in a dialogue with H.B. Mallalieu who, if the war had not intervened, would have become an associate editor of the magazine in its next issue.

Here Mallalieu argues that Symons has laid undue emphasis on individuality and privacy; too many poems had been printed which were wilfully obscure, and placed unnecessary barriers between poet and audience. Although Symons defended himself with a reiteration of his familiar position, concentrating upon the importance of individuality and aesthetic standards, the conversation tacitly implies that Symons was prepared to countenance change by accepting Mallalieu as an associate editor. These changes were never put into practice, however, because the war broke out and the magazine folded. But the direction of Mallalieu's argument is significant because it opposes the myth that poetry of the late 1930s and 1940s is inward-looking, private, and a retreat into extremes of 'Neo-Romanticism'. Mallalieu was not alone in advocating a more public poetry; his thinking was shared by many poets of the 1940s.

Much, but not all, of the poetry that Symons published in *Twentieth century verse* attests to the accuracy of Mallalieu's criticism. The tone was set by Symons's own poetry, for, like Grigson, Symons chose to publish more work by himself than by anybody else in his magazine. In many of his poems Symons attempts to develop highly cerebral arguments to express a fundamentally private vision. The tone is serious without ever approaching the sublime, and ellipsis to the point of impenetrability is often a weakness. But in other poems, Symons strives for, and achieves, a more lucid expression; a style of relatively plain speaking shared by such of his friends as Ruthven Todd and D.S.

Savage, both of whom appeared regularly in the magazine.

Some other poets who frequently appeared in Twentieth century verse could also be found within the pages of New verse, again demonstrating that Symons and Grigson shared various tastes. Both editors printed much of Philip O'Connor's verse; an irony because O'Connor has subsequently admitted that his work was largely of that 'automatic' Surrealist kind which both Grigson and Symons said they despised.[20] The precise tones of Gavin Ewart could be heard in both magazines, together with the less well-known Geoffrey Taylor. And it should be noted that both George Barker and Dylan Thomas also appeared in Twentieth century verse. But despite these hints of catholicity no Audenesque poems or poets appeared; Symons published those poets whose cut of jacket and colour of tie most resembled his own.

That Twentieth century verse, like New verse, came to a close at the outbreak of the war has encouraged the notion that what was written in the 1930s was somehow radically different from, and incompatible with, the 1940s. Symons himself has encouraged this view by writing retrospectively that the literary magazines of the 1930s 'belonged peculiarly to their time, and came to an end with that time'.[21] He has also, as we noticed earlier, implied that his magazine existed in the shadow of New verse.[22] Both these remarks seem to me to be over-statements. Some of the poetry he published, not least that by himself, Savage, and Todd, prefigures much of the best work of the 1940s. And although Symons shared some of Grigson's tastes, his magazine gave a hearing to poets who did not share the public-school and Oxbridge ethos which could be found in much of what Grigson printed. Most importantly for my purposes, it provides further evidence against the myth that the decade's poetry was predominately left-wing and was pervaded by the Audenesque.

II

The poetry of Julian Symons, Derek Savage and Ruthven Todd has been ignored in the literary-historical myth of the 1930s. Although two of them, Symons and Todd, were born within the fourteen-year span by which Hynes delineates his 'Auden generation', neither poet is mentioned in his study. Derek Savage, in Hynes's view, belongs to a different 'generation', being born in 1917. But it is not primarily birth-dates which distinguish these poets from others writing in the decade, but differences of class and educational background which give rise to a different ideological orientation and style in their work. The most striking common denominator shared by Symons, Savage and Todd is that none of them attended those bastions of the establishment: the universities of Oxford and Cambridge. Indeed none of them went to a university at all. As we have already noted, Symons attended an elementary school which he left at the age of fourteen. Savage similarly attended an obscure school in Edmonton on the outskirts of London where, as he succinctly puts it, he 'learned nothing'.[23] Also like Symons, Savage left school at an early age and proceeded to a commercial college from which he graduated to become an office clerk. Todd's case is somewhat different as he had an undistinguished career for three years at a public school, Fettes College in Edinburgh.[24] I have not been able to ascertain to which schools Todd went before the age of fourteen when his time as a boarder at Fettes began. Since he was one of ten children it is not impossible that he too went to an elementary school. However this may be, it is clear that Todd came from the middle class and had a middle-class education, but nevertheless like Symons and Savage he stands outside the mainstream of the upper-middle-class educational progression from prep to major English public schools, and from there to Oxford or Cambridge.

Further biographical information about both Savage and Todd is sparse. Savage was born in Harlow, and although his parents came from the working class, his father 'became a small business man and prospered'. Savage speaks of his reaction to this semi-rural, lower-middle-class background thus: 'There was no love of art in our family. We children were brought up to "know the value of money" and to appreciate something called "security". My temperament is fundamentally rebellious and freedom loving, and as a consequence I have always lived in poverty, and have a certain contempt for security'.[25] Savage rejected the commercial and material values of his parents and worked his way towards a position of extreme poverty. Having been an office clerk for a time he then worked in a bottle factory, a copper refinery and a bookshop, before retiring in 1937 to a condemned cottage without sanitation or water supply where he lived on the dole for some time until eventually gaining work in a hospital.

Todd's father was an architect in Edinburgh, and it was thought that on leaving school Ruthven might follow in his father's footsteps. But after a brief period of employment in his father's office, the young man decided to go to art school instead. This also proved unsatisfactory to him, and so in the early 1930s he left the mainland of Scotland to work for a crofter on the island of Mull. After a time Todd returned to Scotland, and spent the second half of the decade between Edinburgh and London pursuing a variety of activities including a relatively impecunious career in literary journalism working for the *Scottish bookman*. Although Todd's background and career are slightly different from those of Symons and Savage, it is, I think, possible to assert that their occupations in the 1930s were not so solidly bourgeois as the upper-middle-class poets we have considered, and that all three saw themselves as standing socially and intellectually apart from their Oxbridge-educated contemporaries.The consequences of this are various and crucial.

It is my contention that the three poets to be dealt with here felt themselves to be dislocated from the ruling, preaching and teaching English upper-middle class. They do not seem to suffer the same sense of guilt which led Auden and friends to attempt answers to the political problems of their time. Symons, Savage and Todd do not seek palliatives either in an identification with a supposedly 'superior' élite or in a negative identification with the working class. Like Kenneth Allott they attempt to assert the importance of the individual. But just as such an assertion proved a struggle to Allott, so it does with Symons, Savage and Todd. There is a marked sense of powerlessness in their work; they register a consciousness of being manipulated by forces beyond their control. And, they reject any religious, political or Romantic metaphysics, which might provide solutions to their public and private dilemmas. The imagination, dreams, heroes and legends, are all treated with dismissive irony. There is no place for myth and religion; all that is tentatively affirmed is the individuality of the poet, the speaking 'I'.

It might be tempting, from what I have said so far, to assume that Symons, Savage and Todd recorded without equivocation the materialistic, sceptical, laissez-faire, conservative values that they inherited. But this is not the case. Just as other poets we have discussed express an ambivalent reaction to their inheritance, so too do these poets. The resulting ideology constitutes a variety of right-wing anarchism. The poets react against their own background, registering an immense dissatisfaction with society, and with their powerlessness within that society. Their assertion of the importance of the individual is an answer to, rather than an affirmation of, state capitalism. Theirs is a critique, however, which does not show any faith in the efficacy of right- or left-wing revolutionary action as a force for positive change. The individual, with his or her very limited sphere of influence, is to be valued amidst the disintegration and impending violence of European society.

And how is this ideology expressed? Interestingly, like Allott, both Symons and Todd in their earlier work write under the stylistic influence of modernism. Both take up Eliot's championing of the metaphysical poets, and write dour, costive, cerebral and often unintelligible poems. But this manner does not prevail, and they, together with Savage, develop a hybrid from their modernist and Georgian inheritance which is quite distinct from the Audenesque, and also distinct from the styles of other Oxbridge-educated poets. In the work of Symons, Savage and Todd we encounter modernist attitudes of relativism, disintegration, anti-Romanticism, but they are expressed in a far less aristocratic way than in the poetry of, say, Yeats or Eliot. The imagery and tone of the poems we are about to look at are more demotic, local and familiar than in any of the poetry we have considered so far. There is a willingness to write with more overt emotion in a lyrical line than one finds in the cooler tones of the more academic poets. The style of Symons, Savage and Todd is paradoxical, for they express anti-social attitudes of individualism, but in a style which, like that of the Georgians, offers itself to an audience more readily than the supposedly publicly-oriented poetry of say, Auden or Spender.

Having said this much, it is salutary to recall Symons's debate with H.B. Mallalieu in the closing number of *Twentieth century verse* wherein Mallalieu accused Symons of printing too much poetry which was deliberately obscure. For this charge can be readily brought against some of the poems in Symons's only volume of the 1930s, *Confusions about X* (1939). Upon scrutinising the lesser poems in this volume, the unkind might be disposed to remark upon the aptness of the title. At his worst, in poems like 'Stone and ghost', 'Ice-ambush', and 'The last question', Symons adopted a style in which outrageously oblique arguments are developed through abstract conceits. Symons is clearly and self-consciously in these poems espousing Eliot's notion that modern poetry had to be 'difficult' in order to deal with the complexities of modern society. In other poems, however, Symons eschews the creation of meretricious 'difficulty', and strives for a more compelling lucidity.

'Garden poem' lies at the heart of Symons's book, for it is the longest poem therein, and gives voice to his recurrent themes. The poem is personal without being resistantly private. It has an appropriately conversational tone as it is addressed to Symons's friends Herbert and Marjorie Mallalieu. Symons begins 'sitting in the garden' imagining himself to be 'a hero, a martyr or a sea-rover;' one of those, he says, 'who are not disposed of but dispose'. Yet the poet is aware that behind such 'heroic', autocratic figures as 'Napoleon, Roosevelt, Henry Ford', there lurks a less attractive reality; time is seen as a great leveller, treating all alike, and revealing the shabby, violent politics which such figures depend upon for their enhancement. Symons not only expresses his consciousness that political leaders have feet of clay, but also implicitly renders a critique of his own imaginative vision of himself in the role of 'hero'. This does not, however, threaten the poet's autobiographical speculations, but rather acts to endorse his questioning of other aspects of belief and imagination. The poet wonders, for instance, 'why or whether':

Love is not Beauty or Creation
But vacant as a railway station
Is existent only in the will of the lover.[26]

The bathetic metaphor is a trick learnt from Auden, but the statement that 'love' is vacant or merely a matter of 'will' goes further than Symons's mentor; Auden clung to various ideas of love as a positive personal and social force. But Symons can only express what he does not believe in. It is, he says, 'too late' for 'uncomplicated faith / The raised fist marching and the missionary death'. Neither the 'wonderful illusion' nor 'simple life' are possible anymore.

'Garden poem' ends with intimations of approaching war, in which Symons prefigures his wartime stance as a Conscientious Objector, before going on to offer his addressee certain gifts:

I can give you the heart's eagles and the singing bough,
The swan song of a dying world, its clatter and row.
What an eye can see and a brain record
And a hand put down in a halting word,
Sitting in the garden I can offer you now.

The overt Romanticism of 'heart's eagles' and the 'singing bough' are ironically deflated by the 'row' of a dying world. Bathos is compounded by the closing lines which make abundantly clear that Symons has little to 'give' or to celebrate other than himself in the present.

Two further poems in Symons's volume conclude with 'gifts' and these, together with 'Garden poem' make a telling comparison with MacNeice's 'Train to Dublin' in which the Irish poet fills four stanzas with exuberant and sensuous 'givings'. For Symons and his friends the later 1930s offered no such consolations. Even when recording the birth of a child, Symons's tone is sombre. In his 'Poem for a birthday', he gives to the child 'whatever may be good', and continues :

I wish you now, to go
Scatheless among all eyes,
Unpeopling desire,
And fishing by the weir
When papers announce war,
That looking at the sane
You finally resign,
While they are counting ten
Be stressed and single, one.[27]

The wished-for resignation here, constitutes a retreat both from the public world of action and event and from personal emotional entanglement. 'Desire' should be 'unpeopled'; a kind of existential aloneness is advocated. But there is little conviction in Symons's affirmation of individuality. 'Fishing by the weir' strikes one as an image of hopeless futility in the face of warfare, and that the alternative for the sane is counting to ten, underlines the powerlessness of the individual.

It is precisely this sense of ennervation, of nothing to celebrate and everything to mourn, which informs poem after poem in Symons's volume. In 'Country week-end' we meet 'defeated and disillusioned ghosts' who people a privileged bucolic world where 'Nothing will disturb', but 'everything', according to the poet, is 'pleasantly wrong'. In other poems we hear that 'love ... is still a sham'; we find that the contemplation of nature, the 'summer bird' and 'intricate leg' cannot 'stop our thirst / Or stay our hunger'. And in another poem, revolution constitutes no answer to the human predicament. In 'Colour absent' we are told that there is 'no chance of the wished-for ending'; human experience is a 'familiar pallor', and colour a 'false brightness'.

On the few occasions when Symons does express affirmations these are always tentative and eventually undermined by a sense of pleasure's triviality. In 'Poem about evening', for instance, evening represents to the poet a time to escape the exigencies of day, to indulge in reverie, and in the 'comradeship of pub and snooker table'. 'Evening', he asserts, is the friend of the personal, and yet the personal apparently amounts to very little:

Whatever I give you now as a parting wish,
Whether the cold futility of your separate island,
The engaging escape from the possible land of love,
Or the power to handle words like pigeons or merely
To swim the Channel and be able to run five miles,
I hope you will decorate evening with your smile.[28]

This is heavily anti-Romantic. There is no cleaving to the idea of willed isolation as a means to imaginative vision. On the contrary, individuality is described as a 'cold futility', and the handling of words, the creation of art, is reductively likened to handling racing pigeons. Individual achievements are merely decorative, and as transitory as the wished-for smile.

As one contemporary reviewer put it, Symons shows 'a thorough dissatisfaction with society'.[29] In this respect he may be likened to other of his more famous contemporaries like Auden or Dylan Thomas. But unlike them he cannot find hope or consolation. He resists any flight into Romantic metaphysics, and fails to locate value in liberal or Christian notions of love. All that is left is the expression of wry disillusionment:

Things are no longer mythical: I am undoubtedly
On the beach at Clacton, my incalculable feet
On a time's quicksand dizzying the air,
I am undoubtedly in my Croydon room, waiting for
The house to fall. I am steady though unstable:
And for the moment I am not able to be afraid.

And horror begins now, it is with horror I see
All your faces are like mine, you are
Puppets like me in the iron fist of money,
Taking the financier's heavy downward step ...[30]

This is a long way from the writings of MacSpaunday. The overt anti-Romanticism, the demotic locations, and the sense of individual powerlessness here are rendered without decoration. The anarchic individualist paradoxically reaches out to an audience with whom he can share no comforting intelligence.

Derek Savage's work, like that of Symons, is devoid of political idealism. In more lyrical and elegiac tones than Symons, Savage gives voice to his own dark vision of decay and disintegration. The epigraph to his book, *The autumn world*, which contains poems written between 1934 and 1938, is Yeats's 'Things fall apart; the centre cannot hold...'. But Savage, unlike Yeats, cannot find any consolation in imaginative vision, rather he is oppressed by his comfortless present. And, although much of Savage's imagery is taken from nature and the seasons, no comforting transcendentalism transforms his perceptions. Savage's 'autumn' encapsulates the decrepitude not only of society, but also that of the imagination.

'Fall of leaves' and 'The autumn world' are both poems which compare the lives of men to scattered autumnal leaves. These poems appear on succeeding pages in Savage's book, and this serves to emphasise both their differences and similarities. 'Fall of leaves' is dated 1934 and presumably was written before 'The autumn world' as it takes precedence in the book. The poet perceives 'autumn's tapestries / fall into rust', and as he watches the Thames he thinks

of the ragged lives that hopelessly

confront me now, cold in the fall of leaves
and decaying winds. Their blood fumbles flesh
frayed and grown sick with living; deciduous
they drift like leaves from squares to square, denied
Society's thinning sap, loosed from the tree
almost without remorse, till finally,
shredded by rain and cold they crumble, sink

and are forgotten.[31]

This is a moving description of the dispossessed; those who are 'denied' by society, the vagrant and unemployed. The poet concludes that their plight is the penalty of 'our adolescence, while man's brain is still "confused with dreams"'. We have, by implication, to stop dreaming and grow up. But what does this mean in terms of political belief? There is an unresolved tension in the poem between seeing the processes of society as somehow 'natural' and inevitable, and asking individuals to act responsibly in order to change society. The poet separates himself from the 'ragged lives' that 'hopelessly' confront him. They are like leaves falling from a tree; society's 'sap' is 'thinning'. The metaphor implies a natural process of ageing and decay. But then Savage changes tack, and, using the inclusive pronoun, indicts himself and his audience for adolescent dreaming. This metaphoric introduction of 'adolescence' into the poem, mixes Savage's initial metaphor. If society is adolescent, how can its sap be thin? But the poem also carries the implication that in the course of time 'we' will 'naturally' grow up, stop dreaming, and then all will be well.

The dominant tone of 'Fall of leaves' is then one of resignation. Yet there is a sense of the poet offering a critique of himself and of society. Perhaps aware that he had not resolved the problems confronted in the poem, Savage broaches similar matters in 'The autumn world'. But here the tensions articulated in 'Fall of leaves' are resolved. From the beginning he uses the second-person pronoun; 'Our world is ruinous and falls about us / like the autumn world, whose leaves bewilder'. We are like leaves driven by the 'slipshod wind':

In autumn mazery so much entangled,
confused with print and dreams our hasty
lives driven by huge winds will leave no trace
beyond the impermanent corrosion of leaves
choking stone fountains in deserted gardens,

and brimming quiet-circled winter ponds.
This century, blown against the future's walls
by war and hunger has only oblivion,
in winter's weather stamped into the soil
like the driven leaves, the driven leaves.[32]

There is no ambivalence here; Savage's vision is one of hopelessness. Our lives are driven by huge forces beyond our control. Nothing of our endeavours will last, and the century will be enshrouded in an ignominious oblivion. Society is conceived of as a natural process beyond man's volition. There is no redeeming principle either personal or political articulated. All we are left with is a sense of individuals drifting through life like leaves swirling from a tree.

Both 'Fall of leaves' and 'The autumn world', are highly impressive performances from a seventeen-year-old, and much of Savage's writing in the 1930s shares their tenor. He consistently expresses his sense of the individual's helplessness in the face of society, and he insists upon the uselessness of dreams and the imagination. 'Rhapsody' is securely located in 'drenched suburban groves' with 'Brahms pumping from the radiogram'.[33] The poet goes on to contemplate death, before urging his audience to 'sleep and forget tomorrow'. We are, he says, puppets 'Jerked by the strings of money or love' in the 'complex dance' of society. The poem closes with a series of negative injunctions in which we are urged to 'live no longer' in 'projected worlds / The simplified cities of the communist', and to avoid the traps of memory and romantic nostalgia. There is self-directed irony here, for the syntax of the poem returns us to the poet's present wherein he is apparently indulging in the 'projected world' provided by Brahms's music. This, together with the language of the poem, signals Savage's attraction to wistful participation in nostalgic melancholy. Hence the poem implicitly becomes a critique of the poet's own procedures.

It is abundantly clear that if Savage is sceptical about the operations of nostalgia, he also is equally wary of the 'simplicities of Communism', by which, presumably, he means the utopian visions of some of his contemporaries. Elsewhere the poet makes equally plain political statements that place him firmly to the right of centre. In 'Galahad' Savage gives utterance to his own ironic version of the grail legend. The quest of Galahad and Lancelot is made into a tale of hardship, homesickness and failure. The slightly archaic language used bespeaks Savage's imaginative involvement in his subject-matter. But what seems at first to be an implicit celebration of heroism is transformed at the close of the poem into condemnation. The 'visions of an improvident king', we are told, send 'true knights' to die for nothing, and 'few survive to tell the tale / In delirium of their mad imagining'. Imagination, including his own, is again castigated by Savage.

The poem closes with the poet drawing the moral from what has now become a political allegory:

Those kings were wise who kept their knights at Court,
Their lands in peace and order, and matins said,
The labouring folk in villages, untaught,
Content with custom and their daily bread;

That men might work the day and sleep the night,
Find comfort in familiar ways of toil
And by mere solidity put dragons to flight,
Entrenched, like oaks, in the coarse, common soil.[34]

That 'labouring folk' should remain untaught, customs be preserved, and men be entrenched in the 'coarse, common soil' is, of course, an enormously conservative expression of nostalgia for a legendary past. But it is also clear that Savage, in attempting to escape the dilemmas of contemporary industrial society, himself experimented with a retreat to the life of the soil. It seems that reaction against society led him to experiment with an alternative lifestyle in the later 1930s.

There are two poems in The autumn world which relate directly to this. One of these, 'Song (II)', indulges in self-pity, as the poet, 'cold and miserable' in bitter reflection, speaks of still owing last week's rent, and not having 'tuppence for a meal'. The sky, it is said, 'will never clear again'.[35] Savage prefigures the middle-class drop-outs of the 1960s by choosing poverty and self-sufficiency. But he finds in such a lifestyle little comfort. His 'Winter offering' is addressed to a beloved. All the poet has to offer is 'a cracked china jug', and potatoes 'grown with tedious sweat and toil' from the 'back garden'. The poet recognises that it is useless to regret 'living like a peasant', but the poem concludes with an ambivalent quatrain:

We'll make no virtue of enforced economy,
Strike no impressive plaster or tin attitudes.
Poverty's fixed, archaic physiognomy
Projects only through masks where nothing else extrudes.[36]

There are two opposed ways of reading this. The first two lines plainly express a determination not to indulge in any poses of martyred self-righteousness. The difficulty lies with the following two lines. Is Savage saying that he is exempt from poverty because something else (implicitly the poem) extrudes from his 'mask', and that poverty is therefore not merely a matter of materialism, but encompasses poverty of spirit as well? Or is he implying that he is not materially poor enough to strike attitudes, because if he were, nothing else could extrude from him; material poverty with its concomitant hunger being a condition which precludes all other concerns or activities?

Whichever way one chooses to read the poem there are aspects of self-congratulation here. But more important for my argument is the expression of dissatisfaction in the poem. What Savage 'offers' in 'Winter offering' is perceived by the poet to be very little, and is hardly rendered attractive. The poem does not celebrate an anarchistic escape or retreat from society but rather a bitter sense that a way of life which offers water and potatoes as its staple diet is not entirely satisfactory either. Savage's dislike of society is unalloyed, but finally he sees no answer to disintegration and decay. Imagination, politics, love hold no reconciliation for him, and implicitly his art is also of no help. Although his poems often exhibit an imaginative relish through their overtly Romantic language, over and over again he asserts that 'dreams' and 'visions' are destructive. It is not then entirely surprising to find Savage writing a poem late in the 1930s entitled 'On defeat'. Here he argues that time leaves us with only memories of happiness or grief, and that

These are but litter in an empty room
(Our friends gone home) that gapes to vacancy,
Calling to mind a woman's weary gesture at
Departure, one day's end, so much of failure, and
The dirty china cluttered in the kitchen sink.[37]

The domestic, familiar and bathetic final image here, helps to measure the distance between Savage and the Oxbridge poets of the 1930s. And it was a distance that he was thoroughly aware of; we recall that it was Savage who wrote to New verse complaining that the editor encouraged the writings of an 'Oxbridge Clique'. Savage was not of the working class, but the world he portrays in his poetry is clearly not that of the Oxbridge poets; he is in touch with grimmer realities which lie beyond the sheltered and sheltering walls of public schools and universities. His voice is far more down to earth in its despair, more sceptical, less confident than his upper-middle-class contemporaries. He perceives social evils, but has no answer to them. He can find nothing to praise in society, and his retreat from it is self-consciously defeatist rather than defiantly celebratory.

Ruthven Todd's poems of the 1930s broach similar themes to those we have identified in Savage's work. But Todd, unlike Savage, managed to locate positive value in individualism. Although there is a tension in his work between imagination and the threat of public events, Todd, at least until 1939, created a somewhat less despairing voice than that of Savage. But he shares with Savage two interesting and significant impulses: an attraction to simple, alternative lifestyles and to simplicity of poetic style. In an autobiographical note written in 1939, Todd says, 'My poems try to be poems, and to be simple'.[38] And the themes that Todd broaches in his poems between 1937 and 1939 will be by now familiar. Here we find a concern with legends and heroes, we find a private world of nostalgia and imagination juxtaposed with threatening political realities, and finally, with the outbreak of the Second World War imminent, Todd registers the conquest of imaginative idealism by warfare. But Todd distinguishes himself from Symons and Savage because he exhibits the surest and most sustained talent as a poet. His work combines music, image and clarity of statement in tones which are genial and urbane. His appreciation of fine art is evidenced by the colour and focus of his visual images. And, unlike Symons and Savage, Todd continued to write and publish poetry well into the 1950s.

Todd's eminently recognisable accents of the later 1930s, however, developed from his much more anonymous and less compelling voice of his earlier published poems. In his work written between 1933 and 1936 he shares with Symons an attraction to the English Jacobean and metaphysical poets, which results in a poetry of enormous obliquity clotted with images of the charnel-house. Bones, viscera, ghosts and worms take their place in poems obsessed with metaphysical notions of decay and resurrection. Fortunately none of this work was printed in book form, and it is best left to the obscurity it deserves. One would only wish to note in passing that these poems exhibit a similar extravagance to those of Kathleen Raine, and that they represent an impulse to escape from the exigencies of society. They may be seen as part of Todd's reaction against his social background.

But here I will concentrate upon his more representative poems of the later 1930s, which show a very clear development of idea and attitude, and which were published in his first volume Until now. Todd's poems of 1937 are concerned with problems of memory and imagination in conflict with a disturbing present. In 'Northward the islands' and 'In September 1937', the poet looks back to celebrate his time on Mull, and attempts to come to terms with a fearful present and more fearful future. 'In September' begins with three stanzas which describe the seasonal life of farmers, and recalls the poet's time 'lifting potatoes and stacking peat / On Mull ...'. We are reminded here of Savage's retreat into toiling for spuds in his back garden. But Todd is nostalgic for the life of the soil. His memories of Mull, of 'reaping' or 'lambing' seem 'out of place beside the chip-shop / And the cockney voices in the pub.' And the 'drab newspapers / Telling of wars, in Spain and in the East' make the poet wish he was back on Mull living the simple life. Here in London he is alienated; he is the 'unwanted guest'. In the final stanza, however, Todd is able to achieve an escape, though not into memories of Mull, but into a domestic haven:

In September, we lit the fire and talked together
Discussing the trivialities of a spent day
And what we would eat. I forgot the weather
And the dull streets and the sun on Islay,
And all my fear. I lost my carefully-kept count
Of the ticks to death, and, in September, was content.[39]

The pleasures of the moment, companionship, food and 'trivialities' triumph over both nostalgia and fear. The poet is quite unashamed of this confession of private felicity. Although Todd is capable of rendering the quotidian life of chip-shop and pub in a way that upper-middle-class poets of the 1930s were not, he nevertheless wishes to avoid public responsibilities, and finds no solace in any collective political activity, but celebrates privacy, individuality.

'Northward the islands' has a similar movement to 'September 1937' in so far as it progresses from lyrical memories of Mull to the less palatable present. And, although the poem does not conclude with such unequivocal 'content' as 'September 1937', its final lines defiantly confess Todd's fear that the future may intrude upon his individuality, and spoil his nostalgia and 'romantic leanings to the land'.[40] It is transparent that he is not interested in political engagement; rather here and in other poems he investigates strategies for the avoidance of politics. But the 'turmoil of Europe' is never far from the poet's mind. In 'Poem' (which was later re-titled 'Personal note') the poet addresses his beloved from whom he is temporarily parted. Ensconced in a 'quiet spot' away from Europe, from the 'flurried engine's noisy start / And the bomb-smashing hope', Todd evokes images of natural beauty to share with his beloved. These, however, are not enough to stop the 'minutes tapping' at his ear:

I wait the morning paper –
How many killed in Spain?
Yet, now, before the deeper
Knowledge of pain,
I give you the minutes of this hour;
All that I have, so treasure them, my dear.[41]

Like 'gifts' offered in poems by Symons and Savage, Todd's here is a minimal gesture; a few moments of felicity pitted against the knowledge of war and pain. There is no sense here, or in any other of his poems, that he could or should do anything to combat the march of threatening political events. Implicitly he expresses his sense of powerlessness. Nevertheless, as in other poems of 1937, there is at least some consolation offered in this poem.

The majority of Todd's poems of 1938 exhibit both a change of subject-matter and a change of approach to his writing. His output of this year is divided between poems dealing with leaders and heroes, and those which take the work of other artists as their starting point. In all these we find the same lucid formality of his previous year's work. But the first-person pronoun is significantly absent. Under pressure from the events which led to the Munich Crisis, Todd's confessional style no longer suffices.

'Delusion of grandeur', 'Lust for power', and 'Apotheosis of a hero', are short narrative poems which investigate various aspects of heroism and tyranny. The force of the poems is to deflate the Romantic notion of the *Übermenschen*, and clearly, given the historical context, have a close relationship to the rise of the European dictators. Both 'Delusion of grandeur' and 'Lust for power' are sonnets which use the octet to establish a tyrant, and the sestet to deflate the portrait ironically. 'Delusion of grandeur' charts the progress of a 'small man' who was 'a cobbler' and who, in fighting for power, 'crushed out his comrades', and 'intoxicated the young' until 'His deeds and face were parcel of a fable'. The sestet follows:

Now in the neat white house that is his home
He rules the flowers and birds just like a king,
And, Napoleon by the sundial, sees his fame
Spread through the garden to the heap of dung;
'All that I do is history!', he loudly cries
Seeing in his shadow his romantic size.[42]

The insubstantial quality of human grandeur and fame is forcefully rendered here. The small man casts a long shadow all the way to the dung-heap with its stink of mortality. Todd perceives that the power of a tyrant depends upon the imagination; he becomes no less a 'fable' to his followers than he is to himself. But the hopeful implication of the poem resides in the 'reality', that the natural order will inevitably supervene to reduce the Napoleons to their true size. The poem then is both a warning and a consolation.

'Lust for power' shares this element of hope, which in the light of subsequent events is apt to seem naive or even callous. But, in the historical context, Todd was not alone in hoping that the Fascist dictators would fall without taking the rest of Europe and millions of lives with them. The poem describes a 'village god' who 'dreams' of blowing up land in order to seize power. The tin 'god' thinks he can also control the elements. But the poem concludes with a vision of impotence: '. . . tomorrow when he goes with lighted lamp / He'll start no fires, for all his powder's damp'. Again nature is the healing force which is opposed to the imaginative 'dreams' of the would-be tyrant. 'Trees' are said to interrupt the protagonist's dream, and at the close of the poem, it is a thunderstorm which dampens his powder and destroys his plot. Todd expresses a conservative hope that natural forces will inevitably triumph over evil imagination.

It might be tempting for critics seeking to demonstrate Auden's domination of poetry in the 1930s to liken these sonnets technically to those Auden wrote in his sequence 'In time of war'. And, similarly, it might be thought that Todd was following Auden's lead in writing several poems (some of them sonnets) about other artists towards the end of the decade. But Todd's poems were written before he could possibly have been influenced by Auden's. Five of Auden's sonnets from 'In time of war' were published in December 1938, but the rest did not appear until 1939. Auden's poems about other artists, 'Rimbaud', 'Voltaire at Ferney', and 'A.E. Housman' were not composed until December 1938, and not printed until 1939. If the dating of Todd's poems in Until now is accurate (and there is no reason to believe otherwise) it makes any question of Auden's influence in their writing untenable. The style of Todd's writing is, in any case, quite distinct from Auden's. In Todd's poems like 'Jonathan Swift', 'For Joan Miro' and 'The drawings for Guernica', there are none of Auden's habitual stylistic traits. Todd's syntax is more supple than Auden's; his rhythms more expansive.

Todd's 'For Joan Miró' is one of his finest poems of the 1930s. Strangely it expresses a darker vision than his poems about tyranny. For here he is dealing with the imagination as a creative rather than a destructive force, and lamenting the imposition of a savage reality upon the benign operations of the artist. The poem begins with a celebration of Miró's paintings, and the point is subtly made that art may describe pain and violence without physically hurting or harming anyone. It is the realm of magical creativity. But the poem's conclusion describes the effect of war upon that world:

Once he had a country where the sun shone
Through the enchanted trees like lace,
But now it is troubled and happiness is gone,
For the bombs fell in that fine place
And the magician found when he had woken
His people killed, his gay pots broken.[43]

This signals an end to the optimism of 'Delusion of grandeur' and 'Lust for power'. In those poems nature conquers the evil imagination, but here there is a recognition that neither nature nor art can withstand the reality of man's destructive impulses. The 'magic' of art cannot transcend bombs. We see the public world disrupting and destroying imaginative vision.

'Jonathan Swift' has an equally sombre tone, and though the poem pretends to a dramatic reconstruction of Swift's state of mind, one cannot help but feel that Todd's own response to the darkening state of affairs in Europe is directing the utterance:

Even the little children had inherited the evil
That mankind had made itself, the blame
Was no one else's: man was himself the devil,
Hell was the odour of a powerful name.
Alone at last, the horror grew and his brain bled
Till he was glad that he would soon be dead.[44]

It is impossible to believe that Todd had anything else in mind but the
European dictators when he speaks of the 'odour of a powerful name'.
And, I think, we should not be dismissive about the bathetic effect of
the rhythm in the last line of the poem. It would, of course, be going
too far to suggest that Todd himself felt genuinely suicidal, but the final
couplet is effective in placing stress on the horror of living which
makes death seem welcome. The comparatively jaunty rhythm of the
last line is ironically appropriate.

Predictably Todd's poems of 1939 continue in the sombre tones of
'For Joan Miró' and 'Jonathan Swift'. What was feared in 'September
1937' by September 1939 had become a grim reality. The latter date
also constitutes the title of a poem, addressed to the poet's wife, in
which Todd speaks of the 'mischief of words', and asserts that 'the gold
of tomorrow is tarnished / already . . .'. 'Dreams', he says, are found
to be dreams, and have 'proved only tissue paper', failing to combat
political turmoil. What is left to console in this situation? If one could
live for the moment Todd says, or for 'precious moments / like beads
on a string', all would be well. But this too is impossible. We are left
with 'the world we build ourselves', the hope that 'some good may
come of all this evil', and the fact that whatever he says or believes,
'the future is certain to arrive'.[45] The weight of negativity in the poem
adds intensity to the lack of faith in his own words here. The
'contentment' in domesticity, the 'romantic leanings to the land' of
earlier poems, have been overtaken by events which the poet is forced
to face.

This too is the burden of 'It was easier', a poem which begins with
images of warfare. Todd articulates the difficulty in recognising that
bullets are being fired in Spain and boys dying. It is, he says, 'easier
to avoid all thought of it / and shelter in the elegant bower of legend'.
Todd continues to enumerate other 'easier' strategies: it is easier to
collect anecdotes, tell tales and 'discuss the rare edition over tea', than
to confront the realities of war. But the irony of the poem is powerfully

underpinned by the contrast between the present tense utilised in the poem – it is easier – and the past tense of the title. Todd implies that he has been guilty of such 'easy' avoidance of political issues. At the close of the poem this becomes explicit when he says he can 'no longer hide in infancy', and concludes:

Time may have answers but the map is here.
Now is the future that I never wished to see.
I was quite happy dreaming and had no fear:
But now, from the map, a gun is aimed at me.[46]

The poem plangently expresses the poet's horrified realisation that the comforts of the imagination cannot protect him from the consequences of war. Escape from society into the bastions of individualism cannot remove the potent reality of the threat of death.

But despite this threat, Todd, like Symons and Savage, and significantly like Kenneth Allott, became a Conscientious Objector during the war. In a poem, 'Letter about war' Todd explains himself by arguing that he refuses to 'play the hero in a dream' or die to 'increase the fame of old men'. He is uninterested in dying for those who 'have forbidden / Life for the living'.[47] Like Savage and Symons, Todd is a disgruntled and finally sceptical individualist; an anarchist. The registration of these poets as Conscientious Objectors at the outbreak of the war is entirely in keeping with this position. They will not serve a society whose values they consistently oppose; they will not defend the bad against the worse.

And yet, as I remarked earlier, all three poets evolved a plain-speaking style in the course of the decade, which owes more to their Georgian inheritance than it does to modernism. They all strive to express their sense of the mundane, the reality of the world they perceive and it is a world quite different from that to be found in Auden's poetry. It is a world which encompasses pubs, chip-shops, poverty, the kitchen sink. However tempted they may be to escape into the dreams of imagination, the demotic social world and the world of political action and event continually intrude and bring them down to earth. Theirs is a poetry of attenuated hope and minimal gratification. In this they are, I believe, more seminal than has been recognised before. Their work prefigures much of the best poetry of the war years, and it is surely not too much to suggest that the ennervation and minimalism of Larkin's poems has a relationship to the poetry I have dealt with here.

Notes

1 J. Symons, Notes from another country, London, 1972, p. 65.
2 J. Symons, The thirties: a dream revolved, revd. ed., London, 1975, p. 71.
3 For this and other biographical information see Symons, Notes from another country.
4 Symons, Notes from another country, p. 46.
5 Ibid., p. 45.
6 Ibid.
7 Ibid., pp. 54-7.
8 Ibid., p. 59.
9 J. Symons, Editorial, Twentieth century verse, No. 1, Jan. 1937, p. 2.
10 J. Symons, Editorial, Twentieth century verse, No. 2, March 1937, p. 22.
11 J. Symons, Editorial, Twentieth century verse, No. 3, April-May 1937, p. 42.
12 Ibid.
13 J. Symons, 'Twentieth century verse', The review, Nos. 11-12, autumn 1964, pp. 22-4.
14 Ibid.
15 J. Symons, Editorial, Twentieth century verse, No. 6-7, Nov.-Dec. 1937, p. 105.
16. W. Lewis, 'Letter to the editor', Twentieth century verse, Nos. 6-7, Nov.-Dec. 1937, p. 106.
17 J. Symons, Twentieth century verse, No. 14, Dec. 1938, pp. 136-7.
18 D. Hawkins, 'Poetry and broadcasting'; R. Fuller, 'The audience and politics', Twentieth century verse, No. 18, June-July 1939, pp. 35-9 and 50-2 respectively.
19 G. Barker, 'A note on narrative poetry', Twentieth century verse, No. 18, June-July 1939, p. 48.
20 S. Spender, Introduction to P. O'Connor, Memoirs of a public baby, London, 1958, pp. 13-14.
21 Symons, The Review, Nos. 11-12, autumn 1964, p. 24.
22 Symons, Notes from another country, p. 65.
23 See D. Savage, 'Derek Savage', Twentieth century authors, ed. S. Kunitz (1st supplement (1955)), New York, 1967, pp. 872-3, and Contemporary authors, vol. 104, ed. F. Locker, Detroit, 1982, p. 415.
24 Letter of the Registrar, Fettes College to the author, 24 March 1986.
25 Savage, Twentieth century authors, pp. 872-3.
26 J. Symons, Confusions about X, London, 1939, pp. 20-2.
27 Ibid., pp. 32-3.
28 Ibid., pp. 39-40.
29 R. Fuller, 'Poems by editors', Twentieth century verse, No. 17, April-May 1939, p. 24.
30 Symons, Confusions about X, pp. 9-10.
31 D. Savage, The autumn world, London, 1939, p. 9.
32 Ibid., p. 10.
33 Ibid., p. 12.
34 Ibid., pp. 17-19.
35 Ibid., p. 14.
36 Ibid., p. 24.
37 Ibid., p. 31.
38 R. Todd, Poets of tomorrow, London, 1939, p. 45.
39 R. Todd, Until now, London, 1943, pp. 7-8.
40 Ibid., p. 10.
41 Ibid., p. 11.
42 Ibid.
43 Ibid., p. 18.
44 Ibid., pp. 14-15.
45 Ibid., pp. 24-5.
46 Ibid., pp. 22-3.
47 Ibid., pp. 26-7.

8

Contemporary poetry and prose, Surrealism, and the poetry of Gascoyne, Barker and Thomas

I

The literary-historical myth of the 1930s ignores poets like Symons, Savage and Todd, and it attempts to bring writers like Raine and Allott under the umbrella either of the Audenesque or of objectivism. But the writers I wish to deal with here, David Gascoyne, George Barker and Dylan Thomas, have a different position within the mythology, for they are considered by the myth as a 'new generation' of writers reacting in a 'Romantic' way to the supposed austerities of the Audenesque. Gascoyne, Barker and Thomas are centrally placed in the mythology of action and reaction which has hitherto governed our literary-historical perspective of the later 1930s and the 1940s. But as I have demonstrated, the poetry and poetics of 'MacSpaunday' are themselves derived from Romanticism; the mythological view will not suffice. It remains here to re-assess the place of Gascoyne, Barker and Thomas's work in the 1930s. In order to do this it is salutary, first of all, to look at Roger Roughton's magazine Contemporary poetry and prose, its relationship to the English Surrealist movement, and its relationship to Communism. For the achievement of the three poets that I wish to deal with here has been clouded by association with this magazine, and what it has been said to represent. I do not, however, intend to deal extensively with the Surrealist movement in England, as Paul C. Ray has already provided such a comprehensive survey of the subject.[1] But some comment upon the theory and practice of Surrealism and its relationship to Communism will be inevitable when dealing with Gascoyne's work since he was a pioneer of the movement in England, and arguably its most able poetic practitioner.

Contemporary poetry and prose was published from the Arts Café, No. 1 Parton Street, and ran for ten numbers between May 1936 and autumn 1937. The Arts Café was situated opposite David Archer's bookshop from where he ran the Parton Press which was responsible for publishing the first volumes of Gascoyne, Barker and Thomas. The Arts Café and the bookshop were well-known haunts of 'left-wing' intellectuals, and since not only Gascoyne and Barker but also Thomas, when he was in London, were habitués of the café, it is perhaps not surprising that they have come to be seen as a 'group' of poets with distinctively Surrealist leanings.

But identification by association is the stuff of mythologies, and as we shall see, Gascoyne, Barker and Thomas developed their poetry and poetics independently of each other, and in the case of Barker and Thomas independently of the Surrealist movement as well. Furthermore, it is a mistake to assume, simply because the three poets contributed to Contemporary poetry and prose, that they were necessarily writing Surrealist poetry; the editorial policy of the magazine was not as homogenous as it is often said to have been. Lastly, the relationship between Surrealism, Communism, and Contemporary poetry and prose is complicated. Most English Surrealists in the 1930s claimed to be Communists or fellow travellers, but their theoretical position could not bear close scrutiny. Marxist critics like Anthony Blunt and Alick West, writing in Left review, disapprovingly pointed to the Romantic, bourgeois, individualism inherent in Surrealist theory and practice; it was a charge that the Surrealists never satisfactorily countered. Roger Roughton, himself a member of the Communist Party, also failed in his magazine to articulate a position which would convincingly unite his political belief with his artistic or editorial practice.

A.T. Tolley has written that 'there could be no doubt about the magazine's policy which was to publish Surrealist verse and prose'.[2] But this is far too sweeping a statement, and accepts at face value the reception of the magazine in the 1930s. Roughton himself was obliged to clarify matters in a policy statement in the last issue of Volume I where he denied that Contemporary poetry and prose was an 'official Surrealist magazine', pointed out that only twenty of the fifty contributors so far were Surrealists, and made it clear that the politics of his magazine were not necessarily those of the English Surrealist Group.[3]

This seems to me an accurate assessment of the magazine, for beside the translated contributions of European Surrealists like Luís Buñuel, René Char, Salvador Dali, André Breton and Paul Eluard, one finds the decidedly un-Surrealist work of Gavin Ewart, Francis Scarfe, Ruthven Todd, Roy Fuller, Edgar Foxall, Wallace Stevens, Jack Lindsay and others. It should also be noted how very few of the English contributors, apart from Gascoyne, could be called genuine Surrealists.

Kenneth Allott contributed six poems which displayed his occasional penchant for irrational imagery, but such images were quite obviously integrated into structures governed by intellectual design; an ordering process at odds with Surrealist theory proper. Otherwise there were Roughton's own contributions, 'Animal crackers in my croup', and 'Lady Windermere's fan dance', which have since gained some small notoriety, not, I think, because of any quality in the writing but more so as curiosities in the history of English poetry; they are two very rare examples of what at least seems to be an attempt at genuine automatic writing. Other English contributions remained stubbornly anti-Surrealist.

Contemporary poetry and prose contains surprisingly little in the way of editorial commentary or theoretical debate. Apart from the policy statement quoted above, the nineteen-year-old Roughton only provided two further editorials in the course of his magazine's short existence. Both of these deal with politics, and one of them specifically with 'Surrealism and Communism'. In the fourth number of the magazine, Roughton expressed what has been called 'a credo for left surrealism':[4] 'Surrealist work, while not calling directly for revolutionary intervention, can be classed as revolutionary in so far as it can break down irrational bourgeois-taught prejudices, thus preparing the mental ground for positive revolutionary thought and action'.[5] Roughton goes on to argue that this 'revolutionary essence' should not be 'adulterated' by individual Surrealists. This seemingly confident expression of political commitment is interestingly modified towards the close of the article where Roughton seems to be aware of the attacks mounted upon Surrealism by some members of the left. Here Roughton calls for 'compromise with all progressive parties', which does not 'entail any betrayal of principles'. He goes on to suggest that even Christianity might have a role to play in fighting Fascism. He concludes that 'As long as the Surrealists will help to establish a broad United Front ... there is no reason why there should be any quarrel between Communism and Surrealism'.

Roughton, then, was in the curious position of advocating the revolutionary essence of Surrealism, whilst at the same time calling for compromise and a United Front. And his assertion that Surrealism breaks down bourgeois prejudice, and lays the ground for revolutionary thought and action, remains hopelessly glib without some discussion of how all this is to be achieved. But these are issues to which we will return when discussing Gascoyne's work. My purpose here is to demonstrate that Roughton's position with respect to both Surrealism and Communism was never very coherent. Like many others in the late 1930s he was anti-Fascist, but his attitude to politics and art are never refined any further. The anti-Fascist position is, however, articulated clearly in the magazine. His second editorial, published in the sixth number, was provoked by the murder of Lorca, and entitled 'Fascism murders art'. Here Roughton asserted that intellectuals, poets and poetry magazines could sit on the fence no longer – 'they must choose between fascism and anti-fascism'.[6] Roughton also published a 'Declaration on Spain' which called for the government to end their policy of non-intervention, and supply 'Arms for the People of Spain'. The declaration was signed by eleven members of the 'Surrealist Group in England'.[7]

In spite of such drum-beating pronouncements, the contents of the magazine wavered from Surrealism to the publication of traditional English folk ballads, and continued to include the liberal and conservative mainstream, thus showing that Roughton himself was sitting on the fence. And in an exchange with Ezra Pound on the issue of Surrealism, this lack of certainty in Roughton's position is clearly signalled. Pound had written a letter attacking the 'coward surrealists' for their ignorance of history, and their 'dim ditherings' which he likened to those of 'the aesthetes in 1888'. Roughton published this together with his reply in the seventh number of his magazine.[8] Pound suggests that the breaking down of bourgeois prejudice might be better undertaken by using words 'with a clear and unequivocal meaning' rather than by the methods of Surrealism. Roughton has little answer to this, and admits that the Communist Manifesto is 'a brilliant pamphlet using words with clear and unequivocal meaning, containing nothing but true statements, based on a correct and rational analysis of capitalism'.

Roughton, understandably, does not continue to explore the implications of this remark with respect to his supposedly Surrealist aesthetic. But as Werner has remarked, he concludes his response with 'a much more modest claim for surrealism'[9] than he had made a few months earlier:

Too much is often made of the directly revolutionary significance of present day surrealism: the part it has to play in helping to bring over a small section of that small section of the bourgeoisie which in times of capitalist crisis joins the class-conscious militant workers, that part in comparison with the direct impact of economic circumstances is very very minute; but the role exists and the revolutionary sincerity of its players is usually genuine.[10]

The hostility of the left to Surrealism seems to have dented Roughton's enthusiasm, and engendered a lack of confidence in his position. The close of the magazine was announced in issue number ten wherein the editor pointedly remarked that he was 'going abroad'. In the following year, 1938, the tensions prefigured in Roughton's magazine between the CP, with its preference for 'realism', and Surrealism were cemented by André Breton's visit to Trotsky in Mexico. The resulting 'Manifesto' called for 'freedom' in art and was deliberately anti-Stalinist, arguing that art was by its very nature revolutionary, and that prescribed themes would not do.[11] Roughton had correctly perceived that his membership of the CP and his interest in Surrealism were incompatible. Roughton was later to commit suicide in Dublin in 1941.

II

Gascoyne, Barker and Thomas all contributed to Contemporary poetry and prose, but as we shall see had differing relationships to Surrealism and Communism. Before looking at their individual achievements, however, it is necessary to discuss what these poets had in common. For it is their collective identity which has been mythologised. Barker and Thomas were born in 1913 and 1914 respectively, and therefore qualify for Hynes's 'Auden generation'. That Gascoyne was born in 1916 is hardly enough to validate Day Lewis's claim that the three poets constituted a 'new generation reacting against the New Signatures group'.[12] Furthermore, the documentary fact that Gascoyne, Barker and Thomas published their first volumes in 1932, 1933 and 1934 respectively, makes the idea of them reacting against the Audenesque or the New Signatures group extremely unlikely. The sixteen-year-old Gascoyne would have had to have read Auden's Poems (1930), and immediately decided that here was a force to be reckoned with and react against. A similar process would have had to occur with the slightly less youthful Barker and Thomas. This seems to me implausible, erasing as it does any development of the individual poets pre-1930, and predicating their creative endeavours entirely upon Auden. In the case of Dylan Thomas we have his early notebooks which demonstrate that Auden was largely irrelevant in the development of his style; there is no reason to suppose that Gascoyne and Barker were any more affected by Auden's early writings than was Thomas.

It is not that they reacted against the Audenesque that associates these poets with each other, but that they all stand further outside the public school and Oxbridge traditions than any of the other poets we have so far encountered. They share striking similarities of background, education, career, and attitude to poetry and poetics. Gascoyne, Barker and Thomas did not attend public schools and were unencumbered by a university education. All three left school before the age of sixteen, and published their first poems at a very early age. All three adhered to Bohemian lifestyles in the 1930s, and their distance from the literary establishment may be measured by the fact that their early volumes were published by the small, private Parton Press, as opposed to Faber and Faber who published Auden, Spender and MacNeice.

Barker and Thomas came from lower-middle-class families. Thomas's father had risen into the middle class by becoming a schoolteacher; Barker's father was a police constable and some time later an insurance agent. Both poets were aware not only of their class background but also of the specifically non-English aspect of their inheritance. Barker's mother was Irish, and although he was brought up in London, as he says in a poem of the 1930s, he 'wore the shape of Ireland' on his mind. Thomas took from the Welsh tradition the image of the poet as bard, and his position as the 'Rimbaud of Cwmdonkin Drive' has passed into the 'Dylan' mythology. Gascoyne's background was also provincial, but possibly slightly more elevated than that of Barker or Thomas. His father was a bank clerk who eventually achieved managerial status via various transfers and promotions. This meant that Gascoyne's childhood and youth were peripatetic; the family lived for various periods of time in Edinburgh, Bournemouth, Salisbury and Fordingbridge. Gascoyne spent some three years as a chorister at Salisbury Cathedral Choir School, before leaving at the age of fourteen to complete his education at the Regent Street Polytechnic. Like Thomas and Barker, from an early age Gascoyne looked away from England for artistic mentors. Perhaps inspired by the derivation of his surname, Gascoyne cultivated Francophilia in the 1930s.

The somewhat anti-English bias in the work of these poets is, I think, part of an extreme reaction not only against their own class background but also against society as a whole. Gascoyne, Barker and Thomas take the position held by poets like Symons, Savage and Todd to a further extreme. They do not suffer the pangs of a guilty liberal conscience, and, because they are closer to the realities of working-class life, they do not seek to identify in their work with the proletariat.

Rather, in the poetry and poetics of Gascoyne, Barker and Thomas we encounter a more intense impulse than we have seen in any of the other poets I have discussed to adopt a radical, anti-social, déclassé position which emphasises the spiritual, emotional, and vatic dimension of their role as poets, at the expense of materialism and reason. In the face of the perceived disintegration in society, and as a response to their feelings of alienation, they attempt the development of a personal organic vision, thereby implicitly embracing the notion of a spiritual aristocracy in a similar way, and for the same reasons that Kathleen Raine did. When politics are encountered in their work, they are so in terms of the visionary and metaphysical.

But Gascoyne, Barker, and Thomas are more radical than Raine in their reaction to society, and more ambivalent. This is evident not only in the stylistic extremes to which they went but also in their attitude to politics. Whereas Raine was apparently untroubled by the adoption of an extremely conservative position, Gascoyne, Barker and Thomas showed some interest in revolutionary left-wing politics. But this did not deter them from pursuing a visionary, individualistic poetry and poetics which tended ideologically towards the anarchistic. Their respective styles eschew any Georgian influences, and stem directly from their High Romantic and modernist forebears. Few concessions are made to an audience; the notion that 'difficulty' is a prerequisite of serious poetry is unashamedly embraced. There is little trace of the vernacular in their work; both tone and language tend to be elevated and self-consciously poetic. Their ambivalence towards society is not then expressed in their poetry but in the disjunction between their poetry and their stated political affiliations.

III

David Gascoyne was born in Harrow, the son of an aspiring actress and a bank clerk. As I have already mentioned, his father's career with the Midland Bank ensured that the poet's childhood was itinerant, until at the age of eight some stability was afforded by his enrolment at the Salisbury Cathedral Choir School. Here Gascoyne stayed until he was fourteen, imbibing a religious ethos which was highly influential in his later development. By the time his voice broke and he was obliged to leave, his father had been removed from his position as manager of the Fordingbridge Branch and transferred back to Head Office in

London. And so Gascoyne was sent to the Regent Street Polytechnic to complete his education in the City. Gascoyne's career at this establishment seems to have been rather less than distinguished. He left at the age of sixteen after the Headmaster advised his father that there was little chance of David passing any exams.[13] Despite or because of this lack of academic success, Gascoyne had already written a volume of poems, and had begun work on a novel: his talent was nothing if not precocious.

From the scant biographical information available, it is difficult to gauge Gascoyne's reaction to his education and family life. But it seems likely, given his obvious intellectual capacities, that he found school unhelpful and tedious, hence his presumed inability to pass exams. And, although apparently his parents did not oppose his aspirations towards art, in his journals 1937-9, he speaks of intending to leave the family home for good, and of his parents as 'perfectly indifferent, engrossed in their own fatigue'.[14] In his partly autobiographical novel, Opening day, the hero is an adolescent who is portrayed reacting in a similar way to Kathleen Raine against the 'stifling meanness of middle-class, suburban existence'.[15] Certainly Gascoyne's career in the 1930s (and subsequently for that matter) vigorously repudiates the values of the society into which he was born, and which his parents upheld. From the time that he left school, Gascoyne pursued the vocation of a writer to the exclusion of all else. Often short of money, this led him towards a Bohemian existence which was in sharp contradistinction to the carefulness and securities of his petit-bourgeois background. In the 1930s he rejected not only his class but his country also. And it is possible to argue that being outside the educational mainstream of the English upper-middle classes enabled Gascoyne a freedom to follow the impulses both artistic and social which led him away from England and towards Europe.

However in his first, self-financed, book of poems, Roman balcony (1932), this 'European' quality is felt only indirectly through the influence of Ezra Pound's Imagism, and in the young poet's unwillingness to admit anything of English society into his work. But in 1933, Gascoyne used the advance on royalties for Opening day to finance his first visit to Paris, a city which he revisited in 1935, and in which he lived for a considerable period between 1937 and 1939. This gave him a knowledge of contemporary French literature greater than any of the young poets of the 1930s, and encouraged him in the direction of Surrealism. By late 1933 Gascoyne was publishing translations of

European Surrealists in *New verse*, and this continental influence is also evident in his own poetry from this time forward. In 1935 Gascoyne used his trip to Paris to research *A short survey of surrealism*,[16] which was published in the same year, and the following year his translation of Breton's *What is Surrealism*[17] appeared.

Surrealism, Communism and finally a variety of Christian mysticism are Gascoyne's aesthetic and intellectual landmarks during the 1930s. This development, no less than his attraction towards France, were all constituents of a struggle to escape his English background. In a 'Letter to Lawrence Durrell', printed in his *Paris journal 1937-39*, Gascoyne speaks with reference to Durrell's *The black book*; Gascoyne praises Durrell's 'wonderful objectifisation or projection of the absolutely universal spiritual squalor and disintegration of the inhabitants of the British Isles', before going on to speak of his own relationship to 'the English Death':

It seems obvious doesn't it, that there has been a conflict going on? And it occurs to me now that this struggle can be explained in two different ways. Firstly, it is between the side of my nature which by instinct, heredity, environment, circumstance, what you will, is altogether *implicated in the* English Death, and the other side, which somehow, blindly, is trying to struggle towards absurdity and life. And secondly, though not so clearly, it is between me as a whole and the English Death as a whole ... I have been pretty conscious of the existence of the E.D. all along.[18]

The 'English Death' is Durrell's coinage, but clearly Gascoyne empathises strongly with the virulent opposition to English values and mores which this phrase implies. By the time Gascoyne wrote this he had turned away from Surrealism, and had been aware of the 'insufficiency of Communism' for quite some time.[19] But his initial attraction to both this aesthetic theory and political doctrine were integral to his struggle with the 'English Death' mentioned above. They both constitute an extreme rejection of the bourgeois, and, in the case of Surrealism, a flight towards the absurd.

It is in his second volume, *Man's life is this meat*, containing poems written between 1933 and 1936, that the impact of Surrealism upon Gascoyne may be seen at its most intense. The theory of Surrealism pushes Romantic notions of inspiration and integration to an extreme. Breton hypothesised that there existed a point in the mind where all antinomies ceased to be perceived in terms of contradiction. The way to access this realm, where dream and reality were resolved into a 'super' reality, depended upon 'psychic automatism', the free play of the mind without the controlling intervention of reason or any moral or aesthetic considerations. Such ideas were applied politically in terms of 'freedom' and 'revolution'. To give rein to impulse, to fight psychological repression, was to free the individual from the dominant capitalist ideology which perpetuated itself as the only reality.

But the more we scrutinise the theory of Surrealism, the less substantial it appears. To their detriment, the Surrealists ignore Freud when they posit a dialectical opposition between dream and reality, and they ask for a leap of faith when they speak of psychic automatism. In Freudian terms the id is always modified by ego and superego, so that even if we concede that it is possible to raise images from the unconscious these are always going to be modified by the act of writing them down. The mental forces of repression at work are precisely those the Surrealists aimed to transcend, i.e. received ideas of morality and taboo. This, of course, points towards the major theoretical problems in the marriage of Surrealism and Communism. If the unconscious aspect of a Surrealist poem is inevitably modified and transformed by repressive bourgeois ideas of taboo and morality, how can it then express revolutionary ideas? One might also ask of Roughton, how irrational prejudices are to be 'broken-down' by another, different, but equally irrational procedure. And, furthermore, how are we to equate that point in the mind where antinomies cease to exist, with Marx's theory of dialectical materialism? How can an aesthetic bent upon transcending material reality express a Marxist materialist vision, or embody a materialist critique of capitalism? Lastly, and most obviously, Surrealism represents an extreme of individualism which clearly runs counter to the aims and aspirations of Marxism.

Such fundamental contradictions in the theory were often exposed in practice. At its worst Surrealist poetry tends towards a turgid stream of imagery graced with neither form nor thought. In Gascoyne's poems like 'And the seventh dream is the dream of Isis' or 'The diabolical principle', one encounters something of this; we find lists of images which resist any but the most empathic and intuitive interpretation. But in most of his poems Gascoyne, like Paul Eluard, retains some vestiges of narrative to impose a pattern upon his imagery, and thus steers away from the reefs of automatism.

'Rites of hysteria' and 'The cubical domes' are both poems which are dominated by a plethora of intense images; some entirely belonging to the curious world of dream association and Freudian symbology, others having a clearer relationship to the public world. By juxtaposing the private nightmares of the psyche with those of the public world of history, Gascoyne subtly suggests the relationship between the two. The poems communicate a vision of both the individual and a society that are crazed and unhealthy. They imply that a world full of political terrors and personal misfortune is bound to be perceived in terms of the absurd and irrational. In 'Rites of hysteria' the atmosphere of dementia informing the public and private worlds is quickly established:

In the midst of the flickering sonorous islands
The islands with liquid gullets full of mistletoe-suffering
Where untold truths are hidden in fibrous baskets
And the cold mist of decayed psychologies stifles the sun ...[20]

The opening lines introduce us to a resonant geography, suggesting not only the provenance of truth in the British Isles but also the self-deceiving of the individual ('no man is an island') who consigns truths to the waste basket. The stanza develops with images which validate the notion of 'decayed psychology', with the Freudian phallic arrow of desire being continually foiled. The poem unfolds further the 'rites of hysteria':

A cluster of insane massacres turns green upon the highroad
Green as the nadir of a mystery in the closet of a dream
And a wild growth of lascivious pamphlets became a beehive
The afternoon scrambles like an asylum out of its hovel ...

Lines like these, wherein the world of warfare and political activity is imaged with frightening intensity, seem to me Surrealist writing at its most effective. A dialectic is achieved between the internal psychic nightmare and the nightmare of political event. As well as being Surreal, it also implicitly explains Surrealism as the concomitant of prevailing political and cultural conditions. The world that Auden observes as a superior outsider – 'this England where nobody is well' – is given direct, emotive expression from within. This, of course, does not mean that such a poem can justifiably be said to be left-wing in its orientation. The powerful sense of inner and outer disintegration and the sense of the absurd are not necessarily politically helpful. They return us to the predicates of Freudian psychology, Eros and Thanatos, the basic human hungers, which have to be both accommodated and tamed in order for political progress to be made.

To be fair to Gascoyne, from as early as 1934, he was troubled by the relationship between Surrealism and Communism. In a question-naire published by Grigson in *New verse* Gascoyne answered queries about the influence of Freud on his work, and about his political beliefs. Here Gascoyne says that he has been influenced by Freud, 'indirectly . . . through the Surrealists', but goes on to remark that he no longer finds 'this navel gazing activity at all satisfying'. For a poet with increasing political convictions, he says, such activity 'must soon become impossible'. On the question of whether or not he took his stand with any political party or creed, Gascoyne responded un-equivocally: 'I have the strongest possible sympathy with left-wing revolutionary movements.'[21]

It is an irony of the literary-historical myth that Auden, Spender and MacNeice, supposedly the leading literary left-wingers of the 1930s, all refused to respond to the *New verse* questionnaire. Grigson perspi-caciously commented upon this circumstance, that 'the English Liberal Romantic dislikes the categorical prod of any question'.[22]

Gascoyne was less liberal and more Romantic than the Auden gang, and poems like 'Rites of hysteria' are plainly an attempt to give Surrealism some tangible political direction. But in consonance with his remarks in the questionnaire quoted above, there are other poems of the early 1930s which aspire to a clearer surface than 'Rites of hysteria'. In poems like 'Yves Tanguy' or 'Charity week' the develop-ment of Gascoyne's style from 1936 onwards is prefigured. Here, abstract nouns are introduced to support imagery rendered in highly emotive language:

Hysteria upon the staircase
Hair torn out by the roots
Lace handkerchiefs torn to shreds
And stained by tears of blood
Their fragments strewn upon the waters

These are the phenomena of zero ...[23]

These lines from 'Charity week' communicate Gascoyne's vision of a sick society, riven by the violence of misdirected desire. An immense pressure of feeling directs the utterance, amply distinguishing it from the Audenesque. There is nothing slick or self-consciously clever about this, and there is a telling absence of irony. It is in terms of 'feeling' that Gascoyne increasingly sought to define his work against that of other poets, as he progressed away from Communism and Surrealism towards a radical Christianity.

Gascoyne's sympathy with Communism did not last long. He joined the party in September 1936 under the pressure of the outbreak of the Spanish Civil War. But in the same breath as he records joining the party he also remarks sceptically upon the 'smugness in the use of the words C.P., Direct action etc'.[24] Nevertheless, a month later, with the help of £20 from his publishers, Gascoyne left for Spain to work in the propaganda Ministry. Gascoyne didn't stay long, and the reasons he gives in his journal for returning to England – that he needed to deliver a collection of Spanish war posters for an exhibition, and that he had a previous engagement to speak at Oxford University about Surrealism[25] – hardly convince one of passionate commitment to the cause. Indeed Gascoyne's disillusion with Communism can be traced to his experience in Spain. Despite his membership of the CP, he speaks of finding the anarchists 'very sympathetic'[26] and goes on to register the disunity of the so-called United Front. That the Communists 'hated the Anarchists and the P.O.U.M. much more than they hated the Fascists', was, he says, the beginning of his 'disillusionment with Communism'.[27]

Gascoyne increasingly came to believe that a 'spiritual revolution'[28] was required, rather than the revolution of the proletariat. As a corollary, he sought a poetry which could embody such a visionary possibility. This led him away from the bulk of his compatriots, and away from the London literary scene. Speaking of his attendance at a dinner-party given by Geoffrey Grigson early in 1937, Gascoyne remarks upon the 'horribly fatuous world' of the 'young poets and critics', and declares that he wants 'no more to do with it'.[29] If he was out of sympathy with the 'world' of Grigson and his contemporaries, it can hardly be expected that he would enjoy the poems which emanated from that world. Referring to Auden, Spender and MacNeice, Gascoyne writes that he admires Auden for the 'sincerity'of his 'best works', Spender because of his 'real passion', but MacNeice is rapped for 'slick technique', 'trivial imagery', and 'cultured whining'. Gascoyne continues:

Poetry is not verse, it is not rhetoric, it is not an epigrammatic way of saying something that can be stated in prose, nor is it argument or reportage. In England the whole question needs to be cleared up and restated. What I call poetry is not understood in England, but I believe it to be of far greater value than what is at present understood there. The tradition of modern English poetry is really something quite different from the tradition of Hölderlin, Rimbaud, Rilke, Lorca, Jouve. I belong to Europe before I belong to England.[30]

This makes clear Gascoyne's distaste for the English liberal tradition, and his enthusiasm for the vatic, visionary, European symbolist and post-symbolist tradition. This last is a tradition which willingly and unequivocally embraces High Romantic notions of the poet as seer and saint, and which glories in the superior loneliness of the poet, whose distance from the rest of society is necessary to the truth of his vision.

As the 1930s progressed Gascoyne increasingly saw himself in the role of prophet. In Paris between 1937 and 1939 he lived out the extremes of poverty and suffering, moving amidst the low-life, the drunks, prostitutes, vagrants and artists so admirably and movingly described in his poem 'Noctambules'.[31] He speaks of the compensation for this existence as a sense of belonging to 'a kind of spiritual aristocracy';[32] of being able to write poetry which is 'the product of a real contact with spiritual truth'.[33] He speaks of his conviction that 'we' must 'learn to think with our hearts and to feel with our minds'.[34] And he is bent upon persuading himself of his prophetic role. Back in London in 1939 he writes of sitting on a park bench and realising that he has 'definitely "been called", to be one of those who are to announce the true underlying event taking place during this century'.[35]

The poems Gascoyne wrote from 1936 onwards seek to enunciate spiritual 'truths', and to express clearly his feelings and vision. The best of his work combines an intensity of image and statement which convinces one of the impassioned depths from which he is writing. But, although we are aware of a magnificent oratorical resonance when Gascoyne calls upon the 'Christ of revolution and of poetry' to guide 'us' in our 'long journey through the night',[36] we nevertheless are obliged to recognise the distance between such a vision and any left-wing politics. Gascoyne in the mid-thirties turned away from politics to pursue his own spiritual adventure. And, though he turned back from the extremes of Surrealism, his style still pursued the heights and depths of individual experience:

It is the endless night, whose every star
Is in the spirit like the snow of dawn,
Whose meteors are the brilliance of summer,
And whose wind and rain
Are all the halcyon freshness of the valley rivers,
Where the swans,
White, white in the light of dream,
Still dip their heads.
Clear night!

He has no need of candles who can see
A longer, more celestial day than ours.[37]

It hardly needs to be remarked how far this is from the urbanities of
the liberal conservative tradition. In his journal Gascoyne writes that
it is 'not done' for a modern English poet to 'believe what he is saying;
it is understood that his fingers must permanently be crossed'.[38]
Gascoyne's fingers are not crossed. He means what he says. Manifestly
he turns away from society as he turns away from irony in order to
attempt a consolatory vision which would save him from the 'English
Death'. Auden et al. cleave to their class and to a society from which
Gascoyne in his life and work attempted to escape via his European
affiliations.

IV

Neither George Barker nor Dylan Thomas needed to look to Europe
to find a tradition of Romantic bardic poetry. For their Celtic
backgrounds of Ireland and Wales respectively provided cultural myths
which encouraged imaginative aspirations to escape from any urban
and suburban environs. Barker was brought up in London, the son of
an English father and Irish mother. In his poetic autobiography, 'The
true confession of George Barker' he speaks of being 'cast a little low
/ In the social register',[39] and recalls his childhood playing in 'the yard
of the tenement', whilst his father 'Trudged London for a job'. We also
here of his learning being, 'like the rent, in arrears…'[40] However much
this was true, he certainly left his formal education at a Chelsea
elementary school behind him at the age of fourteen to pursue a
miscellany of jobs which included designing wallpaper and working
as a garage mechanic. It was a highly impecunious life, not unlike
Gascoyne's in Paris, and Barker records being so poor that he was
'reduced to sleeping on Putney Common wrapped in newspapers'.[41]
Despite this raffish, cockney background, and Barker's involvement
with David Archer and the young poets and 'revolutionaries' of the
Parton Street bookshop, it was the Romanticism of Ireland which
informed his extravagant early poems. Barker's 'Poem on Ireland'
written in the later 1930s, charts his imaginative involvement with his
mother's birthplace. He was, he says, exiled from Ireland 'in the
womb', but still that country shapes his mind:

I can brush Lake Sligo when I take
The tear from my eye, or when I talk
Hear the foiled tongues of the streams
That cannot convert rocks to their water.[42]

But this is written in the clearer style which Barker developed in the later 1930s, and which reached its apotheosis in arguably his finest volumes, *Eros in dogma* (1944) and *The true confession of George Barker* (1950). His early style, though it shares the passion, the concern for imagination, and the self-orientation of the later work, is marred by contorted involutions, and, at its worst, a profound abstraction of both image and statement.

Unlike Gascoyne, Barker was not tempted towards political commitment, and only wrote poems with overtly political subject-matter towards the end of the decade under the pressure of public events. Barker's affiliation with Surrealism was also slight, and amounted to little more than an early enthusiasm for extravagant language and imagery. In response to the *New verse* questionnaire of 1934, Barker said that he 'did not' take his stand with any political party or belief, that he was 'extremely sceptical of Freud', and that he equated the 'use' of poetry with the 'process of spiritual unravelling'.[43] Although it is not until the poems of the later 1930s that Christianity becomes a central concern, this overt soul-searching is evident in Barker's first three volumes.[44] These books have attracted much justified criticism (and some from Barker himself) precisely because, though they seek to unravel, tend rather towards a labyrinthine ravelling. The use of dense alliteration and internal rhymes in badly 'sprung' rhythms indicate not only Barker's debt to Hopkins but also an enormous verbal exuberance which has not yet been properly harnessed. The following stanza from 'On first hearing Beethoven' typifies the problems in Barker's early work:

Whose absolute dumbness circumscribed by sound
Dumbfounds and profoundly confounds the boundary
Of my sense, I hear, in dense silence founded
By supernal sound, the immense harmonic like mountains
Intensely embedded in moon in agony bound and drowned.[45]

The insistent internal rhymes, coupled with impenetrable abstractions communicate Barker's striving to express intangible responses to Beethoven's music. There is a sense of straining to reach beyond the confines of language, and certainly to encounter areas of experience beyond the quotidian. The lack of interest in social and political issues is symptomatic of all Barker's early work. But it was not this, so much as the vagueness imparted by abstraction, which led Grigson to review Barker's second volume under the brutally simple headline, 'Nertz'.[46] There is some justification for this, but in my view it is far too dismissive. There certainly are too many poems written before 1937 which are self-indulgently involuted, and Barker's preoccupation with his emotional ambivalence towards women is somewhat tedious. But there are moments of focus and clarity in which Barker attains a sonorous grandeur:

Against the interminable grieving of the sea
I raise my voice, silence the miserable
Breakers, while upon my inward winter break
Messengers in the budding of these lines…[47]

The greater control apparent here is also to be found in Barker's work of the later 1930s. But his insistence upon the centrality of imaginative vision to poetry is always a constant even when political themes are broached. In an essay published in 1937, Barker speaks of the 'process of the poetic on the externally real' as one of 'intensification and exaggeration'. The 'whole poem', he says, may be described as 'a metaphor on reality'.[48] The transforming power of imagination is central to this poetic which has its origins in the writings of the High Romantics. And so it comes as no surprise to find in Barker's poems, written between 1937 and 1939, which articulate a visionary politics, continual reference to Blake, Wordsworth and Shelley.

All three of these writers are involved in Barker's long five-part poem 'Vision of England '38' which to my mind is one of his finest achievements of the decade. Here Barker adopts the Romantic commonplace of a dream-vision which allows the poet to register his sense of both the history and geography of England, whilst maintaining a sustained attack of the cash-nexus upon which all contemporary ills are blamed. The heritage of St George, William Langspee, King Arthur and Alfred is now in need of a Blakean revolution of the spirit in order to be redeemed. The poet in his dream encounters a lamb which speaks in the voice of Blake, telling the poet that England is not yet fit for 'the foot of Christ', and admonishing: 'How can your word or sword sleep / While the Thames is the sweat of the people?'

The division of England into two nations, the prosperous South and the ailing North, is personified by Barker in terms of a husband who deserts his wife. The metaphor ingeniously records the foundation of English wealth upon Northern industry, together with the abandonment of areas in the same region during the depression. Although the verse is feelingly dramatic, Barker's penchant for the vision splendid ensures that the poem never touches the reality of social conditions in the North:

> Not less strong than the indomitable rock,
> Not less lovely than the lake and the star,
> The wife of England roves in the North,
> Among the derelict cities and the memories of war ...[49]

The idealised vision of the wife of England in the last stanza is so abstract and elevated that the afflatus obscures the political point. Like Yeats, Barker has no time for passive suffering, and seeks, through the operation of imagination within the poem, to make such suffering heroic, and build upon the heroism a hope for spiritual revolution. In the closing stanzas of the poem, the means and direction of any such revolution are carefully obscured by a passionate rhetoric. A 'Political Prince' is invoked to 'cut the health and wealth of England loose'. The 'equitable stars' are called upon to 'hasten that liberation'. One can readily appreciate the passionate hope expressed in such a poem, but the 'metaphor on reality' is finally too transcendental to make the poem an effective, left-wing, statement.

'Elegy on Spain' follows a similar pattern, and makes an interesting comparison with Auden's poem about the Civil War. Whereas Auden's utterance is cool, analytic, Barker's is impassioned and rhetorical. Like Auden, however, Barker sees the conflict in Spain as one involving archetypal spiritual antagonisms. But the 'good' in Barker's poem is more clearly identified with the cause of the politically oppressed than it is in Auden's poem. Barker cites the Tolpuddle Martyrs, the Hungerford Hundred and the Easter Irish as antecedents of the Republicans' moral and spiritual struggle in Spain. But Barker can blithely speak of 'heroes' battling Satan, to 'level out' the 'crags of hate', and of friends 'shaking hands over the break of evil' without ever suggesting that all this might entail some struggle and pain. The 'reality' of the war is abandoned by the transforming imagination. Like the jingoistic poems written at the outbreak of the First World War, Barker's enthusiasm, albeit directed in a more palatable direction, tends retrospectively to sound not only callous but also facile:

So close a moment that long open eye,
Fly the flag low, and fold over those hands
Cramped to a gun: gather the child's remains
Staining the walls and cluttering the drains;
Troop down the red to the black and brown;
Go homeward with tears to water the ground.
All this builds a bigger plinth for glory,
Story on story, on which triumph shall be found.[50]

This has all the emotional appeal of a skilled public rhetorician. But the final lines are very telling: triumph is to be found in 'stories'. Barker implicitly elevates the pen at the expense of the sword, hoping like Shelley that the poet might be a 'legislator'; an idea which looks hopelessly forlorn when one considers the grim political history of our century. The 'triumph' of the final line has a horribly hollow ring placed as it is against the remains of the slaughtered child.

By 1939, Barker was understandably less ready to identify absolute good with the Republican cause in Spain. In a funeral eulogy for Lorca, Barker says that he would prefer to see the Spanish poet as a 'martyr who died because he had no cause', rather than regarding him as a hero who died for the Republic. Later, Barker qualifies this, making it clear that the cause Lorca died for was not that of political faction, but for 'the imagination militant after mystery'.[51] The 'antithesis of poetry', he says, is not science but warfare.

In another short essay of the same year Barker extends the notion of martyrdom to poetry and poets in general. The 'Theology of poetry', is described as 'following the process of dying', and poets are 'martyrs to a darkness... more formidable than fire'.[52] Barker then went out of the 1930s no less of a militant Romantic than he was in 1930. And by 1939 Christianity was openly dealt with in his sequence 'Holy poems' which prefigures the 'Sacred elegies' written in the early war years. His style was progressively refined through the 1930s, but his adherence to the conservative world of the 'spirit' and 'imagination' was undiminished. Barker wished to transcend the world of material reality, to escape society, and to avoid politics. The pursuit may be courageous, the product though is not always satisfactory.

V

Dylan Thomas's poems, despite much scholarly support, have never quite gained as secure a reputation as those of Auden. Although eleven of Thomas's poems appeared in *New verse*, Grigson was one of the first to raise the by now familiar cry that Thomas's poems had sound but little sense. That Thomas chose to publish poems in *Contemporary poetry and prose* may have encouraged the detractors to read his poems without even trying to make sense of them, since so much Surrealist work that appeared there was entirely impenetrable. However this may be, it is clear that Thomas had, and still does have, readers who find his style and manner antipathetic, and others for whom, in both his life and work, Thomas represents the 'type' of the bardic poet.

Constantine Fitzgibbon and Paul Ferris have written cogently of the nineteenth-century Welsh traditions into which Dylan Thomas was born.[53] Not only are these traditions those of non-conformist religion, the dark puritanical God whom Thomas reacted against, but also traditions of poetry wherein, as Fitzgibbon says, 'it was no odder for a cobbler to be a bard than it is today for an industrial worker to be a Trade Union leader'.[54] This second strand of his Welsh inheritance is clearly one that Thomas took very seriously. His idea of himself as 'Poet', and of what 'Poetry' constituted developed very early on and did not waver. They are ideas which by now are familiar as they were shared by Barker and Gascoyne. In a letter written at the age of nineteen Thomas writes:

I am in the path of Blake, but so far behind him that only the wings on his heels are in sight. I have been writing since I was a very little boy, and have always been struggling with the same things, with the idea of poetry as a thing entirely removed from such accomplishments as 'word painting', and the setting down of delicate but usual emotions in a few, well-chosen words. There must be no compromise …

Neuberg blabs of some unsectarian region in the clouds where poetry reaches its highest level. He ruins the truth of that by saying that the artist must, of necessity preach.

There is no necessity. He is a law unto himself … I do not want to express only what other people have felt; I want to rip something away and show what they have never seen.[55]

There was no compromise, either towards his readership or towards politics; Thomas pursued his goal of ripping away surfaces in an attempt to penetrate to what he saw as the truth of things. This procedure had as its corollary an attitude to language and to metaphor. Thomas emphasised over and over again in the course of the 1930s his dedication to the formal aspects of his art. In this way he distinguished himself from the Surrealists, and likened himself to the metaphysicals, and to the theorists of modernism, Pound and Eliot. He compared his craft to that of a sculptor; he insisted on his technique of letting images develop from each other in an endless dialectic. His aim was to be 'rid of the sophistication which is a disease';[56] to stretch, tear, and wrestle with language to disrupt ordinary usages, to get beyond the veneer of colloquial usage and plumb the depths of his own vision.

But his commitment to an elevated, self-oriented, vatic utterance was not merely something he straightforwardly inherited from his literary antecedents. His ambivalent attitude towards his provincial upbringing also played a part. Thomas was highly conscious of his own background describing himself as '"lower-middle-class" in attitude and reaction'.[57] But this does not necessarily imply a happy acceptance of his origins. Early on he was aware of the *ennui*, hypocrisy, and the false, snobbish norms of politeness which were endemic to his family life in Swansea. He was brought up in a semi-detached suburban villa, the son of D.J. Thomas, a master at the local grammar school. Both the poet's parents were descended from families who had eked out small livings upon the land, until industry and its trappings offered alternative employments. Dylan's grandfathers both worked on the railways. His parents were therefore acutely conscious of their new middle-class status, and of the need to keep up appearances.

Aged seven, Dylan was sent to a local 'dame school' which, was 'one of those private establishments that still cater for ambitious parents in the suburbs'.[58] In four years here, by all accounts, he learned very little, but somehow managed to gain a place at the local grammar school. It is likely that his father had to pay for this privilege, and certainly D.J. was less than pleased when Dylan left school at the age of sixteen with no tangible academic achievement to his credit. Like the other poets in this chapter, academe was not for Dylan. Ironically, his father had something to do with this, for it was at D.J.'s knee that Thomas first heard poetry read aloud, and it was his father's enthusiasms that informed Dylan's early reading. Furthermore it has been suggested that D.J. was himself a frustrated writer; Dylan was to fulfil his father's ambition, but at a cost that D.J. could hardly have predicted.

Dylan left school in July 1931 and worked during the next eighteen months for the local newspaper, the *South Wales daily post*. At the same time he was assiduously writing poems in the first of the four Notebooks which provide the basis for all his books published in the 1930s. As time went on, the only part of journalism that Thomas seems to have enjoyed were regular drinking sessions, and after about eighteen months he and the paper parted company by mutual agreement. From then on he lived a precarious life earning what he could from his poetry, and for the rest begging, borrowing and occasionally stealing.[59]

Between 1933 and 1937 he moved restlessly from Wales to London and back again, always uncertain and ambivalent as to which place he preferred. Significantly, Thomas wrote very little outside of Wales, as if he needed the security of the familiar in order to create. Certainly the period 1931-34, most of which was spent in Swansea, was the most creative period of his life. During these years he wrote 'all the poems in his first volume, *Eighteen Poems*, most of those in his second, *Twenty-Five Poems*, and, in embryonic form at least, a considerable number of his later ones'.[60] Nevertheless his view of Wales and the Welsh is hardly rosy. In his long self-revelatory letters to Pamela Hansford Johnson of 1933 and 1934, Thomas continually returns to the theme of his provincial Welsh upbringing :

... each town [is] a festering sore on the body of a dead country...

All Wales is like this. I have a friend who writes long and entirely unprintable verses beginning, 'What are you, Wales, but a tired old bitch?', and, 'Wales my country, Wales my cow'.

It is impossible to tell you how much I want to get out of it all, out of narrowness and dirtiness, out of the eternal ugliness of the Welsh people and all that belongs to them, out of the pettiness of a mother I don't care for and the giggling batch of relatives.[61]

When Thomas did 'escape' to London, however, just as when he later 'escaped' to America, he was lonely and homesick for Wales. It was an ambivalence he never reconciled, and one apparent in his writings. His poetry is a reaction against suburban provincialism, and attempts to develop a natural supernaturalism which Ralph Maud aptly describes as 'a personal religion of the organic processes'.[62] But in his prose, *Portrait of the artist as a young dog*, *A child's Christmas in Wales*, no less than his verse drama, *Under Milk Wood*, Thomas celebrates with great warmth the vigorous life of the 'never to be forgotten people of the dirty town' who 'had lived and loved and died and, always, lost'.[63]

It is not surprising, given such feeling for the people, that Thomas, despite his disavowal of any relationship between poetry and politics, should express an interest in revolutionary Communism in the 1930s. Again his early letters provide ample evidence of this; one goes so far as to suggest that if constitutional methods prove insufficient, then revolution by force is the only alternative.[64] This, of course, might be written-off as braggadocio, but his interest in Communism was, at least for a time, real. Answering Grigson's *New verse* questionnaire, Thomas, like Gascoyne, answered the enquiry about politics in the affirmative: 'I take my stand with any revolutionary body that asserts it to be the right of all men to share equally and impartially, every production of man from man, and from the sources of production at man's disposal, for only through such an essentially revolutionary body can there be a possibility of a communal art'.[65]

The revolution then, was to precede a communal art, and until such time as the revolution occurred, Thomas continued in his belief that difficulty was a sure sign of serious poetry. He was also quick to see through the veneer of 'intellectual Communists' whom he met in London:

I dislike all of them. Not so much as persons; ... but *as* revolutionaries and as communists, for born in fairly wealthy middle-class or upper-middle-class homes, educated at expensive prep-schools, public schools and universities, they have no idea at all of what they priggishly call the 'class struggle' and no contact at all with either any of the real motives or the real protagonists of that class struggle. They are bogus from skull to navel.[66]

This was written in 1935, and perhaps helps to explain why Thomas shows very little further interest in Communism for the rest of the decade. Certainly Thomas's view of upper-middle-class 'Communists' did not mellow as the decade progressed. Writing to Henry Treece in 1938, Thomas is no less acute than he is waspish about the development of the Audenesque:

Today the brotherhood of man – love thy neighbour and, if possible covet his arse – seems a disappointing school-society, and I cannot accept Auden as head prefect. I think MacNeice is thin and conventionally minded, lacking imagination, and not sound in the ear; flop Day Lewis; and Spender , Rupert Brooke of the depression, condemns his slight, lyrical, nostalgic talent to a clumsy rhetorical death. I find his communism unreal: before a poet can get into contact with society, he must surely be able to get into contact with himself, and Spender has only tickled his outside with a feather.[67]

It should be made clear that Thomas is hardly less acerbic about David Gascoyne and George Baker; the Welshman was an individualist. Nevertheless it is certainly no wonder that Spender and Day Lewis wished to consign him to 'another generation'.

Hostile critics, however, might be tempted to suggest that in Thomas's first volume, *Eighteen poems* (1934) the poet gets into contact with himself far too often. The images of onanism in 'I see the boys of summer in their ruin' do not help his case in this regard. But there is, I think, enough in this first book to justify some of Thomas's confidence in making dismissive remarks about Spender and Day Lewis. The themes established here were to be Thomas's perennial concerns; they are the great themes of individual human existence. As Maud says, the antithesis of faith and despair, the world of waking action as opposed to dream, and love as against sexual waste, 'can all be seen as part of a universal antithesis of growth v decay'.[68] The style has been developed from Thomas's diverse influences. Thus a Romantic language developed from Blake, Beddoes, Clare, Tennyson and D.H. Lawrence is utilised in a manner derived from the Elizabethans and Metaphysicals. Audacious images are juxtaposed and developed, sometimes with a density of texture that defies all but the most determined reader. Yet in the finest poems like 'Before I knocked', 'Our eunuch dreams', and 'The force that through the green fuse', Thomas achieves a fine lucidity which does not preclude the expression of complex ideas.

'Before I knocked' imagines the Christ child, already suffering the woes of the world in the mother's womb preceding birth. Since it is written in the first person, the poem also makes the by now familiar identification of the poet with the spiritual martyr. The poem concludes with the birth and death of the Christ/poet:

And time cast forth my mortal creature
To drift or drown upon the seas
Acquainted with the salt adventure
Of tides that never touch the shores.
I who was rich was made the richer
By sipping at the vine of days.

I, born of flesh and ghost, was neither
A ghost nor man, but mortal ghost.
And I was struck down by death's feather
I was mortal to the last
Long breath that carried to my father

The message of his dying Christ.

You who bow down at cross and altar,
Remember me and pity Him
Who took my flesh and bone for armour
And doublecrossed my mother's womb.[69]

Here there is magnificent sound and sense. The first stanza quoted demonstrates Thomas's impulse towards a celebration and rejoicing in the paradoxes of mortality; the concluding stanzas constitute a balancing lamentation, in which one may perceive not only a rejection of conventional Christian teaching but also something of Thomas's complex psychological relationship with his father which engendered the great 'Do not go gentle' as well as the final, unfinished 'Elegy'. The sense of being abandoned by the father, yet pitying him because he is mistaken in trying to make the son a protection from mortality, is powerfully communicated. The sense too that the mother is twice cheated, by both father and son, may also be read on the level of psychological confession as well as an inversion of Christianity.

But, however far 'Before I knocked' moves from accepted Christian theology, its religiosity cannot be doubted. In a letter of 1933, Thomas wrote, 'God is the country of the spirit, and each of us is given a little holding of ground in that country, it is our duty to explore that holding'.[70] When he compiled his Collected poems in 1952, he said in the preface that his poems were written, 'for the love of Man and in praise of God'.[71] His sense of a pervading creative energy in the world, which united all organic nature, was very strong, and nowhere does he more resonantly express this than in the justly famous 'The force that through the green fuse', from Eighteen poems.

This poem, typically, deals in antithesis and paradox. The poet's closeness to nature is juxtaposed with his inevitable isolation from it. Though the same force is perceived to dictate the growth and decay of all created nature, including the poet, the force is ultimately seen to be mysterious. Thomas seeks to resolve these contradictions, and an apparent tranquility is registered in the fourth and last full quatrain where time is associated with the fountain-head or God. Love emanates from this source and Christ's fallen 'blood' offers a salvation from the pain of temporal existence. A faith in heaven is proclaimed and synthesis is achieved through the acceptance of paradox: time is the destroyer and healer; the instrument of God. But it is not unusual for Thomas to remain uncertain of his conclusion. And the poem ends with two further lines which express a poised ambivalence: 'And I am dumb to tell the lover's tomb / How at my sheet goes the same crooked worm.'[72] A sense of loss for the dead with whom we cannot communicate, and an intimation of hope that since we share the same end we may share the same after life, is encapsulated succinctly.

None of the poems in Thomas's first volume broach social issues. And his second book is also dominated by what Maud has called 'process' poems; work which, like 'The force that through the green fuse', seeks to articulate Thomas's sense of the organic connections between mind and body, between human nature and the rest of creation. There are, however, in his second volume, Twenty-five poems (1936), two poems which look outwards to the immediate public world of action and event, and thus prefigure his great poems of the war years dealing with the London Blitz. But it should not be supposed that this circumstance had anything to do with the worsening international situation of 1935-6. For many of the poems in the volume, and certainly the two in question, were begun in 1933 and predate much of the material in Eighteen poems. Nevertheless, both 'I have longed to move away', and 'The hand that signed the paper' are poems in which revolution, Fascism and war are very much part of the poet's consciousness. Thomas looks at various aspects of the contemporary political situation in their widest possible context.

'I have longed to move away' is a poem which obliquely expresses both a fear of the status quo and a fear of change. Although the poet expresses a desire to 'move away' from the 'hissing of the spent lie' and of 'the old terrors' continual cry', he is 'afraid' that

Some life, yet unspent, might explode
Out of the old lie burning on the ground,
And, crackling into the air, leave me half-blind.[73]

Thomas does not want to 'fall to death's feather' through the agency of 'convention and lies'. The poem may be viewed as expressing a conflict between conservatism and revolutionary change. Thomas's attitude is typically ambivalent and paradoxical. And, as Maud says, there are more than political issues at stake here; the 'conventions and lies' may also be related to the class values, aspirations and pretensions of Thomas's parents, which Dylan had to fight against all his life.[74]

'I have longed to move away', though its central idea is interesting, has some unusually loose and vague lines which strike one as padding. But 'The hand that signed the paper' is more successful, developing a central metaphor which explores the awful damage and suffering the hand of a politically powerful individual can incur. The poem is a lament for the loss of pity, and demonstrates implicitly the distance between the sources of power in a state, and the consequences which follow from that power's decisions. At the close of the poem Thomas widens his perspective to include the metaphysical:

The five kings count the dead but do not soften
The crusted wound nor stroke the brow;
A hand rules pity as a hand rules heaven;
Hands have no tears to flow.[75]

The 'five kings' are the fingers of the hand, which sign the papers which in turn cause 'murder', 'famine' and fallen 'cities'. Such dictatorial power is then equated with the notion of a dictatorial God, who has the potential for pity but chooses not to exercise it. The poem thus moves back to the weeping human being as the source of pity; a pity which, as Thomas realises, is defenceless and useless, unless it has some relationship to the 'hands' of action and power.

The themes of death and power encountered in this poem are those which Thomas was further drawn to in his war time poems. Given his interests and poetic development in the 1930s, it is not surprising that Thomas could build great poems out of the war years. Concerned already with the warring antinomies of decay and generation, death and sex; the war, as it were, was a living symbol of the reality of his major concerns. Already in his second volume where we also find his magnificent 'And Death shall have no dominion' there is a movement towards the lyrical lucidity of his later and finest utterances, 'Fern Hill', 'Poem in October', 'The refusal to mourn' and 'Do not go gentle'.

In 1951, answering a student's queries, Thomas wrote of 'treating words as a craftsman does his wood', of hewing, carving, and polishing words into 'patterns, sequences, sculptures' which express 'some spiritual doubt or conviction, some dimly realised truth'.[76] There was 'no compromise' in Thomas's pursuit of these ends during the 1930s. Even after his marriage to Caitlin MacNamara in 1937, Thomas like Gascoyne and Barker, lived the life of the anti-bourgeois Bohemian, whilst often craving for precisely those middle-class securities which his upbringing had taught him to appreciate. But the latter values sit uneasily with poetry, and it was his commitment to his art that meant that he and his family were poor often to the point of destitution. He spent the rest of the decade in typically peripatetic fashion moving between Cornwall, his mother-in-law's house in Hampshire, and Wales. He worked sporadically on poetry, but his early facility had deserted him never to return. His last volume of the 1930s, The map of love, contained short stories and sixteen poems, most of which were 'process' poems and which had had their beginnings in the notebooks written between 1930 and 1933. Between the publication of Twenty-five poems in 1936 and The map of love, he only completed five new poems, and it was left to his experiences in London during the war to inspire a further energising of his talent.

Kathleen Raine writes approvingly of David Gascoyne that there is nothing remotely suburban in the kind and quality of his imagination. This is true of all the poets in this chapter. All of them sought a language of imaginative vision, a language which breaks the bounds of convention both literary and vernacular. They were more radical than the poets of the upper-middle class, but despite some sympathy with working-class movements, the direction of their radicalism may be legitimately questioned. For in turning away from politics and the life of the people to the realms of the imaginative and transcendental they implicitly allied themselves with a spiritual aristocracy antipathetic to Marxism. Like Roger Roughton, like the Surrealists, Gascoyne, Barker and Thomas did not forge a radical left-wing poetry or poetics.

Notes

1 P. C. Ray, The Surrealist movement in England, New York, 1971.
2 A.T. Tolley, The poetry of the thirties, London, 1975, p. 227.
3 R. Roughton, Contemporary poetry and prose, No. 8, Dec. 1936, p. 143.
4 C. Werner, 'Contemporary poetry and prose', British literary magazines, vol. IV, the modern age, New York, p. 87.
5 R. Roughton, Contemporary poetry and prose, Nos. 4-5, Aug.-Sept. 1936, p. 74.
6 R. Roughton, Contemporary poetry and prose, No. 6, Oct. 1936, p. 106.
7 'Declaration on Spain', Contemporary poetry and prose, No. 7, Nov. 1936, between pp. 130-1.
8 R. Roughton, Contemporary poetry and prose, No. 7, Nov. 1936, pp. 136-8.
9 Werner, British literary magazines, vol. IV, p. 89.
10 R. Roughton, Contemporary poetry and prose, No. 7, Nov. 1936, p. 138.
11 P.N. Siegel, ed., Leon Trotsky on literature and art, New York, 1970, pp. 115-21.
12 C. Day Lewis, A hope for poetry (1934), revd. ed., Oxford, 1936, p. 79.
13 P. Gardner, 'David Gascoyne', Dictionary of literary biography, vol. 20, ed. D.E. Stanford, Detroit, 1983, pp. 140-2.
14 D. Gascoyne, Paris journal 1937-1939, London, 1978, pp. 13, 27, 39, 44.
15 Gardner, Dictionary of literary biography, p. 142.
16 D. Gascoyne, A short survey of Surrealism, London, 1935.
17 André Breton, What is Surrealism, trans. D. Gascoyne, London, 1936.

18 Gascoyne, *Paris journal, 1937-1939*, pp. 30-1.
19 Ibid., p. 63.
20 D. Gascoyne, *Collected poems*, London, 1988, p. 56.
21 D. Gascoyne, *New verse*, No. 11, Oct. 1934, p. 12.
22 G. Grigson, *New verse*, No. 11, Oct. 1934, p. 2.
23. Gascoyne, *Collected poems*, p. 45.
24 D. Gascoyne, *Journal 1936-7*, London, 1980, p. 24.
25 Ibid., pp. 48-9.
26 Ibid., p. 45.
27 Ibid.
28 Gascoyne, *Paris journal, 1937-1939*, p. 124.
29 Gascoyne, *Journal 1936-7*, p. 56.
30 Gascoyne, *Paris journal, 1937-1939*, p. 55.
31 Gascoyne, *Collected poems*, pp. 118-21.
32 Gascoyne, *Paris journal, 1937-1939*, p. 120.
33 Ibid., pp. 120-1.
34 Ibid., p. 136.
35 Ibid., p. 124.
36 Gascoyne, *Collected poems*, p. 94.
37 Ibid., p. 76.
38 Gascoyne, *Paris journal, 1937-1939*, p. 126.
39 G. Barker, *Collected poems*, ed. Robert Fraser, London, 1987, p. 175.
40 Ibid., p. 181.
41 Barker is quoted by Jo Marie Gulledge, 'G. Barker', *Dictionary of literary biography*, vol. 20, ed. D.E. Stanford, Detroit, 1983, p. 52.
42 Barker, *Collected poems*, p. 112.
43 G. Barker, *New Verse*, No. 11, Oct. 1934, p. 22.
44 G. Barker, *Thirty preliminary poems*, London, 1933; *Poems*, London, 1935; *Calamiterror*, London, 1937.
45 Barker, *Thirty preliminary poems*, p. 37.
46 G. Grigson, 'Nertz', *New Verse*, No. 15, June 1935, pp. 17-18.
47 Barker, *Collected poems*, pp. 20-1.
48 G. Barker, 'Poetry and reality', *Essays*, London, 1970, pp. 80-1.
49 Barker, *Collected poems*, pp. 65-75.
50 Ibid., pp. 114-19.
51 G. Barker, 'Funeral eulogy on Garcia Lorca', *Essays*, p. 43.
52. G. Barker, 'Therefore all poems are elegies', *Essays*, London, pp. 64-6.
53 C. Fitzgibbon, *The life of Dylan Thomas* (1965), London, 1968, pp. 9-27, and P. Ferris, *Dylan Thomas* (1977), Harmondsworth, 1978, pp. 1-39.
54 Fitzgibbon, *The life of Dylan Thomas*, p. 15.
55 Letter of Dylan Thomas to Pamela Hansford Johnson, 15 Oct. 1933, *The collected letters of Dylan Thomas*, ed. P. Ferris, London, 1985, p. 25.
56 Letter of Dylan Thomas to Pamela Hansford Johnson, 25 Dec. 1933, *The collected letters*, pp. 81-2.
57 Letter of Dylan Thomas to Henry Treece, 16 June 1938, *The collected letters*, p. 304.
58 Ferris, *Dylan Thomas*, p. 35.
59 Ibid., pp. 44-5, 73-4, 86-7.
60 Fitzgibbon, *The life of Dylan Thomas*, p. 68.
61 Letter of Dylan Thomas to Pamela Hansford Johnson, Oct. 1933, *The collected letters*, p. 30.
62 R. Maud, *Poet in the making: the notebooks of Dylan Thomas*, London, 1968, p. 25.
63 D. Thomas, *Portrait of the artist as a young dog* (1940), London, 1964, p. 254.
64 Letter of Dylan Thomas to Pamela Hansford Johnson, 20 July 1934, *The collected letters*, pp. 159-60.

65 D. Thomas, *New verse*, No. 11, Oct. 1934, p. 9.
66 Letter of Dylan Thomas to A.E. Trick, Feb. 1935, *The collected letters*, p. 185.
67 Letter of Dylan Thomas to Henry Treece, 23 March 1938, *The collected letters*, pp. 280-1. See also pp. 299-300.
68 Maud, *Poet in the making*, p. 33.
69 D. Thomas, *Collected poems*, 1934-1952, London, 1952, p. 7.
70 Letter of Dylan Thomas to Pamela Hansford Johnson, Jan. 1934, *The collected letters*, p. 86.
71 D. Thomas, Author's Note to *Collected poems, 1934-1952*, p. vii.
72 Thomas, *Collected poems, 1934-1952*, p. 8.
73. *Ibid.*, p. 58.
74 Maud, *Poet in the making*, p. 23.
75 Thomas, *Collected poems*, p. 56.
76 Quoted by Fitzgibbon, *The life of Dylan Thomas*, p. 336.

9

The left

I

It will by now be clear that in my view English poetry and poetics of the 1930s were not dominated by Auden, the Audenesque, or by an interest in left-wing politics. In the political and aesthetic ideologies of the poets we have considered so far, nowhere have we encountered any sustained attempt to develop a Marxist poetic or a Marxist poetry. So now we may legitimately enquire: where was the literary left in England in the 1930s, and what was it doing? In attempting to answer these questions we must discuss work which the literary-historical myth of the decade either erases or subsumes in order to perpetuate its privileging of the liberal conservative ideology that it represents. Looking leftwards, it will become apparent that voices were raised against the burgeoning mythology during the 1930s, but these voices have been drowned by liberal literary historians. I begin with a discussion of the magazines *Left review* and *Poetry and the people*, before looking at the poetry of Jack Lindsay and Hugh MacDiarmid.

Left review was not primarily a poetry magazine. For most of its publication span one or two poems were printed in each issue, and these are of interest, but of more importance were its critical perspectives, and its concern to foster working-class writing. The magazine had its beginnings in a 'room over a pub in Fitzrovia' where a meeting took place to form a group of revolutionary writers. Amongst those present were Hugh MacDiarmid, Bert Lloyd, Ralph Fox, Edgell Rickword, Tom Wintringham and Amabel Williams-Ellis.[1] From this meeting held in 1934, a magazine emerged entitled *Viewpoint*, which later became transmogrified into *Left review*, the paper of the British section of the Writer's International. The magazine was a monthly costing sixpence, and was initially edited by Montagu Slater assisted by Tom Wintringham and Amabel Williams-Ellis who 'handled correspondence with aspiring proletarian writers'.[2] From January 1936 to June 1937 Edgell Rickword took over the editorship, giving way to Randall Swingler, who presided over the magazine's decline and eventual demise in May 1938.

In the opening number of the magazine a statement was published declaring the position and aims of Left review. The statement speaks of a 'Crisis in Capitalism', and relates the 'decadence of the past twenty years of English Literature and the theatre' to political and economic developments between 1913 and 1934. The 'collapse of a culture' is said to be a corollary of 'the collapse of an economic system'. The statement goes on to further advertise the association of revolutionary writers who are 'working for the ending of the capitalist order of society', and aiming 'at a new order based not on property and profit but on co-operative effort'. The statement concludes by calling for membership from writers who are anti-Fascist, pro-Soviet, and, who, if they are members of the working class, wish to express the struggles of that class in their work.[3]

Speaking retrospectively about what the originators of Left review meant by revolutionary writing, Edgell Rickword equates such writing with working-class life: 'I think it was literature that expressed and reflected the actual struggle of the down-trodden, as it were, or could convey by realistic treatment, reportage, their actual conditions of work and communicate their humanity and the plight of their position in a flourishing society – you know, a society that was bilious with riches at the top'.[4] This concern for, and encouragement of, working-class writing, together with the pro-Soviet, openly Marxist position of many of the contributors, has led to the magazine's being treated dismissively by liberal and conservative literary historians. The most common complaint is that Left review had a 'party-line', and that this prevented the editors from printing writing of any 'literary-value'. Thus Julian Symons argues that the conscious party line of the magazine made its contributors write 'uncommonly badly',[5] whilst Tolley declares that as a source of literature and 'poetry to be read for its own worth it [Left review] has little to offer'.[6] Hynes' only speaks of Left review when MacSpaunday are under discussion, and then it is to denigrate 'ideologues', and to assert that the ideological censorship in force in Russia was approved by writers in Left review.[7]

An inadvertent irony emerges from all of this. If Left review was so narrow, and toed such a party line, why were authors like Day Lewis, Spender and Auden published there at all? Either they too must be ideologues, or the editors were not. It is my contention that under the guidance of Slater and Rickword, Left review was not narrowly doctrinaire in its approach, and that it published criticism, reportage and poetry of an extremely diverse kind.

It is true that most contributors were pro-Soviet, and most, but not all, were of the persuasion that 'all art is propaganda', but this by no means precluded the publication of a wide range of opinion as to what and how left-wing writers should be writing. Slater ran a column called 'Controversy' which was a successful attempt to encourage debate about the relationship of art to politics, and such debate was by no means always polite. Much of the 'Controversy' in the opening issues of the magazine centred upon what kind of language should be utilised in art committed to the working-class cause. As David Margolies remarks in a useful essay, Alec Brown contributed 'some classically crude judgements' to this argument.[8] Brown argued that literary English was 'an artificial jargon of the ruling class', and called for the 'proletarianization' of language. Hugh MacDiarmid's response to this was swift and sure. He stated unequivocally that Brown was wrong, and continued: 'The literature of the future cannot be "thirled" to limitations that have had their roots in lack of educational opportunity and other methods of mass mutilation'.[9] MacDiarmid, in keeping with his Scottish Nationalism, went on to slap Brown for speaking of 'English this and English that', and to denigrate Simon Blumenfeld's 'quite irrelevant remarks' about the English language being spoken by hundreds of millions of people. MacDiarmid concludes that proletarian culture, like any culture, depends upon quality not quantity, and that there is no evidence to suggest that better work will be done in English rather than any other language just because millions speak it.

Slater's editorial stance also encouraged the notion of quality writing. In issue nine of the magazine, Slater wrote an essay entitled 'The purpose of a Left review' which was a response to a conference of Left review contributors. Here Slater defends himself against the charge that the magazine had 'no clear line'. Amongst other things he says that he imagines most of his readers accept that 'literature is propaganda', but he questions whether it is emphasised often enough 'that the most lasting and persuasive propaganda is literature'.[10] Slater also calls for 'theoretical advance' as one of the 'conditions of literary advance'. He supports 'reportage' as a 'scientific and literary discipline of some value'. He also speaks of a change which is beginning to be noticed in many writers who 'are very far from being revolutionary', yet who have appeared and 'must continue to appear' in Left review.[11]

Edgell Rickword's editorship continued along the same lines with some widening of the magazine's ambit through the inclusion of more international writings than Slater had approved. Rickword recognised the need for literary theory, for debate, and for the inclusion of unrevolutionary writing, and his concern for 'quality' is implicit in his choosing to print poems by Mayakovsky, Neruda, Lorca, Malraux and Brecht.

David Margolies has provided an excellent account of the literary theory which appeared in Left review written by authors such as Alick West, Ralph Fox, David Garman and Rickword himself.[12] Since much of this did not deal strictly with poetics there is little need to reiterate Margolies's summary here. As he says, the work done in Left review, though necessarily limited in its scope by the short essay form, provided a basis for the more developed ideas in the books of Ralph Fox, Christopher Caudwell and Alick West.[13] I would only wish to add that in my view Rickword's essays in cultural criticism, his re-assessment of major authors like Spencer, Swift, Blake, Dickens and Hopkins, and his reviews of contemporary writers, were an outstanding achievement prefiguring as they do, the early work of Raymond Williams. Rickword acutely read authors in terms of their relationship to a Marxist notion of history. He also understood the class basis of literary production: 'What bourgeois education teaches us to call the best art is, I am prepared to agree, what has proved the most successful propaganda at some date in history; and the most successful propaganda is, naturally, that which exemplifies or deoderizes the ideology of the ruling class...'[14]

Despite this acute perception, Rickword actively encouraged writers like Stephen Spender and C. Day Lewis to contribute to Left review. Clearly in his editorial capacity Rickword did not believe in a 'party line', but wished to encourage a United Front against Fascism. He may also have thought that the inclusion of such writers, who had been given so much publicity in bourgeois periodicals, would not only boost sales of Left review, but also provide an example of just how many bourgeois writers were 'coming over' to adopt 'left-wing' positions. However this may be, the consequence of Rickword's decision is that the poetics advanced in Left review tend, for the most part, to have a very liberal colouring. For as we have seen in an earlier chapter, the writings of Spender and Day Lewis about poetry and politics have their basis in nineteenth-century Romanticism.

But this does not mean that Left review remained wholly uncritical of the Audenesque. Only one poem by Auden, and one by Day Lewis, appeared in its pages; MacNeice and Spender contributed none of their verse. Furthermore, reviews of Audenesque work in Left review provided a salutary critique of the myth that Auden et al. were committed to the left. Rickword himself, reviewing Spender's The Destructive Element, notes the failure of the author to progress beyond 'a well intentioned liberalism'. He also perspicaciously diagnoses Spender's difficulties with respect to class: 'In our own society, the most usual stage for the intellectual to be in is one of hesitating to recognise the class-struggle; and the more nakedly and brutally this declares itself the more elaborate are the unconscious defences woven against this recognition. And it is particularly hard for the middle-class intellectual to recognise it, as Spender demonstrates again and again, with disarming ingenuousness, in this book.[15] Rickword concludes the review benignly asserting that if Spender cared to study Communism a little more, then there would be 'nothing to prevent his present inhibitions being broken down'.

Rickword is no less astute in his response to Day Lewis's Noah and the waters; Noah's compromised position is tellingly analysed, as is Day Lewis' implicit insistence upon Romantic notions of poetic vision. Rickword argues that the latter 'confines the poem to being one more statement of the inability of the Capitalist system any longer to use its poets productively, and prevents it [Noah and the waters] being a revolutionary poem'.[16]

Rickword was not the only critic to penetrate the leftist veneer of Auden's mode. In a review, entitled 'The fog beneath the skin', which looked at Auden's and Isherwood's play, The dog beneath the skin, as well as at Day Lewis's Collected poems 1929-33 and his A time to dance, Montague Slater notes that both writers are 'poets of an indeterminancy principle'. The 'muddles' of Day Lewis's criticism are noted, and also perceived to infiltrate his poetry. Auden is criticised because he substitutes 'tabloid headlines' for a sense of history, and both poets are attacked for writing principally for their friends.[17]

Such criticism is cogent, and clearly does not conform to the climate of myth-making praise created by more liberal commentators both then and since. But still there remained for the editors of Left review the difficult task of finding poems suitable for publication in their paper. Hugh MacDiarmid and Jack Lindsay made distinguished contributions, but apart from these, undoubtedly the finest poems came from the international poets mentioned earlier, whose talent was honed in political situations more extreme than most of their English counterparts had experienced. It is lack of such experience, together with lack of tact, which makes much English middle-class Agitprop poetry sound crude and naive like Day Lewis' *The magnetic mountain*. Nevertheless the editors sometimes succumbed and printed such stuff, together with work from writers like John Pudney and George Barker, which at best could only be described in terms of bourgeois anarchism.

But there were some few poems printed in *Left review* which were genuine attempts to break from the bourgeois Romantic traditions of English poetry, and are important for that reason. The manifest difficulties of this pursuit, together with the limited educational opportunities available to the working class, made sure that comparitively few working-class poets emerged in the 1930s. The bulk of the decade's distinguished working-class writing is in the form of the novel or of reportage. But still *Left review* found, in poems by Idris Davies and Earnest English, courageous articulations of working-class experience. Earnest English was a technician at an aero engine works. His poem 'Security' appeared in the fourth number of *Left review*. Here English explores the ironies of his situation as part of a team busy manufacturing war-planes. The extra work means financial 'security', and the opening of the poem describes a couple planning to buy consumer goods, including a motorcycle, 'On the never o' course'. In the final two stanzas, however, the poet twists the notion of hire-purchase and applies it to the government's investment in war machines. An aircraft engine is described, its 'entrails of steel and light alloy / Machined to one ten-thousandth of an inch'. The 'plane' is also fitted with armaments:

And gun gear cunningly disposed
To synchronise with the beat of the pistons
To fire twin machine guns through the propellor's web.
But in the Alcema's nights of sweating self-contempt
I know that all this is on the never.
This is the quid down. The rest is to come.[18]

The poet's financial security is predicated upon international insecurity. The joy of a new motorcycle is dispersed through the ironic contrast with man's capacity to create hugely destructive machinery. And the telling portent of the final lines is informed with the worker's sense of guilt in his compromised position. As English wrote in a note to the poem: 'The issue is, of course, prostitution or starvation'.[19]

English uses a free verse form which juxtaposes highly colloquial language with technical and self-consciously literary registers. His rhythms are clearly an attempt to register the speaking voice regardless of literary conventions. Idris Davies also employs a variety of metric and syntactic configurations to break from the conventions of polite verse and convey his vision of working-class life in the coal mines.[20] The magazine, then, though it was not principally devoted to poetry, served as a forum for debate about literature and politics, and gave space to writers like English and Davies, who would have found it difficult, if not impossible, to find a place in the bourgeois periodicals of the decade.

It is true, however, that in the closing months of its life, under financial pressure, and in an increasingly threatening political situation, *Left review* came more and more to be dominated by the Communist Party and its line. Under Swingler's editorship there is less literary interest and more of the 'simplistic, sentimental Russophilia' of which Bernard Bergonzi has complained.[21] But this should not blind us to the real achievements of the magazine. As Rickword retrospectively says of why the *Review* deserves to be remembered: 'I think on its literary side it demonstrated that there could be a fruitful relationship between literature and politics, which in academic and conventional circles at that time were consciously kept separate: The *Review*, as consciously regarded them as inseparable ... Of course we weren't always successful in what we set out to do...'[22] That the editors of the magazine were bourgeois in their origins is invariably noticed by liberal commentators intent upon denigrating the magazine. Slater was born in 1902, the son of a North-country tailor. He belonged then to either the upper-working class or the lower-middle class, and won a scholarship to Oxford from his local secondary school. Rickword was somewhat older, being born in 1898. He attended a local grammar school in Colchester, and, having served in the First World War, he too went to Oxford but only stayed for four terms. He was not of the upper-middle class. Randall Swingler, born in 1909, was the only one of the editors who came from the ruling class. He was educated at Winchester and Oxford, although he too left the university without completing a degree. Slater may have joined the Communist Party as early as 1928, but it is certain that he was a member by 1930 and remained so for the rest of his life. Rickword joined the party in 1934, because it was the only party 'that was actually doing something' about Fascism.[23] He remained in the party for a considerable period of time. Swingler joined the CP in the same year as Rickword and did not leave it until 1952. Their commitment, then, was not of the 'emotional, sloppy' kind that characterised so much interest in radical politics during the decade.[24] It was not negative identification with the working class that led them to Communism, but a hard-headed intellectual conviction that outlasted mere fashion. Here were members of both the lower- and upper-middle classes who genuinely resisted their inheritance in order to pledge themselves to a revolutionary cause. Part of the cost of that commitment, however, may have been the sacrifice of their respective talents as poets.

All three wrote poetry in the 1930s, but little suggested that any of them had forged a style that convincingly wedded their aesthetic and political concerns. Rickword's satire 'To the wife of a non-interventionist statesman' makes its point well, but only through reversion to an Augustan form with all its Tory aristocratic heredity. This was virtually the last poem he published. Slater and Swingler were more prolific, but hardly more successful. Both of them wrote personal, metaphysical poems crabbed by abstraction and by attempts to break from traditional metrics. Both also assayed the ballad, but here narrative energy, vital to the effective use of that form, was too often surrendered to abstract exhortation. Although no one could doubt the sincerity of their political conviction, none of these writers successfully allied their beliefs to their poetry. It is as if the English poetic tradition was too strong to enable them successfully to forge new forms appropriate to the expression of left-wing sentiments.[25]

However, *Left review*, and the chance it gave to working-class writers, remains a fitting tribute to the commitment of Slater, Rickword and Swingler. In the 1930s the magazine is said to have had the second highest circulation of any literary periodical.[26]

II

Although *Left review* has been caricatured by conservative and liberal literary historians as the purveyor of single- and narrow-minded propaganda, at least it has been found worthy of mention. This is not true of *Poetry and the people*, a little magazine which first appeared in July 1938, and which has been paid scant attention in major studies of the period.

Poetry and the people began as an offshoot of the Left Book Club.[27] Unlike all of the other magazines I have dealt with, this one, in keeping with the democratic and proletarian implications of its title, was not at first professionally printed but consisted of cyclostyled sheets stapled between orange soft-card covers with black lettering. Little is known of its first editor, Philip Ongley, who, in a nicely Trade Union manner, styled himself the 'convener' of the paper. It is not, however, difficult to discern the aspirations of the magazine:

The Poetry and the people movement has a place together with Dramatics and Singing, in providing the entire Labour Movement with a vigorous cultural life … we can say that our organisation has three principle aims:
(1) To stimulate and encourage the poet to write out of his experience, to reflect the life and feelings of his fellow men.
(2) To arouse an interest in such poetry among the people.
(3) To bring the poet and the people into as close a contact as possible for their mutual understanding and enjoyment.[28]

These were broad and generous ambitions for a small magazine, but apparently a positive response to them was entirely forthcoming. As an adjunct to the magazine, and in pursuance of its aims, poetry groups were established on a regional basis throughout the British Isles. By January 1940 there were twenty-five such groups scattered through the length and breadth of the country.[29] The magazine advertised the various groups, and acted as a common denominator between them. And, although the ethos of the magazine and the poetry groups was left-wing, it was not narrowly doctrinaire. In issue seven of the magazine, encouraging the establishment of more poetry groups, Ongley wrote that anyone was welcome to join, '. . . whatever their political opinions, or lack thereof, they can be united on the basis of a desire to revive the tradition of poetry'.[30]

As we might guess from his references to 'Dramatics and Singing' in the editorial quoted above, what Ongley meant by 'the tradition' of poetry was the folk tradition. In the opening numbers of the magazine articles were published by two Australians, Jack Lindsay and John Manifold, which extolled the ballad tradition. These writers were particularly well-placed to mount such arguments, since the burgeoning of a distinctively Australian literary tradition had close connections with the early songs of the convicts and pioneers. Manifold notes this circumstance in his essay on Australian poetry, as he traces his own poetic practice to a cross-fertilisation of the folk tradition with the 'colonial' writings of Leconte de Lisle. He carefully defines his position in contradistinction to the bourgeoisie who, he says, do not consider the ballads to be 'entirely respectable': such poems are never mentioned in literature lessons of expensive schools, and there are no courses in Australian literature at the universities. The 'immense public' for the ballads comes from the 'agricultural proletariat and the smaller bourgeoisie who have the nerve not to be ashamed of being "colonials"'.[31] This is developed further into an argument about the necessity for regionalism, which must have been music to the ears not only of northern working-class writers, but also to those in Wales and Scotland who were busy launching their own nationalist magazines at this time.[32]

Some of the contributors, however, found the exigencies of the ballad form uncongenial, or too difficult. In the seventh and eighth issues of the magazine the editor complains about the poor quality of many of the poetry submissions and suggests that more people should try the ballad form. He speaks of being 'flooded' with contributions to the paper and is pleased to report that readers are 'steadily growing in number'. But he is forced to admit that 'Most of the great volume of stuff we receive is, frankly, worthless as poetry'.[33]

Quality then was a concern as well as ideology. But to the editor's credit, he clearly published some work in order to encourage and give working-class writers a forum rather than insisting upon a uniform standard of achievement. Significantly, a fair proportion of such writing was by women who were suffering in the 1930s the double disadvantage imposed by class and anti-feminism. Poetry and the people opened its pages to Margaret Wilkinson, who forged anti-war poems out of her experiences working in a shirt factory, and to Elsie Newton, who in her poem 'The hope of England' expresses her own angry and embittered version of Love on the dole :

We have to sit and watch the 'smarties' flirt
Or lose our tanners on a real dead 'cert',
Knowing our love a shameful furtive thing
A blighted blossom ere it knows a Spring.
What can we hope for — we who can't be whole,
Degraded by the means test and the Dole.[34]

The technique may not be very pretty, but the sentiments are trenchant; we are a long way from Auden's hopeful musings about the saving power of love here.

Other themes regularly assayed by contributors to Poetry and the people included the divisive nature of class discrimination, the ironies for the militant of working in a society on the brink of what was often perceived as an imperialist war, celebrations of the Republican cause in Spain, and denunciations of the English government, of politicians and capitalists. The most successful poems were ballads written by poets like John Manifold, Jack Lindsay, D.K. Lindow, Idris Davies, William Soutar, Miles Carpenter, Frank Ball and Herbert Peacock. It is, I think, again significant that only three of these writers were English. Soutar was Scottish, Davies came from Wales, and Lindow, Manifold and Lindsay were Australians. Indeed the Australian contribution to the magazine and the movement seems to have been disproportionately large. The editor remarked upon this when he noted the 'astonishing number of our active membership' who were Australian.[35]

The literary-historical myth has it that towards the end of the decade, with the Republicans' defeat in Spain and the outbreak of the war, literary interest in left-wing politics declined and reaction set in. But the progress of *Poetry and the people* directly contradicts this idea. By November 1939 the magazine was selling sufficiently well to justify moving from its cyclostyled format into print, and in the next issue (January 1940), it was announced that the reception of the first printed number had been so good that they were printing twice the number of the present issue.[36] And by February the editors were boasting of having to print ten times the original number in order to meet demand.[37]

The outbreak of war was not then a signal for a general retreat from left-wing positions or beliefs. And John Isserlis made it quite clear that *Poetry and the people* was not going to fall prey to any of the Neo-Romanticism for which editors like Cyril Connolly were crying out:

This magazine has always stood for the acceptance of reality by the poet. We have never supported the poets who write of the beauties of nature, of lonely women, of sunlit gardens, and ignore a world of poverty, of nature ruined by ill-planned industrialism, of women prematurely aged by long hours in the kitchen, factory, by life in ill-lit basements, by poor and insufficient food, and the difficulties of bearing and rearing children on meagre wages.[38]

This was to become a popular theme for Isserlis. He invoked the earliest traditions of English poetry and song produced by the 'peasants, serfs and ordinary workers', to encourage poets to lead the left to a post-war victory.

The magazine continued with the title *Poetry and the people* until May 1940, when, under a different editor, it became *Our time*, a left-wing magazine which ran for the duration of the war, extending its interest from poetry to other literary forms and to political commentary. That the standard of writing in *Poetry and the people* was uneven is undeniable. But its very existence is crucially important to an understanding of the literary history of the 1930s. Like *Left review*, it constituted a forum for committed left-wing writers, and encouraged a militant working-class audience in both its literary and political endeavours. Most importantly for my purposes, it places the work of Auden *et al.* in a new and salutary perspective.

III

In a recent volume of essays celebrating his work, it is said of Jack Lindsay that he is 'not only one of the most important writers of the Twentieth Century; he is also one of the least well known'.[39] Despite having written, translated, and edited well over 150 books, his work is relatively unknown both in Australia and in England. Why this should be so is not, I think, difficult to gauge, and has nothing to do with the quality of Lindsay's writing. His long residence in England, and the European concerns of much of his writing, have offended the nationalistic trend of Australian letters, whilst the English literary establishment has been less than welcoming not only because of Lindsay's nationality but also because of his Marxism and his dealings with the Soviet Union.[40] Lindsay has fallen between two shores. His poetry of the 1930s has been ignored or treated dismissively by literary history, and yet as we shall see, he played a major role in left-wing literary activities in England during the latter half of the decade.

In order to understand this work fully, and see it in relation to the other poets and poetry I have discussed, it is necessary to attempt the same kind of contextualisation that I have offered in my previous discussions. This, however, is rendered difficult in Lindsay's case, because to appreciate his background fully one would have to provide the same kind of potted history of Australia that he himself offers as the opening chapter of his autobiography. Space will not permit such an indulgence. Suffice it to say that Lindsay saw his own background and early development as an embodiment of specifically Australian tensions and traditions. Particularly important to him is the democratic tradition of Australia which makes heroes of the gold diggers of Ballarat who fought for their rights at the Eureka stockade, and which celebrates the fact that 'the first ballot law of the modern world' was passed in Victoria in 1856. Equally of interest to Lindsay is the opposite tension evident in the class-structures he witnessed emerging when he was a boy.

Lindsay was born in 1900 in Melbourne, the son of the artist Norman Lindsay, but his parents separated early on, and Jack was brought up in Brisbane by his mother.[41] Their life during Jack's childhood and youth was not terribly comfortable as they shuffled between a series of boarding houses and rented accommodation. It was a lifestyle which was poised uneasily between petit-bourgeois respectability and working-class deprivation. Lindsay himself best describes his own situation:

The years of my childhood and youth ... were the post-Federation years when Australians felt something of a new sense of national unification, but when the industrialization was still in its infancy. It follows that neither was the proletariat fully founded and grounded nor the middleclass widely extended. A portion of the mobility, confusion or instability of my spiritual positions must be attributed to this fact. The last thing I want to suggest is that my doubts and difficulties are reducible to it; but I can see now that the stage of national development played an essential part in the attitudes I took... For the unstable state of the class to which I belonged, hovering on the edge of a considerable advance but still uncertain of its role between squattocracy and proletariat, could not but help in giving a buffet to my uneasy station ....[42]

He goes on to speak of being able to move easily between the houses of the 'wealthy and esteemed' and those of 'revolutionary Quinlan or carpenter Cunningham'. It is not merely the simple fact of Lindsay's nationality which distances him from the English poets we have looked at so far, but also his ability to move easily between classes is, I suggest, crucial in his later adoption of Communism and critique of capitalism. His background gives him a critical distance from which to view English power, its history and structures.

But this is to jump ahead too far too soon. Just as his class background was 'fluid' so his educational progress was mixed. Due to a very indulgent mother, Lindsay's only schooling until the age of twelve was some little time at a kindergarten. The young Lindsay seems to have taught himself to read, nevertheless when his uncle insisted that he should go to school he began in the infants' class and had to work his way upwards from there. This he did and eventually at the age of fourteen he won a scholarship to Brisbane Grammar School where he found friends among the other scholarship boys: the 'rough tough lads', as he was later to call them. He entered the University of Queensland in 1918, graduating brilliantly in 1921.

It was during his time at university that Jack fell under his father's aesthetic spell. Norman Lindsay, in both his art and polemical prose, was the purveyor of a Nietzschean, Dionysiac vitalism, which opposed the parochialism of Australian art, and which viewed art as the only aspect of society which had any value. As Craig Munro has remarked, Lindsay's creed was 'not only elitist, but also unashamedly racist, sexist, and anti-modernist; in short thoroughly reactionary'.[43] At university, and for some considerable time afterwards, Jack Lindsay embraced his father's beliefs; the artist was an aristocratic anarchist rejecting the 'barbarism' of the Australian petit-bourgeoisie, together with what was considered as the life-denying morbidity of European modernism. In the early 1920s, Jack, now living in Sydney, co-edited a literary magazine, *Vision*, which was dominated by Norman's ideas.

But by 1926 Jack Lindsay had had enough of Sydney in particular, and Australia in general, so, encouraged by P.R. (Inky) Stephenson, a university friend now studying at Oxford, Jack left for Europe and after a time in Paris set up the Fanfrolico Press in London with Stephenson and John Kirtley. Despite the fact that at this stage Stephenson was a Communist, the Fanfrolico Press continued to be dominated by Norman Lindsay's ideas and his drawings. The press produced high-quality limited editions and managed to survive, despite financial problems and the vagaries of its three editors, until it was brought down in the early years of the slump. It was at this stage (1930-1) that Jack retreated from London to the West Country where he lived in poverty as a virtual recluse for most of the decade.

It was during this time that Lindsay began to move intellectually and emotionally away from the Nietzschean philosophy derived from his father towards his own somewhat idiosyncratic, but nevertheless committed, Communism. Both in Australia and in England Lindsay had been somewhat déclassé, but now he turned to make common cause with the working class, and, at whatever distance, to join the radical literary tradition of Australia which has its origins in the anti-establishment ballads of firstly the convicts, and subsequently the gold-diggers and agricultural workers.

Lindsay's was not a superficial conversion to Marxism. In late 1935, with his mind upon what was happening in Europe, he read voraciously in the works of Marx and Engels, 'with a sprinkling of Lenin's theses'.[44] He had also been reading Kierkegaard and Jaspers. He saw in Marxism the possibility of integration:

At the crucial point, reached round the New Year of 1936, the new balance triumphantly asserted itself as a definitely organised system, and I found it was Marxism: not simply the particular system labelled Marxism at that moment, but Marxism the vital stream of thought-feeling which in that system had reached the highest world level then possible. Marxism, as a vital stream broadening into the future and implying an ever greater unity of consciousness, unity of man and nature, unity of man and man. Not that I did not welcome and accept the system as it had evolved up to that moment. To do otherwise would have been to sever potentiality from existence, otherness from self – the primary existentialist errors.[45]

Lindsay was before his time in the way he attempted to fuse existentialism and Marxism in his personal philosophy, and in later years his continuing unorthodoxy occasionally led him into conflict with his comrades in the Communist Party. But in 1936, Lindsay's voice was a welcome addition to the pages of Left review and Poetry and the people.

In the 1920s Lindsay had shown himself capable of writing opalescent lyrics which figured his father's Hellenistic predilections. In the early years of the 1930s, having parted from the Fanfrolico Press, and working away from Norman's influence through his own personal problems, he turned to Surrealism. But in 1936, he wrote two poems which signalled his new direction. Both of them were inspired by newspaper articles, one concerning England and one about Spain. It is in these poems that Lindsay begins to forge his own left-wing poetry and poetics which are unique in the history of poetry written in English. For here he brings together Romantic modernism with the folk tradition to create a passionate voice which is capable at its best of combining lyrical feeling with an uncompromising tough-mindedness.

In early 1936, Lindsay read a review in the Times literary supplement of Alan Hutt's book This final crisis, a Marxist interpretation of the condition of England. The reviewer remarked that Hutt was hampered in his pursuit by 'serious drawbacks' amongst which was numbered the fact that he 'did not understand the nature of the English People'. In response to this piece of reactionary blather, Lindsay wrote a long poem initially entitled 'Not English', which was published in the Left review for May 1936.[46]

The poem opens with the lines, 'Who are the English / according to the definition of the ruling class', and goes on to describe in highly emotive language all the oppressed and exploited who have martyred themselves to preserve the upper classes' notion of 'England' and the 'English'. The casualties of the First World War and slum-dwellers are concentrated upon. It is implicit from the beginning that in appropriating definitions of 'England' and 'English', the ruling class have literally appropriated and exploited both land and people.

In the long middle section of the poem Lindsay turns to an alternative historical view of England and the English. A description is provided of all those who have resisted the ruling classes' definitions:

We'll step back first six hundred years or seven
and call up the peasants hoarsely talking under the wind,
their cattle stolen by the king's purveyors,
their wives deceived by whining hedge-priests.
Peasants, leaving your wattled huts to haunt
the crooked dreams of Henry with your scythes,
unrolling a long scroll you couldn't read
though you knew the word it held, not England,
but justice – come, you peasants with hoof-smashed faces,
speak from the rotting wounds of your mouths, we'll understand,
prompting you with our anger.[47]

This is a fine example of Lindsay's historical imagination at work. The minimisation of metaphoric decoration together with a judicious deployment of epithet enhances Lindsay's narrative method. But the most interesting stylistic feature is the rhythm. Rather like T.S. Eliot, Lindsay uses the iambic pentameter as a basis, and plays all kinds of free variations upon it, lengthening or shortening the line at will. The effect is to approximate to speech-rhythms. Lindsay takes *vers libre* and allies it with the narrative and dramatic aspects of folk art. Those seeking to denigrate his work would doubtless invoke modernist or post-symbolist criteria in order to judge him 'prosaic'. But such judgements seem to me an irrelevance. The real question is whether the writing is effective or not, and in its passionate evocation of a revolutionary tradition it seems so to me.

The poem contrives to invoke not only the peasants' revolt but also the revolutionaries of Cromwell's era, the Anabaptists and Levellers, and from there Lindsay moves through Luddites and Chartists to William Morris and 'the unknown weaver / who wrote in the *Poor Man's Guardian* of 1832/ . . .There is no common interest / between working-men and profit makers...'[48]

Having thus established an historical basis for a radical tradition, Lindsay returns to the present asserting that 'we' are not the English either; the working classes of today, like those of the past, have been dispossessed. In a long lyrical passage Lindsay evokes the beauty of the English countryside, but this is neither to convey a Georgian nostalgia or a reactionary patriotism but rather to point up the birthright of the working class which has been plundered, leaving them only with, 'the field of toil':

... it was all taken away, England was taken,
what little of it was ours in desperate toil
was taken, and the desperate toil remained,
and lanes of dank gloom where the echo of midnight falls
a late wayfarer stumbling, leaving nothing behind
except the gaslight coughing and the crying child,
milk turned sour in the thunder-hour awaiting,
queues at the Labour Exchange while the radio squeals,
in the shop nearby, and nothing remains, nothing
except the mad-faces forming from the damp stains on the plaster ...[49]

Lindsay adroitly shifts his focus from the agrarian to the tenements of the industrial cities, bringing his vision to a dark nadir, before introducing his final rallying call: 'Workers of the World unite'. From this point forward Lindsay moves to an heroic vision of the future in which England is re-inherited by the working class. From the perspective of the present this is apt to sound hopelessly naive, and the relationship between past and future disastrously over-simplified. But at least the poem attempts to encapsulate past, present and future in its radical vision. It is a poem of great breadth, moving easily from emotional appeal to intellectual analysis. To read Lindsay's poem is to perceive immediately the difference between upper-middle-class liberalism and a truly radical left-wing position. None of the English poets of the 1930s expressed a Marxist view of history in their work. For Lindsay it was an imperative.

According to his own testimony, 'Not English' was 'received with such acclamation that it was reprinted in large numbers as a pamphlet'. More importantly, the recently formed experimental Group Theatre asked if they could use the piece, and it was duly performed as a dramatic production accompanied by dance and mime. This, Lindsay says, 'provided the basis of an English form of mass-declamation'.[50]

In an article for Left review, Lindsay outlined a plea for left-wing poets to concentrate upon the writing of declamatory poems which could be performed to large working-class audiences. Drawing upon his extensive knowledge of classical as well as English literature, Lindsay argues that 'poetry has always found its vitalisation in a socially valuable relation to the speaking voice'. The epic, together with Hellenic and Elizabethan drama, were all, he argues, born out of traditional rituals and declamation. Since the Industrial Revolution in England, poetry has been severed both from its sources in folk art and from its proper audience. It has degenerated into bourgeois sophistication severed from the productive world, and constitutes 'nothing but a perverted taste for the complexities and corpse-lights of disintegration'.[51]

Lindsay goes on to attack contemporary English poetry which has attempted to grapple with political issues. Such work, he says, represented a dead-end because it addressed itself primarily to a bourgeois audience and thus 'sought to expand in terms of a narrowing audience, to regain vitality in terms of the debilitated'. The answer to this problem, Lindsay believed, lay in mass declamation; an attempt to revitalise poetry by fusing it with ritual, by 'resuming all the socially valid forms of the past with a new content' and going beyond these 'with an enriched drama and lyric'. The emergent proletariat were to be wooed in this way, and so poetry was to become a revolutionary weapon.

Whatever the limitations of this cursory theoretical position, what may be forcefully demonstrated is that Lindsay's idea worked. When the Spanish Civil War broke out, encouraged by Edgell Rickword, Lindsay wrote another poem in declamatory style entitled 'On guard for Spain'. Like its predecessor, 'Not English', it was first published in Left review, and then reprinted as a penny pamphlet. The poem was first performed at a rally in Trafalgar Square in 1937, and subsequently upon a great number of occasions throughout Britain, often to very large audiences. Don Watson quotes Jerry Dawson, a member of the Merseyside Unity Theatre Group, describing the impact of the poem thus: 'When we did On Guard the impact was almost always enormous. I remember when we played it to a meeting at Garston Baths, I saw people in tears even at the mention of the name of certain Spanish towns ... These audiences didn't see declamations as something arty, as poetry being recited to them, but as an emotional expression of things they'd come across politically in their newspapers.'[52] If some members of the audience did not consider the poem to be 'arty', this does not mean it was written without artistry. Liberal critics have been dismissive in their condemnation of the poem as 'mere' propaganda. But as the following stanzas indicate, the poem is

not without 'literary' as well as political virtues. Here Lindsay is
describing the election victory of the Republicans prior to the outbreak
of the Civil War:

After the February elections
the people sang in the streets of work.
The echoes of time were notes of guitars
and the moons smelt of oranges
amid the jasmine-stars.

Bodies that had been jailed by fear
turned to the slopes of light once more.
The sun tied ribbons in all the trees
when we led the prisoners out of the jails,
thousands of comrades came singing out
while the waves of the sea clicked castanets
from shore to dancing shore.[53]

This celebration is neatly handled with its use of sensuous imagery and
direct statement producing an appropriately emotional texture. The
poem goes on to celebrate the heroism of the Spanish workers in the
face of the Fascist revolt. Lindsay projects the struggle in Spain as an
image of the international working-class struggle against Fascism and
capitalism. It is a plea for solidarity and for courage. It calls upon its
audience to mourn for the Republican dead, but not to lose heart or
belief. The poem as a whole, to my mind, is not as successful as 'Not
English'. But its emotional appeal cannot be doubted. And again we
find Lindsay using modernist *vers libre* together with the demotic
language, syntax and imagery of the folk tradition to produce an
authentic left-wing utterance.

   Lindsay did not confine his poetry of the later 1930s to mass
declamation. He wrote other poems which dwelt upon English history,
and he wrote occasional satire usually using a balladic form as here in
'Ballad of a dean'. This poem was a response to a remark of Dean Inge's
in 1936 to the effect that there was no class-conscious proletariat in
Britain:

O take him away to the Rhondda Valley,
and rub his face in the coal,
strip away his dog-collar,
unstud his immortal soul,
feed him on bread and dripping
and bilge of tea for a year,
then ask him if he's class-conscious yet
or merely feeling austere.[54]

The poem progresses geographically through the United States to Australia, Russia and back to Lancashire and Scotland, in all of which locations are found the militant proletariat fighting against capitalism.

Other of Lindsay's poems, like 'Summering song', and 'Prayer at dawn' deal with his more personal philosophical involvement with Marxism. As his remarks quoted earlier imply, and as these poems express, he saw in the Marxist dialectic the way forward to a sense of unity not only between men but also between man and the means of production, and from there between men and nature. In other words, Lindsay found in Marxism the answer to the Romantic dilemma; the materialist dialectic replaced, as it were, the dialectic between imagination and nature.

His poetry then, accommodates both his emotional and intellectual commitment to the left. It has been ill-treated by liberal critics and literary-historians pretending to make 'apolitical' judgements of purely 'literary value'. But it is Lindsay's politics they object to. The quality of his writing that I have quoted in his defence stands tall against the work of say, Spender or Day Lewis. And Lindsay continued to write out of his political convictions throughout the war years. Joining the army to fight against Fascism, he wrote dramatic narratives in verse, 'written for the understanding of the common soldier'.[55] Courage, comradeship and political hope for the future, remain his principle themes conveyed through vers libre or ballad forms. In his narrative poem 'Into action' Lindsay extended his formal apparatus to include collage. Using accounts of the Battle of Dieppe, and interviews he gleaned, he produced an epic poem. It was first published in 1942, and 'seems to have been issued in at least ten thousand copies within a few months'.[56] Lindsay's work of both the 1930s and the 1940s then, defies the literary-historical myth of the period 1930-45.

IV

Hugh MacDiarmid's work, unlike Jack Lindsay's, has a secure reputation in his native land, and the recent publication of his Complete poems by Penguin may signal a more widespread acceptance of his oeuvre in England than he has enjoyed hitherto. But until 1970, much of his work was unobtainable in England, and the writers of English literary history of the 1930s have ignored him. Compared with Auden's mythological position with respect to the decade, MacDiarmid's participation has been relegated to the status of footnotes. Yet he published eight volumes of poetry in the 1930s and took part in literary debate on both sides of the border. Some of his work appeared in English periodicals. But that he was, and still is, viewed with suspicion by certain sections of the English literary establishment, or worse still not viewed at all, can hardly be a matter for surprise. He was virulently opposed to English imperialism, and allied a vigorous nationalism to his Communist commitment. He represents the antithesis of the Oxonian upper-middle-class London literary scene.

MacDiarmid was born in 1892 in the small town of Langholm not far from the Scottish/English border. He does not then fit into Hynes's chronological definition of the 'Auden generation'. MacDiarmid's paternal forebears were mill-workers, whilst his mother was descended from agricultural labourers. His father, however, escaped the mill, but not the working class: he became a rural postman. This working-class borderer background crucially informed MacDiarmid's attitudes. Speaking of his formative years he says: 'Above all, there was the frontier spirit – the sense of difference from, and not infrequently hatred of, the English, which I certainly inherited to the full, and which later developed into my own life work'.[57] Elsewhere he refers to 'driving' a distance between England and Scotland as 'his fixed and unalterable purpose'; it is 'the key' to his 'whole personality and life story'. 'Anglophobia' is said to be his 'very life'.[58] He also remarks upon his early sense of class-antagonism; Langholm teaches him an 'out-and-out Radicalism and Republicanism' and a 'hatred' of the gentry.[59] 'To speak English' is to speak fine;[60] Scottish language for MacDiarmid was inextricably equated with working-class language.

Yet Langholm provided MacDiarmid with other, and potentially contrary, impulses. The family lived in the same building that housed the public library, and it was the young MacDiarmid's habit to visit the library with a washing basket to fill with books which would then be devoured before another load was collected.[61] He read voraciously and omnivorously, and it seems likely that his attendance at the local school was somewhat less important than his own self-educative reading. Certainly this experience laid the foundations for MacDiarmid's 'highbrow' attitudes, his taste for a life of reading, writing and scholarship. Furthermore, MacDiarmid attributes to his relatively sequestered birthplace the development of an attitude to art (and to some aspects of life) which is Romantic and mystical:

There is an old saying – 'Out of the world and into Langholm', and throughout my life I have applied it in this way. It has been my touchstone in all creative matters: always I derive thence that 'intuitive perception of stillness of some sort, an idea or quality' which is the 'germ of composition'. This – which explains how I reconcile my use of a linguistic medium utterly unintelligible to 'the mob', and my highbrowism generally, with my Communism - the extremes of High Tory and Communist meeting - is, of course, just what Osbert Burdett was getting at in his book on Coventry Patmore when he wrote: 'There is a force in a life removed'.[62]

Of all the poets we have discussed then, it could be argued that MacDiarmid shows the most severe ambivalence towards his class background. On the one hand he is intensely proud to be of the working class, and is deeply committed to its cause, but on the other he despises those members of his own class, the 'lumpen' part of the proletariat, who are inherently conservative and who do not wish to help themselves towards the political ends which MacDiarmid deems to be appropriate. Complementing this tension, and equally apparent in much of his writing, even when it is ostensibly at its most left-wing, is the conflict between materialism and mysticism.

By the time MacDiarmid left Langholm at the age of sixteen, his social, political and aesthetic bearings were well on the way to being fixed. In accordance with his parents' wishes he went to Edinburgh to work briefly as a pupil teacher. But MacDiarmid had soon had enough of this and he left to pursue a more uncertain career in journalism and letters. His anti-imperialist political convictions were given further impetus by his experience as a stretcher bearer on the Western Front during the Great War. After the war he resumed his journalistic and political endeavours until 1933 when he retreated from public life to Whalsay in the Shetland Islands, where he lived very simply in comparative poverty, helping the locals in their fishing boats, and pursuing his poetry and politics.

Language, literature and politics were never separated in MacDiarmid's life and work. His greatest poetic achievement of the 1920s was *A drunk man looks at the thistle*, a work concerned with Scottish Nationalism. In the same decade he was politically very active, and helped to form the National Party of Scotland. In the 1930s his nationalism and his Communism were further developed in the direction of Scottish Republicanism. In the minds of some, however, Communism and nationalism were simply incompatible. In 1932 MacDiarmid was expelled from the National Party he had helped to found for

Communist deviation. He joined the Communist Party in 1934, but was expelled three years later for nationalist deviation. After an appeal he was reinstated, but then thrown out again in 1938. Throughout these now almost risible episodes, MacDiarmid's Leninism and his anti-imperialist Anglophobia did not waver. He reconciled his position by arguing that the social revolution was possible sooner in Scotland than in England, and that to press for a separate Scottish Republic would hasten the disintegration of the British Empire, thereby indirectly aiding the English workers towards their own revolution. This 'Red Scotland' line, MacDiarmid argued, was 'in perfect keeping with the dicta of Marx, Engels, Lenin, and Stalin, and with the practice of the Soviet Union in regard to minority elements'. He wanted Scotland to enjoy what he presumed to be the cultural autonomy of the 'republics of the U.S.S.R.'[63]

Given this uneasy but passionately held belief in both Communism and Scottish separatism, it is not suprising to discover that MacDiarmid's attitude to the English literary establishment was virulent and uncompromising. The following extracts from a letter to John Lehmann, written in 1938, make this abundantly clear. Lehmann had suggested that if MacDiarmid's best work had not been written in Scottish dialect, then it would have been included in Michael Roberts's *New country* anthology. MacDiarmid responded by remarking that he had 'no respect' for Roberts's judgement, and implied that he despised Roberts's pro-Christian attitudes. The letter continues:

I do not think much of Auden, Spender, and Day Lewis as poets, and believe them to be grossly over-rated ... I view with deep suspicion the whole nature and tendency of the left-wing literary-movement in England – knowing that you have only to scratch it to find English chauvinism and a 'superior' inability to believe that any good can come out of anywhere but Oxford and Cambridge... Unlike all the other English left-wing poets and other writers, I have the advantage of belonging to the working-class, have always remained in it, and never earned enough to lift me into any higher category.[64]

This prefigures eight pages of vigorous repudiation of the English literary establishment, and the Auden–Spender–Day Lewis–MacNeice 'school' in particular, to be found in the chapter of his autobiography entitled 'The kind of poetry I want'.

MacDiarmid's poetry of the 1930s was no less forthright than his prose. Like Lindsay, MacDiarmid had the advantage of a close contact with a ballad tradition; the border ballads are amongst the greatest ever written. Also like Lindsay, MacDiarmid was a compulsive reader and

had an encyclopaedic mind. He began writing in full cognisance of the
European symbolist tradition. His first three volumes, *Annals of the five
senses* (1923), *Sangshaw* (1925), and *Pennywheep* (1926) are the least
political of his writings, but already in their combination of lyrical
feeling, tough thought, and clear imagery expressed in MacDiarmid's
own version of Lallans, they show both an appreciation of tradition
and a willingness to experiment which became the hallmarks of his
later, more politically involved, verse. It is also significant that neither
Lindsay nor MacDiarmid were afraid to depart from the short lyric
form and to write long poems combining argument and narrative. *A
drunk man looks at the thistle* is a superb example wherein MacDiarmid uses
the ballad quatrain to develop his complex vision of the failure of the
Scottish people to embrace nationalism.

MacDiarmid's work of the 1930s is arguably his finest. Here he
develops a staggering range of tone and style in order to express his
vision from a variety of angles. His work never descends to the false
optimism of facile propaganda, or easy attitudinising.   Rather it
articulates the intellectual tensions inherent in Scotland's postion, and
in MacDiarmid's complex attitude towards that position. The apotheosis
of his 1930s work is to be found in the three *Hymns to Lenin* where we
find MacDiarmid investigating different aspects of the Leninist
inheritance, in a variety of styles within and between each poem. The
First hymn was published in an anthology, *New English poems*, edited by
Lascelles Abercrombie in 1930. It subsequently appeared as the title
poem of MacDiarmid's volume of 1931.

In this poem MacDiarmid compares Lenin to Christ, and asserts that
conservatives like Churchill and Beaverbrook, when seen in history's
perspective, are no more than the centurions presiding at the
crucifixion. Lenin is the greatest turning point since Christ, and is also
seen as the descendant of the 'unkent bards', who rather than being
concerned with the 'laurel and the bays' deal in the 'mightier poo'er'
shared by all men. This 'mightier poo'er' has little to do with dialectical
materialism, but rather a lot in common with Romantic metaphysics.
It is an elemental force of life and thought, which has been misused,
but Lenin knew how to harness it in the cause of Everyman.

In the final stanzas MacDiarmid articulates a statement of faith:

Here lies your secret, O Lenin, – yours and oors,
No' in the majority will that accepts the result
But in the real will that bides its time and kens
The benmaist resolve is the poo'er in which we exult

Since naebody's willingly deprived o' the good;
   And, least o'a', the crood![65]

The poet's faith is in the inmost (benmaist) power which resides deep
in everyone, to resist deprivations and seek the creative 'good'. But in
equal and opposite tension to this Romantic idealism, is a tough, and
in retrospect chilling, recognition that some sections of the proletariat
are 'as bairns' and need to be 'men'. The possibility of revolutionary
violence is not precluded as a means to a desired end: 'What maitters
't wha we kill / To lessen that foulest murder that deprives / Maist men
o' real lives.' MacDiarmid is determined not to flinch from the
unpalatable aspects of his aspiration. In this he amply distinguishes
himself from the English liberals. But he also lays himself open to
charges of either bloodthirsty irresponsibility or dealing in abstract
ideas without an adequate registration of the gross pain and suffering
which such ideas cause when translated into action.

    Happily, the Second hymn to Lenin dwells upon the creative rather than
the destructive aspects of Leninism. Here we witness the great strength
of MacDiarmid's writing which resides in his ability to combine a
colloquial vigour with intellectual sophistication. And, although his
rhythms are often more prosaic than those to be found in the English
Romantic tradition, his speech is rarely without passion. In this 'hymn'
MacDiarmid sets down his ideas concerning the relationship between
poetry and Leninism, juxtaposing the annunciation of ideas with a
demonstration of them in italicised, balladic quatrains. MacDiarmid
proposes the idea that poetry should be the 'hub of life' and should
become even greater than Lenin's work. This could be interpreted as
an act of self-aggrandisement on MacDiarmid's part, but I take it that
the point he is trying to make is that poetry is a corollary of Lenin's
political vision, in so far as it expresses the rich fullness of experience
which should be the birthright of everybody. Just as Lenin advocated
the pursuance of revolution in a precise fitting of means to ends, so
poetry must learn that lesson and extend it:

Wi' Lenin's vision equal poet's gift
And what unparalleled force was there !
Nocht in a' literature wi' that
Begins to compare.

Nae simple rhymes for silly folk
But the haill art, as Lenin gied
Nae Marx-without-tears to workin' men
But the fu' course instead.[66]

As in the First hymn, we might detect here MacDiarmid's determination to avoid facile utopianism. There is a cognisance that social change is rarely achieved without pain, and there is an insistence upon the need for 'workin' men' to have the full intellectual 'course', rather than any simplistic condescensions.

MacDiarmid continues to register his impatience that 'breid and butter' problems still prevent men from realising their potential. It is the poet's vision which embraces and expresses this full power, 'for a poet maun see in a' thing'. Lenin dealt in the narrow sphere of politics, the poet deals in the totality of experience.

The test of the poet is clear:

Are my poems spoken in the factories and fields,
    In the streets o' the toon?
Gin they're no', then I'm failin' to dae
    What I ocht to ha' dune.

Gin I canna win through to the man in the street,
    The wife by the hearth,
A' the cleverness on earth'll no' mak' up
    For the damnable dearth. [67]

Here, as in the other Hymns to Lenin, MacDiarmid is apparently dealing in self-persuasion and self-accusation. This is a clever ploy to avoid the 'preacher's loose immodest tone' which infects so much Audenesque writing. MacDiarmid projects himself publicly in order to persuade others of the truth and power of his vision. But he is under no illusions as to whom he is addressing. His scorn for fools of any class is always apparent, and all his energy is devoted to raising thinking people to ponder social injustice and to act in order to eradicate it.

That the Second hymn to Lenin was first published in T. S. Eliot's Criterion in 1932 signals something of that ambivalence which results in the coalescence of High Tory and Communist attitudes in MacDiarmid's work. Eliot and MacDiarmid respected each other greatly, and clearly each appreciated the other's art. MacDiarmid was always convinced of the importance of modernism, and admired the works of Joyce and Rilke as well as those of Eliot. In the Second hymn, whilst writing in balladic quatrains, using familiar, demotic imagery, and aspiring to be spoken in the 'factories and fields', there is also a wealth of allusion to intellectual and artistic figures of past and present which appeals primarily to an intellectual élite, and which clearly owes a debt to modernism. MacDiarmid differentiates himself from Eliot, however, by declaring himself to be on the side of 'miner' and 'shepherd', of 'sailor' and 'housewife'. The implication is that the intellectual and poetic traditions which he invokes should be the common inheritance of all.

In the Third hymn to Lenin which was completed by 1938, but not published until much later, MacDiarmid's debt to modernism is clear as here he extends Eliot's experiments with rhythm and collage. Prose extracts from various radical thinkers are juxtaposed with MacDiarmid's own muscular free-verse rhythms.

The poem is centred upon the slums of Glasgow. After an initial celebration of the universal grasp of Lenin's thought, MacDiarmid asserts that Russia before the revolution 'had no hell' like that to be found in Glasgow:

A horror that might sicken your stomach even,
The peak of the capitalist system and the trough of hell,
Fit testimonial to our ultra-pious race,
A people greedy, lying and unconscionable
Beyond compare. – Seize on this link, spirit of Lenin, then
And you must needs haul upwards to the light
The whole base chain of the phenomena that hold
Europe so far below levels worthy of its might.[68]

In similarly stressed, excoriating language, MacDiarmid goes on to lambast his countrymen for their apathy towards alleviating the social conditions he so tellingly describes. He also enumerates the reactionary forces which prevent progress. Apart from the machinery of Church and State, there is also the bourgeois siren of 'culture' which distracts people from what MacDiarmid considers to be their proper task of 'doing some honest service to mankind'. But the most severe criticism is reserved for the English literati. MacDiarmid forcefully sees through their 'pink' veneer to give them a mawling:

Michael Roberts and All Angels! Auden, Spender, those bhoyos,
All yellow twicers: not one of them
With a tithe of Carlile's courage and integrity.
Unlike these pseudos I am of – not for – the working class
And like Carlile know nothing of the so-called higher classes
Save only that they are cheats and murderers,
Battening like vampires on the masses.[69]

It is no wonder that the literary establishment has been cool towards MacDiarmid's writing.

MacDiarmid saves his final invective, however, for the Glaswegian 'hordes', who are characterised as illiterate, 'bogged' in 'mumbo-jumbo', 'wallowing' in 'exploded fallacies' and 'gross stupidity'. The only way to enlighten this darkness is via the quest for 'human wholeness', which in turn requires the inheritance and assimilation of the radical political traditions of Richard Carlile and Lenin. And it is the latter whose spirit MacDiarmid invokes to light the city of Glasgow in a passionate finale.

There is a tension in the Hymns to Lenin between courting a working-class audience and despising the 'ignorance' of the 'masses'. That MacDiarmid was exercised about this problem is attested to in a letter of 1932, in which MacDiarmid speaks of his preoccupation with the problem of 'bridging the gulf between poetry and the people, bringing poetry and power into effective relation again'.[70] Both the balladic quatrains and the declamatory and oratorical mode of the Hymns to Lenin were ways of attempting this without surrendering anything of intellectual sophistication. But MacDiarmid was also capable of writing in much gentler tones. In 'The seamless garment', for instance, the argument is akin to that pursued in the Second hymn to Lenin, but the mode of address is quite distinct. Here MacDiarmid addresses 'cousin Wullie', a worker in a Langholm mill. The object of the poem is to inspire Wullie to look beyond the confines of his work in order to achieve his full potential. MacDiarmid cunningly employs the metaphor of cloth-making to explain the importance of Lenin's thought. Speaking of the mill, MacDiarmid says:

The haill shop's dumfoonderin'
    To a stranger like me.
Second nature to you; you're perfectly able
    To think, speak and see
Apairt frae the looms, tho' to some
That doesna sae easily come.

Lenin was like that wi' workin' class life,
    At hame wi't a'.
His fause movements couldna been fewer,
    The best weaver Earth ever saw.
A' he'd to dae wi' moved intact,
    Clean, clear, and exact.

A poet like Rilke did the same
    In a different sphere,
Made a single reality – a' a'e 'oo –

O' his love and pity and fear;
A seamless garment o' music and thought
But you're owre thrang wi' puirer to tak' tent o't.[71]

It is clear that MacDiarmid, like Lindsay, saw in Marxism the means towards the integration of self and society. In the last stanza of the poem it is equally transparent that MacDiarmid's ambition as a poet is to create 'a seamless garment' through the bringing together of poetry and politics, the spheres of Rilke and Lenin respectively. But the major concentration in the poem is upon Wullie, who is too worried about poverty ('owre thrang wi' puirer') to have time to consider Rilke's work. The answer to this is politics first, art later. MacDiarmid challenges his addressee to be equal to life as he is to the loom, to make 'mair' of himself, implicitly by joining a Communist cell, where men are joined closely like 'threids' of cloth. The poem then surrenders nothing of intellectual complexity, yet retains its demotic tone through imagery and language familiar to the mill-workers. It is a poem full of energetic concern and compassion.

During the 1930s MacDiarmid also did not abandon the lyrical grace he had exercised in his earliest volumes. He produced a series of 'Shetland lyrics' which were included in his volume of 1934, *Stony limits and other poems*. The most famous of these poems is 'With the herring fishers', which is based upon MacDiarmid's experiences with the fishermen of Whalsay. The poem not only celebrates the work of the fishermen but also effortlessly develops a metaphor wherein 'the herrin'' as they 'come walkin' on board' are likened to the human race progressing from darkness into light:

For this is the way that God sees life,
The haill jing-bang o's appearin'
Up owre frae the edge o' naethingness
– It's his happy cries I'm hearin'.

'Left, right – O come in and see me,'
Reid and yellow and black and white
Toddlin' up into heaven thegither
At peep o' day frae the endless night.[72]

To those unfamiliar with MacDiarmid's work it may seem incongruous of him to speak, as he does in 'With the herring fishers', of God and Heaven. MacDiarmid hated institutionalised Christianity and the kirk, and invokes 'God' in his poems as a symbol of unity and creativity. As may be observed in the stanzas quoted above, his specific purpose in this particular poem is to liken the work of the herring fishers to that of God. It is a self-conscious celebration of working life.

MacDiarmid was planning in 1938 to write a book in collaboration with William Soutar which would consist of four hundred lyrics to be entitled 'The commons of Scotland'.[73] The plan was to divide the book into sections dealing with tributes to political heroes, the history and evolution of Scottish democracy, and lastly a section devoted to 'poems on all the most significant operations of human labour in Scotland'. 'With the herring fishers' was to be included in the latter category. The book never came to fruition, but MacDiarmid did indeed write many poems which could appropriately have been accommodated therein. His great and angry poems to the memory of the Scottish radical John MacLean, for instance, fit easily into the first category, and the huge 'Lament for great music', into the second.

Here there is not space to do MacDiarmid's work of the 1930s full justice. What might be asserted are the great strengths of his writing during the decade. His political idealism was fired by the slaughter that capitalist imperialism had given rise to in the First World War, and by anger at the condition of the Glasgow slums, and the Scottish people. It is the expression of this anger and indignation with its concomitant compassionate wish for human wholeness that constitutes the most impressive aspect of MacDiarmid's work. Equally important is his ability to celebrate and communicate various aspects of working-class life in a decade when most of the literati simply did not have the experience of such life upon which to draw.

But these strengths of MacDiarmid's writings might also be said to be close to his weaknesses. For it was surely the depth of his anger at the injustices of capitalism and imperialism, and the depth of his commitment to the working-class cause which led him to the endorsement of revolutionary violence in the *First hymn to Lenin*, and a subsequent refusal to condemn Stalinist atrocities, on the grounds that capitalism was responsible for worse excesses. Such attitudes have not helped his literary cause. Yet there is further irony here. For MacDiarmid's poetry does not bear the stamp of the cultural implications of Stalinism with its party-line and cultural thuggery as administered by Zdhanov. On the contrary, MacDiarmid eschews mere propaganda, and is often as far away from dialectical materialism as he could be. His work combines a debt to the ballad tradition with one to modernism. Popularist ambitions coincide with a rigorous deter-mination to remain highbrow. On the one hand MacDiarmid undoubtedly wished to communicate with members of the working class, but on the other had a deep suspicion of any possible 'talking down', and clearly was unwilling to compromise anything of artistic and intellectual integrity to the demands of ideological purity.His work stands interestingly athwart the debate about the relative merits of Social Realism and modernism which have preoccupied Marxist theorists from the 1930s onwards.

Notes

1 J. Lucas, 'Interview with Edgell Rickword', The 1930s, ed. J. Lucas, Hassocks, Sussex, 1978, p. 4.
2 C. Werner, 'Left review', British literary magazines, vol. IV, The modern age, New York, 1985, p. 218.
3 Left review, vol. 1, Oct. 1934, p. 38.
4 Lucas, The 1930s, p. 5.
5 J. Symons, The thirties: a dream revolved, revd. ed., London, 1975, p. 74.
6 A.T. Tolley, The poetry of the thirties, London, 1975, p. 320.
7 S. Hynes, The Auden generation: literature and politics in the 1930s, London, 1976, pp. 164-5.
8 D. Margolies, 'Left review and left literary theory', Culture and crisis in Britain in the thirties, eds., J. Clark, M. Heinemann, D. Margolies and C. Snee, London, 1979, p. 71.
9 Left review, No. 1, Feb. 1935, p. 182.
10 Left review, No. 1, June 1935, p. 361.
11 Ibid., p. 365.
12 Clark et al., Culture and crisis in Britain in the thirties, pp. 67-81.
13 See R. Fox, The novel and the people, London, 1937; C. Caudwell, Illusion and reality, London, 1937; A. West, Crisis and criticism, London, 1937.
14 Left review, vol. 1, Nov. 1934, pp. 44-5.
15 Left review, vol. 1, Aug. 1935, pp. 479-80.
16 Left review, vol. 2, April 1936, pp. 339-40.
17 Left review, vol. 1, July 1935, pp. 425-30.
18 Left review, vol. 1, Jan. 1935, pp. 116-17.
19 Ibid.
20 Left review, vol. 2, Jan. 1937, p. 866.
21 B. Bergonzi, Reading the thirties: texts and contexts, London, 1978, p. 135.
22 Lucas, ed., The 1930s, p. 12.
23 Ibid., p. 11.
24 Ibid.
25 The same could be said of Julian Bell and John Cornford, both of whom gave their lives for the Republican cause in Spain. Although Cornford was a brilliant young man, and wrote some fine Marxist-oriented literary criticism, his poetry did not develop beyond the liberal bourgeois tradition.
26 Werner, British literary magazines, vol. IV, p. 218.
27 Tolley, The poetry of the thirties, p. 324.
28 Poetry and the people, No. 4, Oct. 1938, p. 2.
29 Poetry and the people, No. 16, Jan. 1940, p.15.
30 Poetry and the people, No. 7, Jan. 1939, p. 15.
31 J. Manifold, 'Australian verse: the other half', Poetry and the people, No. 6, Dec. 1938, pp. 7-9.

32 Keidrych Rhys was the founding editor of *Wales* which ran from the summer of 1937 to the winter of 1939-40. In Scotland Hugh MacDiarmid edited *The voice of Scotland*, 1938-9, and subsequently 1945-9. This magazine in a sense replaced *The modern Scot*, 1930-6.

33 *Poetry and the people*, No. 8, Feb. 1939, pp. 13-14.

34 *Poetry and the people*, No. 6, Dec. 1938, p. 11.

35 *Poetry and the people*, No. 12, June 1939, p. 2.

36 *Poetry and the people*, No. 16, Jan. 1940, p. 15.

37 *Poetry and the people*, No. 17, Feb. 1940, p. 5.

38 *Poetry and the people*, No. 15, Nov. 1939, pp. 1-2.

39 B. Smith, Editor's Preface to, *Culture and history: essays presented to Jack Lindsay*, Sydney, 1984, p. 10.

40 See, N. Lopyev, 'Jack Lindsay's books in the Soviet Union', *Culture and history*, pp. 181-97.

41 J. Lindsay, *Life rarely tells*, London, 1958, pp. 9-66.

42 Ibid., p. 18.

43 C. Munro, 'Two boys from Queensland: P.R. Stephensen and Jack Lindsay', *Culture and history*, p. 42.

44 J. Lindsay, *Fanfrolico and after*, London, 1962, p. 252.

45 Ibid., pp. 262-3.

46 *Left review*, vol. 2, May 1936, pp.353-7.

47 Ibid., p. 354.

48 Ibid., p. 355.

49 Ibid., p. 356.

50 Lindsay, *Fanfrolico and after*, p. 263.

51 J. Lindsay, 'A plea for mass declamation', *Left review*, vol. 3, Oct. 1937, pp. 511-17.

52 D. Watson, '"On guard for Spain" and mass declamations', *Culture and history*, p. 158.

53 *Collected poems of Jack Lindsay*, Lake Forest, Illinois, 1981, pp. 304-5.

54 Ibid., pp. 269-70.

55 J. J. Borg, 'A poet for the people', *Culture and history*, p. 133

56 Ibid., p. 134.

57 H. MacDiarmid, *Lucky poet* (1943), London, 1972, p. 16.

58 Ibid., pp. 23-4.

59 Ibid., p. 225.

60 Ibid., p. 17.

61 Ibid., p. 12.

62. Ibid., pp. 3-4.

63 Ibid., pp. 143-5.

64 Letter of Hugh MacDiarmid to John Lehmann, 6 June 1938, *The letters of Hugh MacDiarmid*, ed. Alan Bold, London, 1984, pp. 594-5.

65 *The complete poems of Hugh MacDiarmid*, vol. I, eds. M. Grieve and W.R. Aitken, Harmondsworth, 1985, pp. 298-9.

66 Ibid., pp. 324-5.

67 Ibid., p. 323.

68 *The complete poems of Hugh MacDiarmid*, vol. II, eds. M. Grieve and W. R. Aitken, Harmondsworth, 1985, pp. 893-904.

69 Ibid., p. 900.

70 Letter of Hugh MacDiarmid to Neil Gunn, 4 August 1932, *The letters of Hugh MacDiarmid*, p. 247.

71 *The complete poems*, vol. I, pp. 311-312.

72 Ibid., p. 437.

73 Letter of Hugh MacDiarmid to William Soutar, 31 May 1937, *The letters of Hugh MacDiarmid*, pp. 157-9.

Conclusion

Valentine Cunningham, in his recent study British writers of the thirties, speaks of his ambition in terms of creating a 'single semiotic' for the thirties. Like Hynes and Bergonzi before him, he charts similarities between writers in order to produce an integrated vision of the decade. The impulse behind this project, and that of both Hynes and Bergonzi, is, I think, both Romantic and liberal-conservative. It is not surprising that the writers they acclaim as 'central' to the 1930s share this ideological orientation. What I have tried to do in the foregoing pages is quite different. I have questioned the myth of the 'Auden generation', and restored the divisions in the literary and social world which are erased in other literary histories. I have attempted to place the writers in terms of their lived experience, and to explore the relationship between this and the tensions in their poetry. In wishing to de-centre Auden and the Audenesque, I have not been concerned to establish another poet or group of poets as 'more central'. My project has been to recover, as it were, a horizontal panorama of the world of poetry in the 1930s, in order to demonstrate the heterogeneity of the work, and of poets' attitudes to their work and that of their contemporaries. I have been anxious to show the breadth of poetry written in the 1930s in order not to consign working-class and lower-middle-class voices and experiences to silence. This seems to me particularly crucial in a time when theoretical debate is pressing harder and harder the claim that our world is created by words. If this is true or even partly true, then of course the power of the word is huge, and which voices are heard and which are not becomes of paramount significance.

The conservatism that politically rules the 1930s also dominates the poetry of the period. Those committed to radical left-wing politics and poetry were decidedly in the minority. As we might expect, the least radical of 1930s poetry was written by the public-school, Oxbridge-educated, upper-middle classes. Degrees of ambivalence to their inherited values differ, but the basic liberal-conservative ideological thrust of their work is a constant. Auden and the Audenesque then represents only a part of the upper-middle-class response to the decade. Poets like Bernard Spencer and Geoffrey Grigson are less conscience-stricken and tense in their styles and attitudes. The mythology which makes Auden 'representative' of the decade, and of the left, is seriously distorting.

Poets from less elevated backgrounds were less accepting of society and its dominant ideology, but very few of them were committed to a left-wing or Marxist political vision. Rather they struck anarchist attitudes which tend, in the final analysis, to be right wing in their implications. Those committed to the left who published in Left review and Poetry and the people mounted just such a critique of the Audenesque and of Surrealism during the 1930s. They also began to develop a seriously Marxist criticism and poetics. But the mythology has attempted to erase them and their achievements through a recourse to dismissing serious left-wing poetry as mere propaganda. The literary establishment has privileged the Audenesque, because the Audenesque is ideologically closest to its heart. They share middle-class perspectives with just a dash of radicalism. The left, on the other hand, has been discredited because of its association with Stalinism. But this should not be an adequate reason for obliterating the part the left played in the literary history of the 1930s, or ignoring the commitment and achievement of such people as Slater, Rickword, Caudwell and West.

The myth not only ignores or dismisses the left but also seeks to erase the heterogeneity of poetry written and published during the 1930s. And it seriously distorts the relationship between poetry of the 1930s and poetry written during the war years. Thus far, literary historians have sought to define poetry of the Second World War as either a pale continuation of 1930s work or as a Neo-Romantic reaction against the 1930s. Neither of these views allows for the complex relationship between poetic production and the society in which that production takes place.

At the outbreak of the war there was no sudden retreat into private reactionary Neo-Romanticism. If anything the debate about poetry and its relationship to an audience intensified as the literati grappled with the proper function of poetry in war time. The political situation was complex with the left facing the obligation to fight Fascism on behalf of their own imperialist government. As Day Lewis trenchantly put it, they were obliged to defend the bad against the worst.[1] This led some intellectuals to make the anarchism implicit in so much 1930s writing explicit in their thinking and writing. Herbert Read's book *Poetry and anarchism*, which was first published in 1938, was reprinted in 1941: clearly there was a demand for what Read described as the 'politics of the unpolitical'. J.F. Hendry and Henry Treece also articulated an anarchist position in their New Apocalypse anthologies.

But stylistically poetry of the war years generally shows a retreat from the extremes of Surrealism on the one hand and Agitprop on the other. This was clearly a reaction to the political uncertainties engendered by the war. But it is wrong to think that the committed left disappeared during these years. It did not. The magazine *Our time*, carried the work of *Left review* forward, and writers like Lindsay and MacDiarmid continued to produce poetry which had a Marxist perspective. Much of Roy Fuller's poetry of the war years also had a decidedly left-wing orientation. Balladry also gained favour during the war years, with many working-class soldiers composing poems which were published in anthologies like *Poems from the desert* and *Poems from Italy*. It is not out of the question that *Poetry and the people* was influential in the flowering of this interest during the war years. In 1945 Lindsay and others edited an anthology entitled *New lyrical ballads*, which contained ballads written from a committed left-wing stance. The political shift which occurred during the war years and resulted in electoral victory for Labour in 1945 was then reflected to some extent in the poetry of the war years.

Other aspects of political and social reality during the war clearly affected the poetry that was written. As Angus Calder has shown in his appropriately entitled book, *The people's war*, civilians were involved and endangered to a very similar degree as the armed forces. The people recognised their own importance and became increasingly determined to work towards a transformed post-war England. As Calder says:

With parliament muted, with the traditional system of local government patently inadequate, with the army conceding the soldiers' right to reason why, with the traditional basis of industrial discipline swept away by full employment, the people increasingly led itself. Its nameless leaders in the bombed streets, on the factory floor, in the Home Guard Drill Hall, asserted a new radical popular spirit. The air-raid warden and the shop-steward were men of destiny, for without their ungrudging support for the war it might be lost; morale was in danger.[2]

Although class distinctions were still very much in place, there was an increased contact between classes, and a broad recognition that the future of England depended to a very large extent upon the working

class. This, together with the increased demand for poetry,[3] led poets
to a greater awareness of audience. Much gratuitous obscurity was
relinquished in the best poetry of the war years, and the development
of a clearer style in poets like Barker, Thomas and Gascoyne is
symptomatic of this.

Poetry of the war years, because of the various and unusual circumstances in which it was written, is far more difficult to categorise than
the work of the 1930s. As I have shown, it is possible to discern in
the work of the 1930s distinct differences of attitude and style in the
work of writers from differing class backgrounds. It is much more
difficult to look at poetry 1939-45 in the same way. There are several
reasons for this, the most important concerning the relationship
between class and lived experience. In the 1930s the experience of
poets can be interestingly related to their class backgrounds. Auden,
Day Lewis and MacNeice all worked in traditional middle-class
occupations teaching in prep schools, public schools and in the case
of MacNeice at universities. Spender divided his time between a
London literary life and extensive travel in Europe. Others from a less
elevated background like Barker and Thomas chose Bohemian lifestyles
on the fringes of society, whereas Lindsay and MacDiarmid lived
reclusive, highly impecunious lives for a good part of the decade; their
dissatisfaction with society seems to have led to their removing
themselves as far as possible from it. During the war, however, the
lifestyle and experience of poets cut across class and geographical
divisions. There were poets from various backgrounds working in Civil
Defence, in the three armed forces at home and overseas, in
propaganda and for the BBC, and finally there were civilian poets living
in exile due to the exigencies of the war, most notably the group from
Cairo and Alexandria. It was this diversity of experience as well as class
difference which helps to make the poetry of the 1940s so diverse and
difficult to categorise. A further factor in this is that there was not time
during the war for a dominant group of Oxbridge-educated poets to
emerge. Attempts were made, but few people were at the universities
long enough to establish themselves as the new 'generation', and many
of them were killed in action before their reputations were secured.[4]

Since the 'People's War', however, and with the emergence of a
'Top People's Peace'[5] literary history takes on a more easily recognisable pattern. Successive 'generations' of Oxbridge undergraduates have
formed dominant 'movements' and 'groups' mythologising themselves and literary history in very similar ways, and to very similar

effects as the Auden group did in the 1930s. With the retrogressive political policies of recent years, the issue of poetry and its relationship to class is still, I believe, highly pertinent.

In a recent article A.D. Moody speaks of contemporary British poetry in the following way: 'By 'British poetry' I mean only the selection which is approved, published and promoted by the small group of London poetry editors who dominate the publishing and reviewing of poetry in the country at the present time. The representative anthology would be the *Penguin Book of Contemporary British Poetry* (1982) edited by Blake Morrison and Andrew Motion.[6]

The implication of Moody's remark is clear. The history of poetry, the making of reputations and movements, is in the hands of a powerful group of contemporaries, many of whom are Oxbridge-educated. Blake Morrison is an exception to this, but Andrew Motion and Craig Raine are not. In the introduction to the Penguin anthology cited by Moody, Morrison and Motion self-consciously ally themselves to the tradition of myth-making anthologies. Michael Roberts's *New signatures*, the Apocalypse anthologies, and Robert Conquest's *New lines*, which launched the Movement, are all named. Motion and Morrison also say that 'it is the privilege of every generation to pride itself on having done something remarkable'; they wish to make themselves representative of a 'generation', in the same way that Hynes and others have made Auden the representative of a generation. Motion and Morrison also speak of their anthology containing a 'new' poetry, but close by asserting that 'a number of young poets today take the view expressed by Keats . . . '. Just how 'new' such a view might be is surely open to some serious debate.

It is true that in the *Contemporary British poetry* anthology there is a very strong Irish contribution, and there are two poets at least in Douglas Dunn and Tony Harrison who have working-class backgrounds, but have broken into the literary establishment. But for those of us who are concerned with both poetry and politics, the myth-making of a dominant literary tradition which represents a dominant ideology rather than 'literary value' must surely be a matter of some concern.

I have written this book not only to shed light upon the poetry and poetics of the 1930s, but also to anticipate a re-evaluation of poetry written during the Second World War. More widely I wished to insist upon the confusion of ideology with 'literary value' which takes place in the creation of literary traditions; confusions which must constantly be acknowledged and grappled with in our literary history. This last point may sound anachronistic given the current state of literary-theoretical debate, but *The Penguin book of contemporary British poetry* demonstrates that such theories have not impinged upon the myth-makers. And doubtless several 'generations' of school and university students will have the book set as a text which is 'representative' of British poetry. Just as I believe it is important to understand exactly what Auden 'represents', so I think it is salutary to critically scrutinise what Motion and Morrison's anthology represents. If this study in any small way encourages such critical perspectives, it will have served its purpose.

Notes

1 C. Day Lewis, 'Where are the war poets', *Collected poems*, London, 1954, p. 228.
2 A. Calder, *The people's war: Britain 1939-45*, London, 1969, p. 18.
3 R. Hewison, *Under siege: literary life in London 1939-45* (1977), London, 1979, pp. 81-3.
4 Among the young Oxford-educated poets who lost their lives during the Second World War are Keith Douglas, Sidney Keyes and Drummond Allison.
5 See A. Marwick, 'People's war and top people's peace: British society and the Second World War', *Crisis and controversy*, ed. A. Sked and C. Cook, London, 1976, pp. 148-65.
6 A.D. Moody, 'Telling it like it's not: Ted Hughes and Craig Raine', *The yearbook of English studies*, vol. 17, 1987, p. 166.

Index